William James

AND

Education

William James

AND

Education

EDITED BY

Jim Garrison
Ron Podeschi
Eric Bredo

Teachers College, Columbia University
New York and London

Published by Teachers College Press, 1234 Amsterdam Avenue, New York, NY 10027

Library of Congress Cataloging-in-Publication Data

William James and education / edited by Jim Garrison, Ron Podeschi, Eric Bredo.
    p. cm.
  Includes bibliographical references and index.
  ISBN 0-8077-4196-5—ISBN 0-8077-4195-7 (pbk.)
    1. James, William, 1842–1910—Contributions in education.
2. Education—Philosophy. I. Garrison, James W., 1949–
II. Podeschi, Ronald. III. Bredo, Eric.
LB875.J32 W55 2002
370'.1—dc21   2001053436

ISBN 0-8077-4195-7 (paper)
ISBN 0-8077-4196-5 (cloth)

Printed on acid-free paper
Manufactured in the United States of America

09 08 07 06 05 04 03 02   8 7 6 5 4 3 2 1

We wish to dedicate this book to our students who have shared with all of us the spirit and meaning of James's philosophy.

Contents

Acknowledgments   *ix*

Introduction   *xi*

1. *The Darwinian Center to the Vision of William James*   *1*
   ERIC BREDO

2. *James's Metaphysical Pluralism, Spirituality,*
   and Overcoming Blindness to Diversity in Education   *27*
   JIM GARRISON

3. *William James's Prophetic Grasp of the Failures*
   of Academic Professionalism   *42*
   BRUCE WILSHIRE

4. *Pluralism and Professional Practice:*
   William James and Our Era   *58*
   RON PODESCHI

5. *James's Metaphysics of Experience and*
   Religious Education   *74*
   SIEBREN MIEDEMA

6. *James's Story of the Squirrel and the Pragmatic Method*   *89*
   CLEO CHERRYHOLMES

7. *A Feminist Re/examination of William James as*
   a Qualified Relativist   *97*
   BARBARA THAYER-BACON

8. *From Radical Empiricism to Radical Constructivism,*
   or William James Meets Ernst von Glasersfeld   *115*
   D. C. PHILLIPS

9.   *Pragmatism's Unfinished Project: William James*
        and Teacher Knowledge Researchers   *130*
        JERRY ROSIEK

10. *James's Concept of Mystical Consciousness:*
        Implications for Curriculum Theory and Practice   *151*
        AOSTRE JOHNSON

References   *173*
About the Editors and the Contributors   *185*
Index   *187*

Acknowledgments

W E WOULD LIKE to thank Virginia Polytechnic Institute and State University for financial support in bringing this book to publication. We would also like to thank Brian H. Ellerbeck at Teachers College Press for his patience and kind assistance.

We the editors would like to acknowledge each other's equally vital roles in bringing this work to press. It was a pleasure experiencing the pluralistic scope of James's philosophy in collegial conversation among ourselves and with our authors.

Introduction

WILLIAM JAMES (1842–1910), along with Charles Sanders Peirce and John Dewey, was a founder of pragmatism, the first distinctively American approach to philosophy. James was also a pioneer in psychology. His classic, *The Principles of Psychology*, ushered in a new approach to the field based on a view of mind as dynamic and adaptive rather than as static. Aspects of his functional approach profoundly influenced the development of American psychology in the 20th century. To this day, James's influence extends to other areas of social science as well as to the humanities and religious studies, with Jamesian scholarship continuing to grow in contemporary philosophy.

In this collection of essays, we offer various interpretations of William James's thought that reveal some of its remarkable complexity and scope, as well as suggesting some of its implications for education. Work focusing on the implications of James's thought for education has been severely limited heretofore. The following chapters begin to address this absence of Jamesian scholarship, especially the relevance of his philosophical perspective to our era. Our hope is to initiate a conversation in education that should have begun long ago.

When James has received attention in education, the general pattern has been to overlook the implications of the deeper and wider aspects of his work. For example, in the 1950s and 1960s, some writers focused on his *Talks to Teachers*, which one called "the most deeply significant and thrilling book ever written for teachers" (Gates, 1967, p. 34). Others saw James as a cultural hero "confronting a changing, challenging world full of risk and adventure . . . [his] greatest contribution to American education" (Larrabee, 1961, p. 86). In the 1980s when James finally became the focus of attention at an American Educational Research Association symposium, the participants treated him merely as an empirical psychologist to be compared with Thorndike. Even a well-known philosopher of education who gave James rare attention during the 1980s limited his scope to *Talks to Teachers*, criticizing James for being condescending to teachers while praising his insight and eloquence about teaching (Jackson, 1986).

The misunderstanding of the importance of James by his admirers is one reason that he became relegated to the fringe of American education, even as his life and work received significant attention in the humanities and the social sciences. But there is a more significant reason as well. Although James received some recognition in education as a forerunner of John Dewey, the latter's giant role in American education overshadowed the work of James. This neglect of James's contributions is paradoxical given his central place in the formation of philosophical pragmatism and his role as a founder of modern psychology, both of which were at the roots of the flowering of progressive education under Dewey and his followers.

Even if educational scholarship had given more comprehensive attention to James's work, there might still have been no consensus about *why* he was important. Certainly there is no consensus on this question in other fields today. A recent annotated bibliography, focusing on writings about James and psychology, categorizes his work as falling into a variety of intellectual frameworks ranging from experimentalism to existentialism (Taylor, 1996). James is viewed by some as a forerunner of behaviorism and by others as a forerunner of phenomenological psychology, gestalt theory, and field theory. Scholarship in philosophy varies as widely in its treatment of James, whose work seems to lend itself to a range of interpretations because of its openness, fluidity, and plurality of perspective.

Pluralism will also be evident in this volume in the authors' varied styles as well as in the range of their interpretations. Some of the authors consider James more from his "scientific" side, others more from his "existential" side, while still others emphasize his concern with "spirituality." Does James reflect the late 19th century or the late 20th century—or both? You will find different answers as well as different approaches to reaching the same answer to this question. You will see a wide spectrum of colorings (some of it blended at times in interpretation): James as psychologist, as philosopher, as educator; James as scientist and as explorer of religion; James as a clear writer and as confusing; James as theorist and as action-oriented; James as a moralist and as a relativist; James as an optimistic meliorist and as one who knows tragedy; James as an individualist and as socially oriented; James as prophetic and as blind; James as open-minded and as patronizing; James as pluralist and as sexist.

As editors, we see this diversity not only as rich in potential for reconnecting James to education but also as reflecting the spirit of William James itself. As an editor of a volume about James's philosophy recently concluded, "A man so passionately devoted to pluralism as he was would have wished to draw attention to plural understandings of his work" (Putnam, 1997, p. 10). There is a metaphor that James (1907/1947) introduced that applies to this collection when he views approaches to knowledge as akin to a corridor in a hotel with rooms branching off:

Innumerable chambers open out of it. In one you may find a man writing an atheistic volume, in the next someone on his knees praying for faith and strength, in a third a chemist investigating a body's properties. In a fourth a system of idealistic metaphysics is being shown. But they all own the corridor, and all must pass through it if they want a practicable way of getting into or out of their respective room. (p. 53)

Although each of our contributors has a "room" of her or his own, they all agree that the "mansion" of James's work encompasses a space of rare complexity and expansiveness that makes a visit with William James invaluable. Although the authors differ in their interpretations of James, they do agree about the importance of James's themes concerning individual uniqueness, pluralism, the centrality of experience, and nondualistic thinking.

We will not attempt in this Introduction to analyze the philosophical similarities and differences in detail among the ten contributors to this volume. Given the uniqueness of each contribution, we are wary of overemphasizing either superficial commonality or categorical difference. James's work is multifaceted and polyvalent, and we urge the reader to appreciate the different facets that are revealed in the chapters that follow.

When it comes to the implications of James's philosophy for education, you will find here that James is used to emphasize active and intelligent self-control with sensitivity to individuality; inject our schools with a vision of multiculturalism that has the depth of metaphysics and the breadth of human diversity; call for educators with their moral freedom to combat the cancer of academic specialization and standardization that spreads through university life; encourage educators to face with courage the ongoing tensions between individuality and community that are encountered in day-to-day professional life; analyze philosophical implications of the importance of religious education in all schools; explore the pragmatic method as a way to clarify meaning in educational disputes; advocate a feminist process of social-negotiating that challenges the fallibility of individual perspectives; remind educators that knowledge needs to be connected to the discovery of reality rather than groundless subjectivity; encourage teacher-knowledge researchers to root their theory into practical consequences; plead for curriculum and teaching that draws from the mystical and ethical dimensions of experience banished in a materialistic culture.

We editors also have contrasting interpretations of James's philosophy and its implications for education. One of the reasons that the collection begins with Eric Bredo's chapter is to ensure that the scientific aspects of James's thought are not marginalized, Bredo insisting that an account of James's work should include both its scientific and ethical-religious aspects. The collection ends with a contrasting emphasis, Aostre Johnson's chapter on James and mysticism. However, James himself would have seen no inherent polarization between the first and last authors, or between them and others in the book. We hope that wherever you choose to begin or end in reading this collection, it furnishes the kind of lively, dialectic process that it has been for us.

For Eric Bredo (Chapter 1), James's focus on the tension between science and religion, and the depth of his concern with both, is what makes him unique. Although noting James's thought did not have just one "center," Bredo explicates in scholarly detail how both James's psychology and philosophy were significantly influenced by Darwin's evolutionary theory. Before doing so, he probes connections between James's personal background and concerns (e.g., the tension between his aversion to closed systems and his desire for a scientific account of things) and the thinking that surrounded him at the time. Bredo's focus, however, is on how Darwinian themes permeate Jamesian psychology, which was an attack on both mechanistic and spiritualistic theories of mind. He also suggests some of the ways these ideas were used in James's philosophy, which was equally committed to attacking mechanistic reduction and absolutist holism. Bredo argues that Darwinian ideas helped James develop an approach that was both scientifically respectable and capable of embracing moral and religious belief as an important aspect of the universe having real effects. The theme unifying James's work in these fields, as well as in education, Bredo suggests, was an emphasis on the dynamics of *life* in both its biological and humanistic aspects.

In Chapter 2 Jim Garrison puts his focus on metaphysics, which most think "too abstruse a subject to have anything to do with everyday educational issues." He believes James's "infinitely pluralistic universe" is just what is needed to understand, and practice, diversity more deeply in education. In such a universe, "we must embrace otherness and difference if we desire to live lives of expanding meaning and value." From a Jamesian base, Garrison contends that all experience is potentially religious and spiritual. He discusses three forms of spiritualism in the context of James's thought, then proceeds to perspectives about practice, and ends beyond the practical with poetry and prophecy. Making connections, that is, creating ameliorative possibilities in an unfinished universe, is a moral and artistic activity. Although never using the word *postmodern*, Garrison shows an appreciation of postmodernists' openness to difference while being at the same time skeptical of their tendency to fracture communities and potential connections.

In his spirited essay, Bruce Wilshire (Chapter 3) extends the perspective of his 1990 book, *The Moral Collapse of the University: Professionalism, Purity, and Alienation*. He explores the prophetic insight of James's "The Ph.D. Octopus," in which James "foresaw the existential crisis into which the professionalization of disciplines and the segmentation and bureaucratization of the university were leading us." Calling for strong winds of freedom to blow into academia, Wilshire focuses on what he knows best, the professionalization of academic philosophy. His alarms ring loudly for those of us in education with their parallels to the institutions in which we work. Wilshire's reflections on James's life and work are clearly swimming upstream in today's cultural currents when market metaphors and certifying standardization drive educational reform. Believing that "to be we must be validated by the universe that evolved us and holds us," Wilshire lays out steps that he thinks will move the university toward the kind of education that William James envisioned—one in which human capacities are touched and developed around the vital questions of human existence.

Ron Podeschi in Chapter 4 also emphasizes a problem that he sees paralleling James's era and our own: "how to enhance creative individuality in the face of societal forces that push us toward narrow standardization and mechanical objectivity." Viewing James as an "existential pragmatist" and as an "affirmative postmodernist," he focuses on experiential tensions in enhancing both an ideal of professional community and an idea of pluralism. Podeschi sees James as rejecting notions of "community" that overemphasize consensus and stability as well as rejecting notions that dismiss the idea of "community" as oppressive. Likewise, James is seen as rejecting concepts of the "individual" as universal and unchanging, as well as dichotomies that straightjacket cultural difference. From an analysis of James's philosophy of the "social self," Podeschi explores dynamics and dilemmas of professional practice. Sharing examples from his own career, he portrays the ambiguity of exercising one's agency in daily institutional life when pursuing an ideal self in a nonideal, pluralistic world.

In Chapter 5, Siebren Miedema, with his interest in William James's philosophy of religion, brings an international perspective from The Netherlands. He sees James's vision centered in a metaphysics of experience that James called "radical empiricism." Miedema thinks "this integrated interpretation of James's work helps prevent us from characterizing his religious writings as dealing only with the subjective and privatized domain of personal experience so that we can see some implications for the public domain." In arguing against Rorty's privatizing James and religion, Miedema presents a reconstruction of James's philosophy as vital for re-

CHAPTER 1

The Darwinian Center to the Vision
of William James

Eric Bredo

WILLIAM JAMES was a brilliant explorer who opened up new intellectual approaches, while making clear their relevance to everyday life. His *Principles of Psychology* helped launch functional psychology, the first uniquely American school of psychological thought. His philosophical writings helped make pragmatism, the most distinctive American contribution to philosophy, widely influential.

The new approach that James helped introduce was an attempt to mediate between polarized positions where one approach denies completely the truth of the other. An advancing and mechanistic way of thinking that was on the advance seemed to contradict an idealistic or spiritual way of thinking that was still valued. The notion that things are governed by empirically discovered scientific law seemed to deny the possibility of human freedom and a role for religious experience, just as religious and ethical thinking seemed to deny the validity of scientific law or its applicability to human affairs. James sought a way between these mutually opposing ways of thinking by considering the practical implications of ideas in context. Focusing on the practical import of ideas helped soften seemingly absolute differences about who was right to a concern with what would be helpful. This strategy was the hallmark of pragmatism, a philosophy that involved more attitude or method than doctrine.

While the basic strategy of a pragmatic approach is simple, it can appear so flexible as to seem vacillating or inconsistent. Pragmatism's situated and flexible approach can be especially frustrating to those who seek a single fixed and certain answer. Those reading James's work, in particular, sometimes come away with a sense of inconsistency and vacillation because he sometimes seems to emphasize one point at one time and another contradictory point later on. To some extent this was characteristic of his way of thinking and expressing himself. As his biographer, Ralph Barton Perry (1935), wrote, "The power of his mind lay largely in its extreme mobility, its darting, exploratory impulsiveness. It was not a mind which remained stationary, drawing all things to itself as a centre; but a mind which traveled widely—now here and now there— . . . making up in the variety of its adventures for what it lacked in poise" (p. 66). James's thinking was open to multiple sides of an issue and his emotional expressiveness sometimes led him to exaggerate one side to make a point while "murdering" the other. Indeed, at times he clearly *was* inconsistent. All of this creates a problem in understanding James, particularly if one adopts a narrow reading of his work.

Some readings of James run into precisely the opposite difficulty, however, by attempting to make him very consistent and interpreting his work in one light while ignoring everything that is inconsistent with this interpretation. This seems particularly likely when James is viewed as aligning with one side or the other in the polarized debates of our own day. Some interpret James from a scientific angle, for example, viewing him as extending the reach of scientific psychology to include ethical behavior and religious experience, just as pragmatism helped extend a scientific and experimental attitude to philosophy more generally. Others interpret James's work from an opposing mystical or spiritual angle, emphasizing his openness to all manner of psychic phenomena, his emphasis on the existential freedom of the individual to choose, and his pantheistic belief in multiple yet finite gods. Although James is often viewed as *either* a scientist *or* a deist, I believe that either reading tends to miss the main thrust of James's work. Because James was primarily concerned with mediating this very conflict, reading James in either of these one-sided ways misses the point, however appealing it may be to those on one side or the other.

Given this tendency to see James either as inconsistent and vacillating or as all too narrowly consistent, how can one get a better understanding of his thought? As James once wrote, "any author is easy if you can catch the centre of his vision" (Lovejoy, 1911, p. 126), but how can we catch the center of James's own vision? This statement suggests that one interpret an author's work in terms of its central emotional concern, or practical interest, and not merely in terms of its formal character or sentence by sentence consistency. When considered in this way, James's work clearly had a great deal of consistency in the way of practical purpose or intent, even though it was (intentionally) not formulated as a closed system of thought. Just as James emphasized that pragmatism was primarily an attitude or method, rather than a dogma, so should we think of his own work when trying to catch its "centre."

Catching the center of an author's work by understanding its central purpose or intent does not mean, however, that one should ignore its central concepts or principles. Rather, the intellectual and emotional sides of an author's work need to be seen in relation to one another, as well as in relation to their practical meaning at the time. In what follows I suggest one way of catching the center of James's vision by interpreting his work in Darwinian terms. Although James has often been viewed as influenced by Darwin, it is rare to follow through in detail the way Darwinian ideas figured in his work. By showing specific connections between themes in Darwin's and James's work, I hope to make James's approach clearer and more obviously consistent in intent, while also relating it to the central intellectual revolution of the 19th century. Finding *a* center to James's work does not, of course, imply that there might not be other centers, other reasonably coherent interpretations of his work. As an admirer of James, I would not want to attempt to reduce his uniquely individual work to my own "closed system." Rather, I would like to offer this interpretation as one among many, and as more useful for some purposes than for others.

The Darwinian interpretation is particularly useful for showing the specific way that James attempted to integrate scientific and ethico-religious concerns. And, as I will suggest, Darwinian concepts helped James find a way of including moral and religious phenomena within a scientifically respectable account, as well as a way of placing science within a broader view of human life. Specific concepts drawn from Darwin helped in thinking through dilemmas of freedom and determinism, individuality and universality, that were central to James's work and part of the genuine moral and intellectual difficulties of the time.

James's attempt to find an intellectually and morally responsible way between the polarized options of his time remains relevant today because the polarized positions of our own time are strikingly similar, although clothed in somewhat different garb. Today we talk about "structure" versus "agency" or "power" versus "agency" rather than "freedom" versus "determinism," but the issue is much the same. We are also more inclined to talk about uniqueness and commonality in cultural terms, as in talk about cultural "difference" or similarity, rather than in terms of "individuality" versus "relation," or "particularity" versus "universality." The issue is, again, remarkably similar.

James's work also remains relevant to education, despite the many changes that have occurred since he wrote. His attempt to find a way forward in the face of social and cultural conflict is relevant because this is precisely the task that educators face today. Educators need to help the next generation find a viable way to link past and future, as well as a way to relate what is unique to their own experience with what they share with others. Showing how these linkages or transitions are possible, despite despairing views that suggest that they are not, is relevant to education's central function of maintaining continuity and coordination in social life. James's work is also relevant to education more specifically because his psychology suggests principles and maxims for teaching and learning that are still helpful.

In what follows I consider James's thought first by describing the way it relates to his central emotional concerns. I then document Darwin's influence on his thinking, contrasting it with other strains of evolutionary thought. The philosophical implications of Darwin's thought are considered next, so that it is clear what it means to be a Darwinian in the philosophical sense. Following this, James's work is described in greater detail, beginning with his psychology and then turning to his philosophy. The educational implications of his thought are brought out in the conclusion.

JAMES'S EMOTIONAL CONCERNS

James invited an interpretation of his work in terms of his emotional concerns when he argued that commitments to philosophical systems are emotional at base (James, 1907/1963). Every philosophy was for him an articulation of an emotional stance, however covert. Finding James's central emotional concerns may therefore be as important as finding the intellectual sources of his ideas. Indeed, it amounts to much the same thing, although coming at it from a different angle.

One of the strongest emotional overtones in James's work seems to have been fear of confinement. Simply put, James was something of a claustrophobe (Perry, 1935, pp. 219, 232). As his sister Alice wrote, "William expressed himself and his environment to perfection when he replied to my question about his house in Chocurua. 'Oh, it's the most delightful house you ever saw; it has fourteen doors, all opening outwards.' His brain isn't limited to fourteen, perhaps unfortunately" (Dewey, 1946a, p. 380). A desire for a way out recurs in James's protest against closed systems and deterministic schemes. As he wrote of Hegel's philosophy, "The 'through and through' universe [of the Hegelian system] seems to suffocate me with its infallible impeccable all-pervasiveness. Its necessity, with no possibilities; its relations, with no subjects, make me feel as if . . . if I had to live in a large seaside boarding-house with no private bed-room in which I might take refuge from the society of the place" (James, 1878/1992, pp. 1018–1019). James's "neurasthenia" may have been a form of panic attack brought on by the thought of being trapped or confined. His bouts with depression likely had similar origins in feelings of entrapment.

Perhaps as part of this tendency, James reacted against any line of thought that denied the uniqueness of the individual. He argued against the notion that a category subsumes the thing categorized, as though one were "in" a category (as opposed to helping to compose it). He argued that people have the right to adopt whatever fundamental beliefs they choose when an issue is undecideable on intellectual grounds, as long as they are willing to bear the personal consequences of their decisions (James, 1896/1956). He also viewed individuals as the source of the novelties that make social progress possible, making being "different" a matter of potential social value (James, 1896/1956, pp. 255–262). In each case, individual uniqueness made one more than a mere stereotypical category member.

In place of closed, deterministic systems James sought to *enliven* and personalize things, noting that his principal "bogey" was "desiccation," or dry lifelessness (Dewey, 1946c, p. 386). Consistent with a rather romantic emphasis on the living and organic, James argued in favor of conceptions that gave a strong role to human activity and spiritedness. He even interpreted the role of philosophy in terms of enlivenment, declaring that "philosophic study means the habit of always seeing an alternative, of not taking the usual for granted, of making conventionalities fluid again, of imagining foreign states of mind" (Dewey, 1946c, p. 388; Perry, 1935, p. 215).

What makes James so interesting is the fact that he combined this emphasis on individual uniqueness, freedom of expression and moral agency with a nearly equal emphasis on universality and constraint. As Dewey astutely noted, "all the determining *motifs* of his philosophy spring from his extraordinarily intense and personal feeling for the work of the individual, combined, however, with an equally intense realization of the extent to which the findings of natural sciences (to which he was loyally devoted) seemed hostile to rational justification of the idea that individuality as such has any especial value" (Dewey, 1946a, pp. 329–393). Because I want to suggest that Darwinian ideas played a large role in James's attempts to resolve this tension, it is important to consider first the degree to which Darwinian thinking influenced him.

DARWINIAN INFLUENCES

Evolutionary thought was pervasive in the United States when James was a young man (Miller, 1968). Three predominant forms of evolutionary thinking were in play, although not always sharply distinguished: Spencerianism, neo-Hegelianism, and Darwinism. Spencer can be seen as a reductionist and determinist. He tended to focus on the adaptation of individuals to the given natural and social environment, viewing their adaption as consistent with sociological laws. Adopting a laissez-faire approach to social change, he rejected social welfare and education as simply prolonging maladaptive ways of living. Social planning should be rejected, as well, because we are not smart enough to understand the subtle reasons that one social structure survives relative to another. Where Spencer emphasized the planless evolution of society, neo-Hegelian holists viewed social evolution as the unfolding of a kind of Idea of God or Absolute Spirit. Humanity was evolving in the direction of increased freedom, rationality, and self-consciousness. In this view all the errors and missteps along the way are ultimately "rational" because they are part of the process of proceeding toward the Good, if only one could see it from the standpoint of the Absolute. What these highly contrasting views had in common was the belief that social evolution was on track toward some ultimate end, as well as a certain passivity with regard to the end to which things are going. Darwin rejected such schemes in favor of more concrete investigations of evolution that left the direction that life might take open and contingent. In his view, neither natural law nor Absolute Spirit set *the* end to be followed.

James was influenced by Spencer at an early stage and even used Spencer's *Psychology* in his first undergraduate course. Conversations with his friend Charles Sanders Peirce lessened Spencer's hold on him, however. As James wrote later on, "I am completely disgusted with the eminent philosopher [Spencer], who seems to me more and more to be as absolutely worthless in all *fundamental* matters of thought, as he is admirable, clever and ingenious in secondary matters. His mind is a perfect puzzle to me, but the total impression is of an intensely two and sixpenny, paper-collar affair" (Perry, 1935, p. 144). Perry (1935) suggests that Spencer's work served James as a "teething ring," which he "outlived as an incident of his philosophical infancy" (p. 154).

James was less touched by Hegelian thinking, even though he was early surrounded by New England Transcendentalists who shared some idealistic tendencies with later neo-Hegelians. Nevertheless, he reacted negatively to neo-Hegelianism for many years, eventually mellowing under the influence of Josiah Royce, a colleague and neighbor.

What incensed James about both Spencerian Social Darwinism and Hegelian Absolute Idealism was their determinism and consequent disvaluing of individual uniqueness. Spencer saw human beings as behaving in conformity to universal laws with natural selection as eliminating unfit ideas (and individuals) that do not conform to the demands of the environment. Arguing against this deterministic view, James (1896/1956) suggested that the "contemporary sociological school" with its "averages and general laws and predetermined tendencies" and "obligatory undervaluing of the importance of individual differences" was the "most pernicious and immoral of fatalisms" (pp. 261–262). Although neo-Hegelians placed greater emphasis on the role of human action, they nevertheless attempted to view everything from a cosmic or ultimate perspective, seeing every tragedy as "rational" because it would ultimately lead to the Good. James reacted against this view, considering it ridiculously insulated from the suffering of others. Both views left no room for the possibility that social evolution might proceed in entirely new directions as a result of the actions of unique individuals. Much of James's work can be seen as defending a Darwinian position, which left the direction of evolution open and gave individuality a valuable role, against these Spencerian and neo-Hegelian competitors.

Harvard was the center of intellectual debate on evolution when James went there and "it was this emancipating influence, among all the forces of his time and place, that most deeply affected William James during the years of his university studies" (Perry, 1935, p. 65). James began his work in chemistry but soon changed to comparative anatomy and physiology with the aim of making natural history his subject (Perry, 1935, pp. 66, 72). He studied for a year under Jeffries Wyman, a professor of anatomy at the Lawrence School of Science, a new school at Harvard. James was attracted to Wyman, who tended to favor Darwin's account, for his "unmagisterial manner" and his "accuracy and thoroughness," viewing him as a paragon of scientific saintliness (Perry, 1935, pp. 67–68). James also came in contact with Louis Agassiz, one of the principal critics of Darwinism. Edward Reed (1997b) summed up the situation recently as follows:

> The only prominent psychologist of his day to have studied comparative anatomy, James had been a pupil of both Jeffries Wyman and Louis Agassiz at Harvard during the 1860's, when they were in the middle of their heated debate over Darwinism. Wyman was the second most important Darwinian in the United States after Asa Gray, who was also at Harvard and also part of this vicious intellectual battle. Agassiz was perhaps America's most distinguished naturalist, and certainly its fiercest anti-Darwinian. When

> James joined Agassiz in a collecting expedition in Brazil in 1865–66 . . . he was repelled by Agassiz's unwillingness to consider Darwin's views. Thirty years later James still remembered the verbal tongue-lashing the distinguished professor gave to the twenty-three-year-old who dared to defend Darwin. (p. 204)

As James wrote to his brother Henry, "The more I think of Darwin's ideas the more weighty do they appear to me, though of course my opinion is worth very little—still, I *believe* that that scoundrel Agassiz is unworthy either intellectually or morally for him to wipe his shoes on, and I find a certain pleasure in yielding to the feeling" (Perry, 1935, p. 102).

After receiving his medical degree, James was unenthusiastic about the drudgery of practicing medicine and was eventually hired to teach physiology at Harvard. He continued to do so for 5 years, replacing Wyman after the latter's death and becoming briefly head of the physiology department. It was only later, after he entered the philosophy department, that he taught psychology. As he recalled, "I originally studied medicine in order to be a physiologist, but I drifted into psychology and philosophy from a sort of fatality. I never had any philosophic instruction, the first lecture on psychology I ever heard being the first I ever gave" (Perry, 1935, p. 78). James's first course in psychology focused on the relation between physiology and psychology (later pursued in depth in *Principles of Psychology*). His work with Wyman is significant because it shows how deeply he was immersed in Darwinian thinking. As Perry (1935) put it, in his teaching "he drew most heavily upon what he had learned from Wyman. The first philosophical problem to which he devoted himself systematically was the problem of evolution, and here also it was the same teacher who had first shown him the way" (p. 68).

Although the 19th-century debate over evolution is usually seen as a conflict between science and religion, the issue was actually more complex than this because the problem of dealing with uncertainty and indeterminism was *inside* of science and not just an external issue raised by those of a religious persuasion (Croce, 1995; Dewey, 1910/1997). Darwin was among those working out an approach that could accommodate uncertainty and indeterminism by using probabilistic and hypothetical reasoning. Rather than seeing Darwin as aligned against religion and in favor of reductive materialism, then, one might better view him as opposing both religious *and* scientific dogmatism. James's affinity for Darwinian ideas can be seen as having deep roots in a shared reaction to dogmatic and deterministic thinking.

DARWINIAN IDEAS

Clearly, there is ample evidence that James was influenced by Darwinian thinking, but what does it mean to be a Darwinian, philosophically speaking? Three ideas seem particularly important for present purposes.

First, Darwin argued that species evolve rather than being immutable. This belief is now a commonplace, but as Dewey (1910/1997) noted, one needs to recognize that it overthrew 2000 years of philosophy. In Platonic and Christian thought, the emphasis was on the eternal and universal form of things rather than on changes or variations in form. The universal, eternal, or final character of a thing (Being) was used to explain its particular, present, or changing character (Becoming). Being was reality, Becoming mere appearance. Darwin reversed this priority, viewing organic forms as emergent within a historical and contingent life process. In so doing he used "Becoming" (varying events) to explain "Being" (structures or forms), rather than the reverse. When Darwin wrote about "the origin of species," he was writing about the origin of form, *species* being the Latin word for form. In effect, his wider target was formalism.

Second, Darwin suggested that change in organic form is the result of a process of variation and selection ["descent with modification through variation and natural selection" (Darwin, 1859/1963, p. 442)]. This point, which is Darwin's central theoretical contribution to evolutionary theory, argued against both traditional Deistic thought, which saw the origin of adaptively useful forms as requiring a designer (God), and traditional mechanistic thought, which saw form as fixed and passive. To develop his argument, Darwin had to separate the source of variation from that of selection, so there could a way both for novelties to enter into a system and for those that were adaptively inferior to be selected out, without either process being reducible to the other. By recognizing that variation could be random relative to selection pressures, Darwin provided a way of understanding how forms useful for certain purposes could arise without a designer through a process that is not mechanical, at least in the Newtonian sense. In so doing he was able to evade the most important dualism of his time.

Third, Darwin conceived of species in populational rather than typological terms (Mayr, 1997). Where someone adopting a typological approach believes that all individuals belonging to a species must possess a set of essential characteristics in common, Darwin suggested that a species is a population of unique individuals that interbreed and share common ancestors, not a logical category of members sharing essential traits. True, the members of one species differ on average from those of another, but there will also be variation among the unique individuals within each species. Seen in this way, a species is a functional and statistical concept, a point elaborated in the modern synthesis in biology, rather than a formal type. One can therefore be considered a member of a species while nevertheless remaining unique as an individual, just as we are all human beings while having unique fingerprints. Philosophically speaking, Darwin's approach was a form of anti-essentialism 140 years before Richard Rorty's current version.

Darwin adopted other principles that also figured in James's work, although they will be given less emphasis here. The principle of continuity meant that a scientific account must explain how organisms change from one form to another without sudden, inexplicable appearances ("saltations"). Darwin suspected that all of life was descended from a single original species from which it evolved step by continuous step. Continuity served as a version of Occam's razor, keeping explanations simple by not multiplying origins. Darwin also used analogical and plausible reasoning (Croce, 1995), arguing that natural selection could be understood by analogy to human selective breeding, and supporting his interpretation by its plausibility rather than its logical certainty.

These Darwinian notions of evolving forms, variation and selection, and populational thinking may seem obvious today, but we may still not appreciate how radical a thinker Darwin was (Mayr, 1997). Defining species in functional and populational terms acknowledged individual uniqueness while retaining distinctions between groups, something that still seems to be hard for us to do when considering the members of different social groups or cultures. Explaining change in terms of variation and selection is still radical in the social sciences, which tend to oscillate between structural determinism and rational choice. In short, Darwin developed an approach from which we still have much to learn.

Darwin's approach can also be seen as custom-made for helping James address his central problems. The Darwinian account was able to integrate individuality and commonality, as well as chance and necessity, within a single perspective. Its emphasis on *life* gave a way of looking at human beings that was natural but did not deny a place for "spirited" action. As Dewey suggested, pragmatism can be viewed as a generalization of Darwinian philosophy to human social and moral affairs. To demonstrate in greater detail how Darwinian ideas figured in James's work, let me turn now to his psychology and then to his philosophy.

JAMES'S PSYCHOLOGY

James's psychology was an attack on both the mechanistic and spiritualistic theories of mind. As he wrote, "This book . . . rejects both the associationist and the spiritualist theories, and in this strictly positivist point of view consists the only feature for which I am tempted to claim originality" (James, 1890/1952, p. xiii).

The mechanistic theory, represented in psychology by associationism, saw complex ideas as assembled out of elementary ideas. This line of thought derived from Locke, who believed knowledge of the external world came from objects impinging on the body's sensory apparatus, creating elementary ideas in the mind. Elementary ideas were then associated, generalized, and abstracted by the mind, using its various faculties, thereby building up more complex ideas. The complex idea of an orange might be formed by associating the more elementary ideas that it is round, soft, orange colored, and sweet, for example.

The "spiritualistic" or idealistic theory of the mind, in contrast, viewed a thought as the result of the operations of an immaterial soul or transcendental ego, much like contemporary views of the inner self. Here the starting point involved the assumptions, relationships, or patterns introduced by the ego that are read into the flux of sensory experience. In this case the mind would start with basic assumptions, such as the notion that experience can be organized in terms of spatial nearness or temporal nextness, and use these premises to interpret the flux of experience so as to constitute different objects. In other words, the first approach saw a thought as built out of basic parts on hand, whereas the second saw it as an instantiation of a general idea or plan to which parts are custom-crafted. Clearly, the former viewed thinking as more determined by the external object, whereas the latter saw the thinker as heavily determining the character of the thought or percept.

James rejected both views. As Reed (1997a) put it, "James wanted to reject both the active-but-unnatural mind of the idealists and the natural-but-passive mind of the associationists" (p. 6). Darwin helped provide the beginnings of a middle way between these two approaches. If mind is understood as a product of natural selection, then "it" must be a natural process and not a mysterious transcendental entity, like the soul. If mind is adaptively useful, it must also do more than merely register and add up external sensory events, like the associationistic view. It must be more actively useful for altering behavior and the external environment. Seen from a Darwinian perspective, mind is both natural and active rather than active-but-unnatural or natural-but-passive. However, this interpretation required an account of the brain and nervous system that was not mechanical in the passive Newtonian sense yet that also avoided smuggling in non-natural entities like the soul or ego to animate the body.

Physiology

A Darwinian approach suggested that mind is a natural *function* evolved to aid human adaptation and survival. As James (1899/1915) put it, "Man, whatever else he may be, is primarily a practical being, whose mind is given him to aid in adapting him to this world's life" (p. 25). Seen in this way, the principal role of thinking is to affect action, and not merely to register the way things are: The thinker is a doer and not merely a spectator.

Viewing mind as an adaptively useful function, rather than as an entity, makes one look at it dynamically, focusing on what it *does* rather than on what it *is*. This eliminates many puzzles, such as the question of where the mind is located, because mind is recognized as a function in behavior and not a thing. If one takes the brain apart, for example, one will never find the mind, just as one will never find "driving" inside of one's automobile engine. The question of where the mind is dissolves when one recognizes that mind is not a thing at all but an activity or a change in the relationship of organism and environment to one another. Such an activity or change in relationship requires mechanisms, such as the brain and nervous system, the rest of the body, and certain aspects of the environment, but it is not the same as these mechanisms, just as any alteration in relationship is not the same as the thing that has been moved.

But how does the mind, viewed as a function, do its job? James (1890/1952) argued that it was "primarily a selecting agency" (p. 91). As he explained, "The pursuance of future ends and the choice of means for their attainment are . . . the mark and criterion of the presence of mentality in a phenomenon. . . . No actions but such as are done for an end, and show a choice of means, can be called indubitable expressions of mind" (pp. 5, 6–7). This notion of mind as a process that selects means for the attainment of ends differed from the mechanistic view because it imputed ends to the organism itself rather than regarding matter as inert and without purpose. It was unlike the spiritualistic view of mind in that the having of ends or preferences was understood to arise from entirely natural origins. James's account of mental life as involving variation and selection among behaviors or ideas was clearly much like the Darwinian idea that species evolve though variation and selection.

Conceiving of mind as a function rather than a thing gave a way of seeing instances of "mind" up and down the scale of behavior. For instance, even isolated parts of the spinal cord select behaviors that help to attain simple "ends," giving them at least a rudimentary "mental" character. As a gruesome example used by Darwin and Huxley, as well as by James, when a drop of acid is placed on the belly of a frog whose spinal cord has been cut, the frog's rear leg reaches up to just the right place to wipe off the acid. If one restrains the leg, the other leg takes up the same job. Even a brainless frog acts in a surprisingly adaptive way, selecting means to bring about "preferred" ends.

After analyzing the kinds of behavioral changes added by each higher level of the brain, James (1890/1952) concluded that "All the nervous centres have then in the first instance one essential function, that of 'intelligent' action. They feel, prefer one thing to another, and have 'ends'" (p. 51). Indeed, the nervous system as a whole is organized so that higher centers (such as those involving the cerebral hemispheres) modify the goals set for lower order centers without intruding into the latter's operation, like officers telling subordinates what to do but not how to do it. The higher centers function as "an organ added for the sake of steering a nervous system grown too complex to regulate itself" (James, 1890/1952, p. 94). James's account can be seen as similar to contemporary views of mind as a cybernetic hierarchy, with governors on top of governors (Powers, 1998). It also combined the cognitive and motivational or emotional aspects of behavior in one account, suggesting that cognition is driven by preference.

James's description of the structure and function of the brain and nervous system provided an account of an organism's behavior that was neither completely determined by its environment nor made up any way the organism preferred. The complexity and instability of the brain allowed for unpredictability and novelty, relative to the observer's expectations, while the success or failure of actions in an environment provided feedback that selected among behaviors (and ideas). James's description of the relationship between higher and lower orders of mind also helped give an integrative account of the relative uses of habit and thought, viewing habit as economical in familiar situations and thought as useful for adapting to novel or complexly contingent situations.

Although James's physiological account of the structure and function of the brain and nervous system went a long way toward mediating the traditional division between mechanistic and idealistic theories of mind, at times he fell back into the more conventional view that there are two types of *entity*, brain and soul, that interact with one another. As he put it, "I confess . . . that to posit a soul influenced in some mysterious way by the brain-states and responding to them by conscious affections of its own, seems to me the line of least logical resistance, so far as we yet have attained" (James, 1890/1952, p. 119). As Dewey (1946c) noted, James was still influenced by conventional thinking about the soul when he wrote his *Principles*.

Phenomenology

The other half of James's psychology was an approach to subjective experience that paralleled his analysis of the structure and function of the nervous system. Here he faced the same two opponents. Associationist psychologists, representing the mechanistic position, thought that complex ideas were assembled out of elementary ideas. Ego psychologists, representing the spiritualistic side, thought that a transcendental ego constituted its objects, giving form and definition to the ambiguous flux of experience. James's problem was how to retain a role for both particularity and universality while avoiding the static character of both of the traditional views.

He attacked this problem most directly in his famous chapter on the "stream of thought" (James, 1890/1952). Here James argued that subjective experience supports the notion that ideas are both individual (unique) and continuous (related). Every thought is individual in the sense that it is a unique whole experienced at a particular time as part of a total personal consciousness belonging to a particular person (James, 1890/1952, p. 147). As a unique event, a thought, considered as a whole, will never be exactly repeated since neither the brain nor the rest of the world will ever be the same again. One should note that this does not mean that one may not think about the same *objects* again and again, but the whole thought, taken with all of its tone and color, will never be exactly the same. On the other hand, James asserted that every thought is also already related to other thoughts, rather than isolated, so it does not require the conscious mind to relate thoughts to one another or to define the thought in terms of some relationship.

To make this apparently paradoxical position understandable James appealed to the metaphor of a stream or wave, sometimes also using the metaphor of a magnetic field. He seemed to view a relatively stable thought, like the thought of an object, as similar to a stable waveform in a pond. Seeing a thought as a pattern or wave made it clear that a given thought could be complex without needing to be composed of elementary parts, because it could be just like a wave that has ripples within it, and ripples within these. The wave metaphor also helps in understanding how thoughts may be related to one another without needing an external relater, or ego, to do the relating. They could be just like the waves in a pond that are clearly related to other waves because all are part of the same dynamics. The very dynamics of the pond, or of the brain and nervous system of a person in contact with the environment, would create these relationships. Just as a wave in a pond is surrounded by other waves that help define it, so each thought is surrounded by a "fringe" of other thoughts that form its background or context.

Earlier and later thoughts are similarly related in this metaphor. If thought of an object is like a dynamically repeating wave, then the transition to a new waveform will involve intermediary forms, each of which will show signs of what came before and what is coming, just as incoming waves at the beach show their relationships in their forms. Thoughts are related, then, by the dynamic rhythms of the whole nervous system as person and environment interact. The relationship between thoughts is a product of the structure of the organism and the structure of the environment as they interact dynamically with one another.

James's stream or wave metaphor characterized thinking as a dynamic activity. When things make sense and behave in predictable ways, thinking is relatively steady, like a bird on a perch (to shift to another metaphor in James's essay), but when they are uncertain or unpredictable, the mind becomes more active, like a bird flying to another perch, as the mind seeks its object. James went on to build a complex psychology consistent with this dynamic metaphor, including an analysis of the role of conscious attention, an interactive theory of the self, and a theory of the emotions that drew on Darwin's account of expressive behavior in animals (Darwin, 1889/1904).

The point for the present, however, is that James's wave model gave a unified way of describing both complex thoughts and the relationships linking them without having to take either elementary ideas or relationships as predefined givens. In his more parsimonious approach one did not need to posit either elementary ideas to be added up in a complex idea or a little thinker or ego inside to impose structure, because "the thoughts themselves are the thinkers" (James, 1892, p. 216). The dynamics of thinking or "experience" involves both objects and relationships without the need for relationship to be created in some inexplicable way.

James's psychology posited a delicate balance between the person as a passive recipient of sensory input and as an agent acting to alter the world. The stimulus of sensory input makes us respond in certain ways. But mental functioning, made possible by the dynamics of the brain, selects and filters and interacts with this input, creating an altered stimulus that alters the response. Processes of attention, or selective focus, are critical in this, as are more specialized processes of voluntary attention, or attention that reorganizes itself despite difficulties, which alters stimulation, however slightly, thereby the resulting response. In effect, the whole difference added by conscious thought and "will" amounts to a slight changes in the sensory field. In this way, and not without difficulties, James tried to balance the notion of the person as externally determined and the person as voluntary agent. Agency and novelty came down, in effect, to the unpredictable dynamics of voluntary attention.

James's psychology was the beginning of the psychology of the act, which was developed further by Dewey and Mead. It foreshadowed field theory in psychology, the holographic theory of memory, as well as contemporary activity theory (Cole, Engeström, and Vasquez, 1997). It also drew on a number of Darwinian themes. The most obvious of these is the notion that mind has evolved for reasons of practical, adaptive use. This implies that one would do well to think of mind as helping to bring about preferred states of affairs, and not merely for contemplation of things as they are, which was, of course, also a tenet of pragmatic philosophy. James also focused on how form emerges within the dynamics of mental functioning, consistent with the Darwinian emphasis on Becoming over Being. His analysis of the stream of thought suggested how both objects and relationships may be equally present in a concrete thought, just as Darwinian organisms are already related to other organisms ecologically and historically and not merely by our classificatory schemes. The metaphor of the stream or "pulse" was also consistent with Darwin's notion of continuity, thoughts being assumed to flow into another just as species evolve without sudden saltations.

Viewing mind as a process for selecting means to ends was consistent with Darwin's emphasis on natural selection. This allowed James to see how ideas serve to anticipate future events without supposing that people have the gift of prophecy, just as it allowed Darwin to explain the origin of adaptively useful organic structures without positing a Designer. If an idea worked in the past, this fact will be remembered and used to anticipate future consequences under similar circumstances, just as the success of Darwinian creatures frequently allows their descendants to survive under similar conditions.

The notion of populational thinking is somewhat less evident in James's psychology, although there are traces of it. He saw thoughts as "waves" or "pulses" that are the aggregated effect of many individual neural firings. His wave model was consistent with Darwin's antitypological or anti-essentialist stance, suggesting that there is no one way to define or capture a unique pulse of thought, because other thoughts will interact with it in many different ways, just as knowing an individual's species does not tell one everything about that individual. As James (1892) put it, "All ways of conceiving of a concrete fact, if they are true ways at all, are equally true ways. There is no property absolutely essential to any one thing" (p. 355).

JAMES'S PHILOSOPHY

It is only a short step from James's psychology to his philosophy. This is at least in part because his philosophy was heavily psychological in character, as evidenced in his emphasis on the emotional basis of an individual's philosophical commitments. Let me first consider James's pragmatism and then his metaphysics.

James's pragmatism was an attempt to mediate between the same two families of opponents. "Tough-minded" scientific empiricists and materialists tended to explain the whole by its parts, whereas "tender-minded" religious idealists and rationalists tended to explain the part by the whole. But as James (1907/1963) suggested, "Most of us have a hankering for the good things on both sides of the line. . . . You want a system that will combine . . . the scientific loyalty to facts . . . but also the old confidence in human values and the resultant spontaneity, whether of the religious or of the romantic type" (pp. 9–10, 12).

Pragmatism was designed to help resolve just such conflicts. James (1907/1963) described his pragmatism as having two parts, the "pragmatic method" and a "genetic theory of truth" (pp. 22–38). The pragmatic method was a way of avoiding fruitless metaphysical disputes, such as when one person says a table is "really" a bunch of atoms and another claims it to be "really" an idea in one's head. Rather than arguing about who is right in the abstract, the pragmatic method suggests that one "try to interpret each notion by tracing its respective practical consequences. What difference would it practically make to any one if this notion rather than that notion were true? If no practical difference whatever can be traced, then the alternatives mean practically the same thing, and all dispute is idle" (p. 23). Focusing on practical consequences brings one back to which way of looking at things is more helpful for what one is trying to do at the moment and away from a fruitless struggle over who is "really" right in the abstract.

The other component of pragmatism, the "genetic" theory of truth, viewed the truth of an idea as the result or outcome of inquiry rather than as something preexistent to inquiry. If a new belief "works" and stands up to tests suggesting that it functions as claimed, and if it proves consistent with previously established beliefs, then it *becomes* "true." In this view, "the truth of an idea is not a stagnant property inherent in it. Truth *happens* to an idea. It *becomes* true, is *made* true by events. Its verity is in fact an event, a process" (James, 1907/1963, p. 89). Using a biological metaphor, James suggested that an idea "makes itself true, gets itself classed as true, by the way it works; grafting itself then upon the ancient body of truth, which thus grows much as a tree grows by the activity of a new layer of cambium" (p. 31). Thus a true idea is one that successfully connects the old to the new, allowing our beliefs to grow.

This "genetic" theory of truth views truth in evolutionary terms, seeing a new truth as like an organism that originates from the mating of prior organisms, survives, and has lots of descendants. Because one cannot know ahead of time which beliefs will succeed, one needs to focus on their "fruits" or "consequences" and not only on their origins. An idea may have good "parents" and still fail to work as expected. The truth of a new proposition, like the adaptive goodness of an animal form, is thus largely prospective. The similarity between this conception of truth and a Darwinian conception of species is obvious.

The main point of James's "genetic" theory of truth was to place claims about the truth of a proposition inside of human experience rather than positing a priori metaphysical givens that are outside possible empirical investigation. By considering truth as a compliment we pay an idea when it functions as claimed, James (1907/1963) placed considerable emphasis on the humanly constructed character of truth. As he put it, "to a certain degree . . . everything here is plastic. . . . When old truth grows, then, by new truth's addition, it is for subjective reasons" (pp. 30–31). This approach contrasted with Dewey's and Peirce's metaphor of a community of scientists testing a proposition's truth by attempting to replicate the results that it implicitly claims can be attained. Although James gave more constrained accounts at times, this emphasis on the subjective or "constructed" nature of truth got James into considerable difficulty, which has been described in many places (e.g., Murphy, 1990).

Radical Empiricism

James's later philosophy, much of which appears in *Essays in Radical Empiricism* and *A Pluralistic Universe* (1912/1971), can be viewed as a fairly direct generalization of his earlier psychology and philosophy. His earlier essays in moral philosophy also contain many of these ideas in germ (James, 1897/1956).

Like more traditional empiricists, such as Locke, James thought that all knowledge came from "experience," although this term can be used in many different ways. According to James (1912/1971), there is only one basic "stuff" of which the universe is composed, "pure experience" (p. 5). By "pure" experience, he meant the feelings and/or sensations one has prior to analyzing an experience and breaking it into pieces. One is likely to have a relatively "pure" experience when losing oneself in the flow of a good movie, for example. The experience has its own flow that may be analyzed later on into various themes or elements, but in itself it contains everything without *explicit* differentiation.

James's empiricism was "radical" because he suggested that even the assumptions of empiricism should be discoverable within experience. Traditional empiricism was wrong, James argued, because one never has an "elementary" sensation, because perceiving any distinct thing involves discrimination learned through great training and effort. Experience doesn't come already chopped and labeled. Traditional empiricism was incoherent because it claimed that everything that can be known comes from experience but did not get its own commitment to atomism from experience! Traditional empiricism's limitation of knowledge to elementary ideas or sense data on which one can reach agreement was also too narrow because it treated relationships as unreal and subjective. In contrast, James (1912/1971) suggested that "everything real must be experiencable somewhere, and every kind of thing experienced must somewhere be real" (p. 84). In other words, if one wants to talk about anything as real, it must somehow be present in experience, even the notion that experience comes already chopped up. On the other hand, everything that we experience must be admitted as in some sense real. If someone in a hypnotic trance experiences something, that experience is "real," even though the person's claim to be out of her or his body and flying over Los Angeles may not be. As a result, the world as James conceived of it was not built out of disconnected atoms, contrary to traditional empiricism, although this was not a dogmatic assertion because the proposition of radical empiricism was adopted as a "methodological postulate."

James's other opponents, neo-Hegelian idealists, went to the opposite extreme, suggesting that every object or event is what it is because of its place in a universal whole making up a rational sequence, like a Godly idea or plan. But, as James pointed out, this absolute whole, being beyond any possible human experience, is also an ungrounded metaphysical invention. Rather than assuming that we can adopt a God's eye view, which is impossible, James suggested a more humble model of human beings as limited and partial knowers. As he wrote, "We may be in the universe as dogs and cats are in our libraries, seeing the books and hearing the conversation, but having no inkling of the meaning of it all" (James, 1912/ 1971, p. 268). If so, then any claim about the ultimate pattern or meaning of history will be a hypothesis based on extremely limited data. We can generate such hypotheses, and they may be consistent with known data, but such a hypothesis will be underdetermined by the data (like a set of datapoints that can be described by many different equations) . By *assuming* that the universe is an integral whole, rationalism was as dogmatic as atomistic empiricism.

Radical empiricism thus cut in between its two opponents, softening the fixed assumptions of each. It widened the scope of empiricism, making the "empirical" consist of all of the sensations and feelings one has in a situation, and not just the standardized bits served up by a narrow methodology. In so doing, James opened the door to relationships, esthetic qualities, and latent possibilities as *real* properties of objects. On the other hand, he also narrowed the scope of knowing relative to rationalism or idealism by arguing that the knower is situated and limited. Any claim about the way the universe is must therefore be recognized as partial and hypothetical rather than derived from a God's-eye view, although it might still be practically useful.

James's *The Varieties of Religious Experience* (1902/1958) furnishes an example of an inquiry informed by the attitude of radical empiricism. In it James considered a wide variety of "religious" experiences that most scientists would likely reject out of hand: theosophy, mind cures, dramatic conversions, mystical experiences, and so forth. For James these were all data to be considered in a truly human psychology that would be sensitive to the psychological function of religious "experience." To omit such things from psychology because they are not suitably well-defined or standardized, or reliably measurable, would be to adopt a nonempirical attitude in the guise of empirical science.

James's thesis was that religious experience, such as belief in a superior being that can act on our behalf, helps give courage to an actor, enabling the person to act more effectively. It also helped unite a divided self by placing its actions in a wider context. In the case of the extreme religious "geniuses" that James studied, such division could be so serious as to be clearly pathological. The unification that occurs as a result of religious experience could be viewed either as a unification of the conscious self with its unconscious elements or as a unification of the person with God. The former interpretation is more consistent with a scientific interpretation, whereas the latter is more like a conventional religious interpretation. James thought it was an open question which interpretation was the more true. But the point for the present is that a radically empirical psychology could study phenomena like mystical experience and religious conversion that traditional empiricism would find intractable and traditional religious thought would suggest are beyond all objective study. James's attitude can be viewed as similar to Darwin's in this regard, because Darwin thought that many issues handled dogmatically in religious thought could be studied empirically and did not have to be relegated to Spencer's category of the "unknowable."

Being oriented to future consequences, James's empiricism was also open to the self-fulfilling character of some beliefs. As he was at pains to point out, some beliefs help create the facts that they declare: "There are then cases where faith creates its own verification" (James, 1896/1956, p. 97). This is particularly true of moral and religious truths, which, in James's view, require human action to become true. If one acts in a friendly manner toward another, for example, this helps create the fact of their friendliness. Similarly, if one acts as though the universe has some force supportive and hospitable to one, as Deists believe, then the added confidence gained from such belief would likely result in experiences that confirm it. In this sense, religious belief may bring about the conditions that make it true, *at least for the believer*. Once again, James had given an important role to voluntarism, while also hedging it.

A Pluralistic Universe

Pragmatism, as Perry noted, gave James a method (the pragmatic method) and his radical empiricism gave him a content (pure experience). Applying the method to the content gave him a universe—one that was both "pluralistic" and "unfinished" (James, 1909).

James's view of the universe can be considered in relation to the longstanding philosophical question of "the one and the many." Is the universe a bunch of unconnected atoms or an integral whole? Is it fundamentally many or one? James argued that such totalistic assertions are meaningless because they have no implications for practice, although they may offer emotional consolation (and therefore a kind of meaning). In order to act we need to know the *specific* way one thing is connected to another, at what place this connection occurs, and when it is active, and not some general notion that things are connected or not in the abstract.

As finite, limited actors we also cannot take all facets and possibilities into account. We develop simple ways of looking at things that are helpful for various purposes, because "no single point of view can ever take in the whole scene" (James, 1909, p. 177). We focus on one aspect of a thing at one point in time, while neglecting many others. In effect, our finite and limited natures imply that our universe will always be pluralistic. There will be ways in which things will be connected and integrated and ways in which they remain separate and disconnected. In this view, we will never find *the* single way things are, and we should accommodate ourselves to this (hypothetical) fact.

In fact, if we have reason to consider ourselves as well adapted to the universe, then our practical need for specific, situated connections and the apparent efficacy of our actions in making a difference in the world provide hints about the nature of the universe itself. If local action really makes a difference, then the universe must be one in which everything is not tightly connected together, for in such a universe nothing could be changed without changing everything. In a universe in which our actions make a difference, there must be a degree of looseness or disconnection between things: "There is something in [a thing] . . . really of its own, something that is not the unconditional property of the whole" (James, 1909, p. 154).

Such a universe has room for chance as well as for possibility among its real features, since it is not a deterministic whole. As James (1897/1956) suggested, it is "for such a half-wild, half-saved universe our nature is adapted" (p. 61).

Because many things are only loosely related to others, our universe is effectively a multiverse. On the other hand, our "'multiverse' still makes a 'universe'" because "every part, though it may not be in actual or immediate connection, is nevertheless in some possible or mediated connection, with every other part however remote" (James, 1912/1971, p. 275). Applying the pragmatic method to pure experience thus implied that the universe is pluralistic. Rather than seeing it as one or many in the abstract, then, we would do better to consider the specific ways things are related or unrelated that are relevant to what we are trying to do.

James's notion of a pluralistic universe clearly projected the situation depicted in his psychology onto the universe as a whole. Rather than taking the individual as a given part to be assembled into various wholes, or the universe as a given whole that constitutes each of its individual parts, James saw individuals as unique participants in the interactive process of composing the universe. He thought the universe could be conceived in terms of a "social analogy" in which there is a "plurality of individuals, with relations partly external, partly intimate, like and unlike, different in origin, in aim, yet keeping house together, interfering, coalescing, compromising, finding new purposes to arise, getting gradually into more stable habits, winning order, weeding out" (Perry, 1935, p. 295).

Seeing the universe in terms of a "social analogy" is not so different from the Darwinian notion that life is the product of local interactions among the members of different species. In such a view there is room for novelty due to the unique contributions of individuals, even though not all novelties survive in interaction with others. Because such a universe is open, its ultimate course depending on the interrelated actions of those involved, there is also room for action that seeks to make things better, unlike a deterministic view that makes morally informed action pointless. There is, in other words, a place for both variation and constraint.

In James's conception, however, the interacting agents affecting the course of the universe could include a superhuman God, or gods, which he insisted must also be finite and limited. As he put it, "The line of least resistance, then, as it seems to me, both in theology and in philosophy, is to accept, along with the superhuman consciousness, the notion that it is not all-embracing, the notion, in other words, there is a God, but that he is finite, either in power or in knowledge, or in both at once" (James, 1912/ 1971, p. 269). This hypothesis James thought consistent with the facts of ordinary and pathological psychology, psychical research, and mystical experience, each of which gave intimations of belonging to a wider life, a kind of wider ocean in which we are but waves.

At this point James clearly diverged from Darwin. One could try to naturalize James's notion by conceiving of these superhuman beings the way Durkheim (1965) did when he thought of society as a kind of real or empirical "superhuman organism" or as Gregory Bateson (1972, 1988) did when he viewed a rain forest as an intelligent being when taken as a whole. James might have tolerated these views given his broad notion of god: The "most primal and enveloping and deeply true might at this rate be treated as godlike" (James, 1902/1958, p. 48). But he would probably have parted company with his more naturalistic brethren and clung to the notion of an "unseen" deity, however finite. That he did so as a hypothesis and as merely his own personal preference, rather than as a dogma or as something to be forced on others, is greatly to his credit. However, the tendency to do so also shows the influence of pre-Darwinian thinking on him. One may speculate that James's god was a holdover from the mystical Swedenborgian beliefs of his father, not to speak of his father's importance in his life, making another source of the "social analogy" of the universe the interaction of the unique individuals in James's own family.

CONCLUSIONS AND EDUCATIONAL IMPLICATIONS

The central tension in James's work was between a tender-minded attitude that cherished individuality and agency and a tough-minded attitude that was sensitive to universality and constraint. Although James often gave more emphasis to the former, he did so with care to ensure that he was not inconsistent with the scientific results or practical constraints involved in loyalty to the latter. To maintain this position with some consistency required great rethinking of conventional ways of understanding.

Darwin's work gave James a way of mediating between these opposing attitudes. It provided the metaphor of the *live* organism acting to get in better relation with its environment. The organismic metaphor was also adopted by romantics, who emphasized life's tendency to burst all constraints, but a more naturalistic, Darwinian view of life gave equal emphasis to constraint. Focusing on the contingencies of living in a world that is uncertain and evolving also gave a way of handling issues of concern to both scientists and humanists. It made the scientific study of mind more lively and dynamic and humanistic concerns more concrete and naturalistic. By looking at psychological and philosophical issues more practically and procedurally, James softened the conventional polarities. Different ways of conceiving of things became partial views, useful for different purposes, rather than *the* way the world is.

The Darwinian notion that variation and selection are two separate processes that work together in evolution was part of this synthesis, helping to give a role for both individual novelty and social constraint, without seeing either as contradicting the other. Populational thinking made clear how a qualitatively unique individual may be part of a group or category yet not subsumed by that categorization. There is no contradiction between the fact that there are differences between groups and the fact that each individual within the group is unique, just as we recognize that there may be variation both between and within groups. The same point applies, of course, to culture, which need not be seen in totalistic or essentialistic terms that deny uniqueness within to nevertheless recognize functional differences between. Seen in Darwinian terms, freedom and constraint as well as individuality and commonality are not mutually exclusive options.

Given James's attempt to mediate between these tough and tender ways of thinking, what are some of the more specific educational implications of his work? His evolutionary view of mind, which saw it as a function for improving practical action, gave a very active view of intelligence. Consistent with this practical and active view of mind, he believed, like Dewey, that one really begins to think only when facing a "live" issue (James, 1896/1956, p. 3). Genuine uncertainty about how to proceed in the face of a committing decision that needs to be made stimulates thought. But thought also needs to lead to action to complete itself. As James (1899/1915) put it, "No reception without reaction, no impression without correlative expression" (p. 33). Instead of preaching to students in the abstract, then, the teacher should "lie in wait rather for the practical opportunities, be prompt to seize those that pass, and thus at one operation get your pupils both to think, to feel, and to do" (p. 71). In this conception, thinking is part of life activity that it helps to reorganize rather than a merely scholastic exercise.

James's psychology also placed considerable emphasis on the student as a unique individual (Curti, 1959). He emphasized the student's individuality by suggesting that a student's interests and background experiences be taken into account by the teacher so that new learning is fused with emotion and understanding. As he put it, the teacher should "begin with the line of his [the student's] native interests, and offer him objects that have some immediate connection with these. . . . Next, step by step, connect with these first objects and experiences the later objects and ideas which you wish to instill. Associate the new with the old in some telling way, so that the interest . . . finally suffuses the entire system of objects of thought" (James, 1899/1915, p. 96). The notion that one should begin "where the child is" may not seem novel today, but it represented a bow to the child as an individual in a day when regimented education was the norm. James was not a mere sentimentalist, however, and did not emphasize such a student-centered approach that student interests defined unilaterally the ends to be achieved.

James's emphasis on the active uses of mind and on the student as an individual resulted, when combined, in a psychology heavily oriented toward self-regulation. When James (1892) discussed habit formation, for example, he offered a number of practical maxims, such as: "Make automatic and habitual, as early as possible, as many useful actions as we can" (p. 144); "never suffer an exception to occur 'til the new habit is securely rooted in your life" (p. 145); "seize the very first possible opportunity to act on every resolution you make, and on every emotional prompting you may experience in the direction of the habits you aspire to gain" (p. 147). What is notable about these suggestions is their emphasis on setting one's own habits. This contrasts, at least to a degree, with Dewey's greater emphasis on collaborative self-regulation, in which people become part of mutually governing democratic communities. It contrasts much more glaringly, however, with the emphasis of most behaviorist psychology on methods for controlling *others*. James's approach was more individualistic than Dewey's, but it was equally democratic, unlike Watson's or Skinner's behavioristic approaches, which were oriented toward developing a science for controlling others.

When James proposed maxims for the teacher, he did not consider them to be dictates to be slavishly obeyed. As he put it, "Teaching is an art; and sciences never generate arts directly out of themselves. An intermediary inventive mind must make the application by using its originality. The science of logic never made a man reason rightly, and the science of ethics (if there be such a thing) never made a man behave rightly. The most such sciences can do is to help us to catch ourselves up and check ourselves" (James, 1899/1915, p. 24). If only professors bent on making teaching a science had heeded these words, much damage to the actions of sensible teachers could have been avoided.

The greatest contribution of James's thinking to education, however, undoubtedly lies in his central suggestion that education should be made a living affair that is part of wider life. His own work furnishes a wonderful example of this, dealing as it does with issues that are genuinely uncertain and important. If this work can stimulate us to reinvent a form of education that is connected to the live issues of our day, allows room for individuality in investigating and proposing solutions to them, encourages active participation and judgment in settling them, and fosters a sense of humility and fallibility by putting proposed answers to practical test, this will be its greatest achievement. Such an education would, moreover, be an integral part of a life that is worth living.

Acknowledgments. I want to thank Ray McDermott for his very helpful comments on an earlier draft of this paper.

CHAPTER 2

James's Metaphysical Pluralism, Spirituality, and Overcoming Blindness to Diversity in Education

JIM GARRISON

MOST THINK METAPHYSICS too abstruse a subject to have anything to do with everyday educational issues. Such attitudes reflect either an allegiance to an irrelevant metaphysics or an underestimation of the depth of educational questions. I believe the pluralism of William James is just what we need to understand and practice education in a pluralistic democracy. Pluralism addresses questions of inclusion and diversity generally; it, therefore, has implications for issues involving educational diversity such as multiculturalism, gender, race, ethnicity, and sexual orientation. All these issues involve questions about the relations between "us" and the "other." In a pluralistic universe, it is impossible to eliminate otherness, which is why such a universe remains perpetually alive and creative.

A pluralistic universe is a multiverse, one filled with an unfathomable number of individuals, some connected to others, and some disconnected. Becoming connected often involves creative activity. Becoming connected well is a moral activity. Becoming connected well involves an active intelligence. However, since an open, pluralistic universe is an unfinished and unfinishable universe, it will remain an open universe containing real, distinct individuals forever. Sometimes, in such a universe, individuals cannot create connections, or cannot create moral connection. Sometimes it is best to let unique beings just be. So, one might ask, why even try?

My chapter seeks to show that in a permanently pluralistic universe we must embrace otherness and difference if we desire to live lives of expanding meaning and value. In securing better relations with others in our environment, especially our social environment, we establish a more intimate relationship with existence at large. James thought all experience potentially religious, or at least spiritual. I believe with James that there is an aspect of the numinous potentially involved in all aspects of inclusion in education.

Paradoxically, those willing to risk reaching out to "aliens" are the least alienated creatures in creation. Only those willing to offer hospitality to strangers will ever know true security within their esthetic, moral, and intellectual home. Finally, only adventurers may fully appreciate the so-lace of shelter. The tensions generated by such paradoxes are reconcilable only to those willing to accept the inclusive "logic" of both/and rather than the exclusive either/or's that usually frame dialogues across differences. Both/and is the logic of connection within a pluralistic universe and the logic of inclusion that honors diversity.

THREE FORMS OF SPIRITUALISM: THEISM, MONISM, AND PLURALISM

James (1897/1956) contends, "The uneasiness which keeps the never-resting clock of metaphysics in motion, is the consciousness that the non-existence of this world is just as possible as its existence" (p. 72). Existential uneasiness before the ultimate existential question, accompanied as it is by the possibility of our own nonexistence, is the source of both natural piety and pitiful attempts at personal grandeur often expressed as the desire to dominate and exclude. Existential uneasiness should make us humble, less egotistic, less likely to hurt others. Needful feelings should make us seek out others who may have what we lack; they should make us more open, not less. The wise response to existential angst is a desire for support and sharing; such feeling should lead to intimacy, to reaching out to make connections, and to including others in our lives. I feel that we find what there is of immortality in our relationships, especially in our children; that is why education is so important.

The influence of Romantic poets, especially William Wordsworth and Walt Whitman, on James is well-documented (see Goodman, 1990). Like the Romantics, he wanted relations that are more intimate with nature including human nature. For James (1909/1996), "Not to demand intimate relations with the universe, and not to wish them satisfactory, should be accounted signs of something wrong" (p. 33). Relations that are more intimate is what environmentalism, multiculturalism, and other forms of inclusion mean; something is wrong with a pluralistic democracy that does not desire them. Intimacy is not identity: Like any good marriage, it means difference, sharing, and creating children of many kinds. James affirms that "we are, ourselves, parts of the universe and share the same one deep concern in its destinies. We crave alike to feel more truly at home with it, and to contribute our mite to its amelioration" (p. 12). James wanted what the Romantic poets wanted; he wanted to sustain intimate relations with the rest of existence such that our creative acts matter in the greater course of cosmic events. Whatever else spirituality meant to him, it meant at least that. What spirituality did not mean to him was the reduction of all difference and otherness to totality, totalitarianism, or monism.

The greatest difference between materialistic and spiritualistic philosophies (like pluralism) is, for James (1909/1996), that the former defines the world "so as to leave man's soul upon it as a sort of outside passenger or alien, while the latter insists that the intimate and human must surround and underlie the brutal" (p. 23). To which philosophy one offers ultimate emotional assent expresses one's fundamental character, wary or trustful, cynical or sympathetic, open or closed. For James monism, theism, and pluralism are spiritualistic philosophies.

"The theistic conception," according to James (1909/1996), "picturing God and his creation as entities distinct from each other, still leaves the human subject outside of the deepest reality in the universe. God is from eternity complete" (p. 25). Such a God is infinitely other and has no obvious need of humankind. For James, "the more intimate species itself breaks into two subspecies, of which the one is more monistic, the other more pluralistic in form" (p. 31). In monism, especially idealism, "we and the universe are of the same spiritual species . . . making us entitatively one with God, attains this higher reach of intimacy" (p. 25). James eventually rejects such a totalizing vision wherein "everything is present to everything else in one vast instantaneous co-implicated completeness" (p. 322). Rejecting monism, James (1897/1956) the pluralist believes "when all things have been unified to the supreme degree, the notion of a possible other than the actual may still haunt our imagination and prey upon our system" (p. 73). We must defer all final meanings forever in a never-resting world. In a pluralistic universe, there are always other, often unique, possibilities. One lover is not the same as another and one unusual student is enough to topple the most comprehensive system of "standardized" testing, if we are perceptive enough to see the difference, and wise enough to honor it.

James (1897/1956) declares, "The difference between monism and pluralism is perhaps the most pregnant of all the differences in philosophy" (p. viii). James contrasts pluralism with monism. First, though, James (1909/1996) does acknowledge that "both identify human substance with the divine substance" (p. 34). There is, nonetheless, a deep difference in how the two philosophies arrive at this identification. Monistic "absolutism thinks that the said substance becomes fully divine only in the form of totality, and is not itself in any form but the *all*-form" (p. 34). Deviations from the "*all*-form" are less divine by the degree that they fail to participate in the divinity of the monistic totality. This thinking assumes a cosmic hierarchy wherein there is only one highest value, one correct standard for thinking, feeling, and acting. Insofar as one deviates downward from this highest value, one is sinful and fallen. Pluralism, by contrast, asserts that "there may ultimately never be an all-form at all," reality "may never get totally collected" (p. 34). In contrast to the "all-form" there is the "each-form." Examples of "*each*-forms" include *individual* forms of life, culture, and interpretation. Every "*each*-form" has an internal quality that no one may universalize beyond the internal limits of the form. This quality limits moral, esthetic, and even scientific generalizations. Too often educators, including educational researchers, ignore this. Assuming what is good and right for "us" holds for all others is the origin of gender, race, and social class bias; it is also the origin of all kinds of colonialism.

The pluralist does not think there is anywhere to stand outside the flux of events to obtain an indubitable perspective; hers is the participant, not the spectator, view of existence. The pluralist thinks that monism is dogmatism. There are always other valuable ways to interpret and connect things and events. Methodological monism in educational research, moral monism in classroom discipline, and value monism in curriculum, are all sources of exclusion, cruelty, and dogmatism. Supposedly monistic essences are fixed, final, and, of course, completely objective. James refutes such nonsense; pluralism, multiculturalism, and environmentalism are all parts of the struggle against dogmatism and cruelty. In schooling, much of this cruelty arises from the putative capacity of "norm-referenced" educational testing to assign essences to students that we may then track students according to "ability" grouping.

James (1909/1996) eventually states the pluralistic thesis thus:

> Pragmatically interpreted, pluralism or the doctrine that it [the universe] is many means only that the sundry parts of reality *may be externally* related. Everything you can think of, however vast or inclusive has, on the pluralis-

tic view, a genuinely "external" environment of some sort or amount. Things are "with" one another in many ways, but nothing includes everything, or dominates over everything. The word "and" trails along after every sentence. Something always escapes. (p. 321, emphasis in original)

Regardless how perfect, internally complete, and totalizing something seems, there is always something other, something external, some other interpretation, something that always escapes the present totality, some alterity that trails along later to alter its meaning. The ultimate meaning of persons, places, or things remains forever deferred in a pluralistic world and everyone and everything eludes a final assignment of perfect identity. Long after you are gone your great grandchildren will, partially, define the meaning of your life. A pluralistic universe is never totally complete; its ultimate meaning, your meaning, and my meaning too is an intimate part of existence, and remains deferred forever. The "and" that always "trails along" implies an indeterminate, although not capricious, continuation. We think, and feel, that something comes after the "and." We expect something more must happen; some alterity must appear. What it will be we cannot exactly say. There is always room to make more meaning and to reach out to other persons, other interpretations, or other possibilities. Nothing should ever dominate over everything.

The Jamesian pluralist ultimately concludes that "nothing real escapes from having an environment" (James, 1909/1996, p. 319). Everything, however large, however totalized, however unified, has *both* internal *and* external relations. Every living "thing," every creature, that wishes to survive and grow must establish relations with aspects of the world external to its existence that is, nonetheless, internal to its functioning. Human beings require food and water to live, mates to reproduce themselves, and educational systems to reproduce their culture.

Individual existence in the metaphysics of pluralism discloses itself as always *both* internally unified enough to be a unique individual *and* externally incomplete enough to be open to connection and change. The universe evolves because each individual form of existence involves endless openness to otherness. The structure of a pluralistic universe is both/and, not just either/or. Overly simplified either/or's are exclusive of others, intolerant of vagueness and ambivalence; it is the logic of standardization and "the normal." Either Roberto is learning-disabled or he is not. Either Katy is included in a "mainstream" class or she is not. Either Ramon passes the test or he fails. Caregivers know that their relations with those who depend on them are characteristically both/and, both loving and exhausting, both bitter and sweet, both rewarding and depleting. Andrew is both gifted and needful. Marie is a mixture of emotional maturity and selfishness. The paradoxes of practice often forbid the drawing of sharp borders, including sharp separations between ourselves and others, subject and object, or knower and known. Both/and is the messy, paradoxical logic of living, and loving, practice. Good teachers like good parents know that children are both connected and disconnected to their self-identity. Only abstract and lifeless theory, and technocrats, can ignore that. The structure of both/and is inclusive; it offers hospitality to others.

A universe wherein we find both internal and external relations, a universe wherein the *each*-form dominates, is one in which some parts do not connect with others. Regarding this consequence of pluralism, James (1909/1996) remarks:

> Our "multiverse" still makes a "universe"; for every part, tho it may not be in actual or immediate connexion, is nevertheless in some possible or mediated connexion, with every other part however remote, through the fact that each part hangs together with its very next neighbors in inextricable interfusion. (p. 325)

Creativity in a pluralistic universe involves making connections. Connected parts need not couple like cars in a train. For example, romance is a "possible or mediated connexion." Marriage *is* an "immediate connexion" requiring constant re-mediation if it is to grow. Many relationships, including teaching and learning, resemble marriage in their intimacy, multiplicity, and fecundity. Creation in a pluralistic universe cannot find completion. For those that delight in the mystery and mystic wonder of creativity, and retain their faith in ideal possibilities, this is good news.

Many readers wildly misunderstand James's doctrine of "the will to believe." The belief is not passive; it is active and seeks to transform the world willfully. In a pluralistic universe, human action makes a difference. James (1909/1996) advises us that in a contingent ever-changing universe our "acting thus may in certain special cases be a means of making it securely true in the end" (p. 329). A pluralistic universe demands an extraordinarily high level of creative faith. Between the way the world is and the way we believe it ought to be lies the "is" of action. One cannot simply assume a quietistic attitude and declare some event "God's will." Indeed, James concludes that we should "be frankly pluralistic and assume that the superhuman consciousness, however vast it may be, has itself an external environment, and consequently is finite" (pp. 310–311). At the very least, one must strive for assurance that God willed the act in a certain way within that part of the divine garden assigned one's stewardship. A pluralistic universe requires reflective, passionate, and, above all, creative action; education in a pluralistic democracy requires the same. Pluralistic democracy requires overcoming blindness and reaching out to others different from us.

THE EPISTEMOLOGICAL PRACTICE
OF REACHING OUT TO OTHERS

The last three chapters of James's *Talks to Teachers* are "talks to students." These are the most "philosophical" of the talks. I will not discuss the first of these. The second talk explores the educational and moral consequences of James's pluralism. Regarding the second talk, "On a Certain Blindness in Human Beings," James (1899/1958) explicitly connects his pluralistic metaphysics with moral relations and individualism. He also investigates this individualism in the third essay, "What Makes a Life Significant." Every different *"each*-form" has its own individual monistic, internal, and unique way of being. Individuality is as unique as one's fingerprints and each form of individuality has a unique and valuable quality James calls "passionate inner meaning" (p. 19). Every one has some blindness to the internal meanings and values of others that are different from them.

James (1912/1976) declares, "The whole question of how 'one' thing can know 'another' would cease to be a real one at all in a world where otherness itself was an illusion" (p. 30). What is wrong with absolutism is that it sacrifices difference to the quest for connection, thereby evading the problem of establishing relationships. Individualism in a pluralistic universe is an epistemological as well as metaphysical inevitability with important moral consequences. In *Talks to Teachers*, James (1899/1958) explores this metaphysical, epistemological, and moral union:

> The truth is too great for any one actual mind, even though that mind be dubbed "the Absolute," to know the whole of it. . . . There is no point of view absolutely public and universal. Private and uncommunicable perceptions always remain over, and the worst of it is that those who look for them from the outside never know *where*. (p. 19)

There are serious limits to what the spectator can know in a pluralistic universe, and even the participant cannot grasp meanings that are truly private and incommunicable. Some things are beyond knowledge, although we may still appreciate and respect them. Our attitude toward the type of individuality that is most desirable has moral and political as well as metaphysical and epistemological implications. James explains: "The practical consequence of such a philosophy is the well-known democratic respect for the sacredness of individuality—is, at any rate, the outward

tolerance of whatever is not itself intolerant" (p. 19). Wholeness characterizes James's thought. For him, our politics and morality is dependent
upon our metaphysics and epistemology, and conversely, our philosophy
of education should not become severed from any of these.

Feelings and ideas confer unique content, and ideals unique contour,
to every "*each*-form" in a pluralistic existence. James (1899/1958) begins
his essay "On a Certain Blindness" by observing:

> Our judgments concerning the worth of things, big or little, depend on the
> *feelings* the things arouse in us. Where we judge a thing to be precious in
> consequence of the *idea* we frame of it. . . . Now the blindness in human
> beings . . . is the blindness with which we all are afflicted in regard to the
> feelings of . . . people different from ourselves. (p. 149)

Each form of life tends to be blind to every other form. Recognizing this
inevitable blindness is necessary for effective dialoguing across differences.

Each individual form of life is a form of practice: "We are practical beings, each of us with limited function and duties to perform. Each is bound
to feel intensely the importance of his own duties and the significance of
the situations that call these forth" (p. 149). These limited practical functions are the limits of finite impassioned creatures, so in themselves fully
forgivable. Dialogues across differences would go on better if participants
recognized they are not just *talking* about different ways of *thinking* about
the world. Too much of our curriculum in multicultural education, for example, is merely intellectual and cognitive. It ignores the fact that we characterize cultures by their distinctive ideals along with the ideas. It fails to
recognize the importance of the social *practices* employed to secure these
ideals and the affective *attitude* participants take toward them. Multicultural
curriculum, along with other forms of diversity education, would do better
if it sought to initiate participants in a plurality of substantial cultural practices over an extended period of time.

It is important, nonetheless, to acknowledge human limits and not
expect too much, especially at first:

> The others are too much absorbed in their own vital secrets to take an inter-
> est in ours. Hence the stupidity and injustice of our opinions, so far as they
> deal with the significance of alien lives. Hence the falsity of our judgments,
> so far as they presume to decide in an absolute way on the value of other
> persons conditions or ideals. (James, 1899/1958, p. 149)

The only general thought is the generous thought. As long as we do not
attempt to absolutize the ideal values of the practices from whence we build

our own individual life, we may avoid blindness, injustice, and cruelty. This does not preclude creating understanding of, or framing alliances with, alien *"each*-forms." Indeed, that is how each individual form of existence grows.

The dynamics of a pluralistic universe devalue the detached and dispassionate attitudes and perspectives of the spectator because they lead to blindness:

> The spectator's judgment is sure to miss the root of the matter, and to possess no truth. The subject judged knows a part of the world of reality which the judging spectator fails to see, knows more while the spectator knows less; and, wherever there is conflict of opinion and difference of vision, we are bound to believe that the truer side is the side that feels the more. (James, 1899/1958, p. 150)

In a pluralistic universe, one cannot feel the full meaning of a practice without participating. Practical reasoning is passionate reasoning. People forget that in practical reasoning we engage in means–ends reasoning to obtain a value (ideal or end) we desire. Nothing is valuable unless desired; ultimate values, or ideals, are orienting; they give direction to thought and action. It is impossible to *know* the value of a practice, of each form of life, truly, unless one feels it. Mere intellectual sympathy is pathetic, and possibly oppressive.

One cannot fully understand another's ideal without participating in that person's practices, without walking a mile with her or him. Furthermore, regardless of how many practices one might participate in, finite creatures cannot know all possible ideals in an interminably pluralistic universe:

> No one has insight into all the ideals. No one should judge them off-hand. The pretensions to dogmatize about them in each other is the root of most human injustices and cruelties, and the trait in human character most likely to make the angels weep. (James, 1899/1958, p. 170)

Sensibly, James asserts, "The first thing to learn in intercourse with others is non-interference with their own peculiar way of being happy, provided those ways do not assume to interfere by violence with ours" (p. 170). Much of the violence directed toward others originates from the assumption that their form of life does violence to "our" values. Still, how does one engage in intercourse without potential interference?

James thought there is a special feeling that comes from participating in a particular practice and the ideal values only it can realize. Such affective recognition provides the basis for the moral perception of alternative practices. James (1899/1958) borrows his description of this emotion from

Robert Louis Stevenson: "For to miss the joy is to miss all. In the joy of the actors lies the sense of any action. That is the explanation" (p. 155). Perhaps not everything, but until we genuinely appreciate the joy in doing something we are not likely to understand it. From without it is not possible to grasp the meaning of an alien form of life entirely. We must see the inner joy and devotion, and that requires seeing the guiding ideals, the supreme values, that others live for:

> We have seen the blindness and deadness to each other which is our natural inheritance . . . we have been led to acknowledge an inner meaning which passeth show, and which may be present in the lives of others where we least descry it. And now we are led to say that such inner meaning can be complete and valid for us also, only when the inner joy, courage, and endurance are joined with an ideal. (p. 185)

We serve our highest values while our shallow values serve us. Both have their inner joy, but it requires courage and endurance to sustain the orienting values that guide and give ultimate meaning to a social practice, and an individual life. Until one serves such values with courage and endurance, they cannot know the joys such action brings. Only until we understand the underlying ideals can we hope to understand the joys, and sorrows, of others. To miss those values is to miss everything.

SPIRITUALITY, OPENNESS, AND INCLUSION

James (1899/1958) recognizes something very important about the practical limitation of the spectator's external perspective: "Yet we are but finite, and each one of us has some single vocation of his own. . . . Our deadness toward all but one particular kind of joy would thus be the price we inevitably have to pay for being practical creatures" (pp. 155–156). The question is can such practical limitations be overcome. James thought so, although it involves a shift from the practical attitude, as valuable as that attitude is:

> Only in some pitiful dreamer . . . or when the common practical man becomes a lover, does the hard externality give way, and a gleam of insight into the ejective world . . . the vast world of inner life beyond us, so different from that of outer seeming, illuminate our mind. Then the whole scheme of our customary values gets confounded, then our self . . . and its narrow interest fly to pieces, then a new centre and a new perspective must be found. (p. 156)

Released from our meager practical interests, ideas, and ideals we might, for a moment, perceive the joy of others in their ideals and practices, thereby growing in perception. The solar system of self may find a new center; we may circumscribe a larger, more inclusive, circle. James thought this ability to expand spheres the virtue of the poet, the seer, and the prophet. More people need to become poets and prophets; that is a more worthy aim for education than increasing test scores. We must be careful here, though. James (1909/1996) hypothesizes that "there is a God, but that he is finite, either in power or in knowledge, or in both at once" (p. 311). It is safe to say that if supernal beings are finite in power, knowledge, or presence, so too are prophets, religious or otherwise.

What is it, though, that prophetic poets see that others do not? They see the joy of life, both their own and that of others, and they see the sorrow. To be more one must see more, but such seeing involves doing, feeling, and, only at the end, knowing. James (1899/1958) concludes, "the occasion and the experience, then are nothing. It all depends on the capacity of the soul to be grasped, to have its life-currents absorbed" (p. 165). Such self-transcending all-seeing moments are transformative: "This higher vision of an inner significance in what, until then, we had realized only in the dead external way, often comes over a person suddenly; and, when it does so, it makes an epoch in his history" (p. 157). The deeper, more numinous, meaning of dialogues across gender, race, and class differences is not just tolerance or understanding. It is the realization that others are a world unto itself (or themselves), and if that world should ever seize us we may transcend our narrow circle and transform our lives. Prophetic poetry imparts new possibilities, new meanings, and a higher vision; they help cure provincial blindness.

James (1899/1958) notes that "to the reader who may himself have had gleaming moments of similar sort the verses in . . . Wordsworth . . . come with a heart-satisfying authority" (p. 158). James understood such moments for in his youth he suffered terrible depression. When he finally came out of it, his father wrote William's younger brother Henry that one cause of the recovery change was "the reading of . . . Wordsworth, whom he has been feeding upon for a good while" (cited in Goodman, 1990, p. 59). Small wonder James thought a diet of other perspectives, of entering the hidden significance of others, might recenter the self and lead to spiritual resurrection.

James mentions many more poets and many other transformational encounters, but his discussion of Whitman is especially interesting. James (1899/1958) pronounces Whitman more than a poet:

> Walt Whitman . . . is accounted by many of us a contemporary prophet. He abolishes the usual human distinctions, brings all conventionalism into solution, and loves and celebrates hardly any human attributes save those elementary ones common to all members of the race. (p. 160)

It is the common aspects of human existence such as hunger, thirst, and loneliness, and the feelings that accompany them, in which we may most readily come to mutual understanding. These we all know, so we most readily understand them in others. It is ideas (including interpretations) and ideals (values) that hold us apart. Dialogues across differences might do better to start with what we all know of loss, increase, and release.

Prophets release themselves from practical interests and conventional social, political, or religious values. This allows them to peer sympathetically into the enabling values of other forms of life. James (1899/1958) observes:

> Only your mystic, your dreamer, or your insolent tramp or loafer can afford so sympathetic an occupation, an occupation which will change the usual standards of human value in the twinkling of an eye, giving to foolishness a place ahead of power, and laying low in a minute the distinctions which it takes a hard-working conventional man a lifetime to build up. You may be a prophet at this rate; but you cannot be a worldly success. (p. 160)

Prophets transvalue conventional values; they often go beyond conventional good and evil to name the ideal we need to transform our lives. That is why they are rarely worldly successes. I am, just now, thinking of Martin Luther King's "I have a dream" speech, and his practice of civil disobedience. Prophets are often dreamers, and the pressures to stay within the contours of conventional ideals and laws, however oppressive, are powerful. Society punishes those who transgress the virtues of conventional practice. Dialoguing across differences is dangerous, and those that do so may expect punishment from those duty bound to each form of life. Everyone must be something of a prophet to see beyond the limits of convention, and like a poet to help us share meaning by creating common metaphors. Fortunately, poets and prophets in the sense required are common. Every day we see them smiling and stopping to talk to strangers. Predictably, they are often those on the edge of each form of practice they occupy. Emissaries of otherness and difference are often mystics, dreamers, and loafers of various kinds. We desperately need more of them. Can the reader conjure up an image of Christ tramping down a pathway with a group of idlers about him, or Socrates in the agora? Such teachers of poverty (Christ) and ignorance (Socrates) have no place in our educational system designed, as it is, to manufacture more economically productive units of human capital. Why were Christ and Socrates not at work, or did they have a higher calling?

Surprisingly, there are important implications for multicultural education, for any education across substantial gender, race, or social class differences, in James's praise of idleness. Multicultural education has yet to come to grips with the difficulty, the hard work, involved in dialoguing across differences. The curriculum seems woefully conventional. How do we educate prophets and poets? Said differently, how do we educate people to transvalue their highest value and create meaning in common with others different from themselves? Perhaps, ironically, we should stop thinking of it as hard work and allow for far more play. If to miss the joy is to miss everything, then we must make sure our students do not miss the joy of learning about others, although there is sadness too. Creating and exploring ameliorative possibility, making connections, is the artistic and moral aspect of problem solving. The arts, practical more than fine, should lie at the center of the curriculum here as elsewhere.

Our culture and school systems devote themselves to enhancing the productivity of existing social and economic practices, and producing human resources to enhance the production function. Because I hold my appointment in a "College of Human Resources and Education," I am reminded of this constantly. Prophets and poets are unwanted; they are unproductive. Are they unproductive? It depends on what one wants to produce. They are very productive of social harmony and understanding. They create insight into others whose feelings, ideas, and values deviate from the so-called norms of standard practice. Mystics, dreamers, and loafers are often punished because they are not on task; what task? Preparing for the standard curriculum and the norm-referenced test is the answer, of course. Mystics, dreamers, and loafers are not normal.

There are many more prophets than we suspect; there are many willing to go beyond conventional good and evil when circumstances demand. Good teachers will sometimes break rules before breaking students. Every teacher who has ever taken time away from preparing for a test to give her students what she thinks they need has prophesied a future that deviates from the norms of American education and poetically acted in the present to better prepare them for it. What happens when a teacher simply decides to play with students, to enjoy some class success, or succor some general disappointment? What happens when we go off task? Much of what most matters in life lies beyond rational planning alone. The same may be said for the curriculum, including the multicultural curriculum, or any curriculum intended to create better understanding across diversity. James (1899/1958) reflects on the values of being off task:

> Surely, a worthless hour of life, when measured by the usual standards of commercial value. Yet in what other kind of value can the preciousness of any hour, made precious by any standard, consist, if it consists not in feel-

ings of excited significance like these, engendered in some one by what the
hour contains? (p. 159)

To miss the joy is to miss everything. Time on task and standardized tests
cannot measure the precious though fleeting moment of marvel, rapture,
and delight. A curriculum that genuinely values diversity, difference, and
otherness is beyond measure by the usual standards of value found on
norm-referenced tests and legislatively mandated standards of learning,
nor is it especially compatible with the commercial values that dominate
the production of human capital. Whose values? Whose norms? Whose
practical interests shall dominate? Must some single practice or some single
value rule supreme? These are the ultimate educational questions in a
pluralistic universe, in a pluralistic democracy, or in a pluralistic classroom.

It is James's (1899/1958) faith that "the religion of democracy tends
toward permanent increase" (p. 178). It is the faith of a pluralist. "Divinity," James believes, "lies all about us, and culture is too hide-bound to
even suspect the fact" (p. 177). He continues:

> Thus are men's lives levelled up as well as levelled down, —levelled up in
> their common inner meaning. . . . Yet always . . . this levelling insight tends
> to be obscured . . . the ancestral blindness returns and wraps us up, so that
> we end once more by thinking that creation can be for no other purpose than
> to develop . . . conventional distinctions and merits. And then always some
> new leveller in the shape of a religious prophet has to arise. (pp. 177–178)

Prophets appear in many guises and places, and are far more common than
we think. When I work with students in Bev Strager's fourth-grade reading and writing workshop, I feel the presence of a prophet appearing as a
pluralistic democrat freeing her charges to creatively and successfully respond to the common inner meaning. She levels down in the sense that
she realizes that all children are morally equal, however different their
talents and abilities. She levels up by demanding the very best of each
child's unique talents. Such democracy teaching is not about voting; it is
about communication, communion, and community. Participatory democracy is ultimately about novelty, creativity, and cocreativity; it begins with
appreciating the social practices, along with the ideas and ideals that guide
them, of others.

Lives in a pluralistic universe are *both* private *and* public; they have
both internal and external significance. Some internal meanings are "private and uncommunicable." A classroom is a pluralistic subuniverse. Some
internal meanings are private but sharable with those special people who
participate intimately in our lives. Some internal meanings may become
public, but only to those that participate in a common practice. Other public

meanings are partially sharable with spectators in a remote, symbolic, and abstract way. In a pluralistic universe all parts, "*each*-form" of life, are "in some possible or mediated connexion." Education in its widest metaphysical meaning involves making connections. It is about growth, that is, living lives of expanding meaning and value, and that means embracing the meanings and values of others. James (1899/1958) declares, "Education, enlarging as it does our horizon and perspective, is a means of multiplying our ideals, of bringing new ones into view" (p. 186). This is the nonstandard spiritual education of prophets and poets, one not found in the refineries of human resources. Making connections, making room for different kinds of folks, is what makes life significant.

CONCLUSION

Education raises the most profound questions about human beings and their relationships. Metaphysics raises the most profound questions about the nature of Being itself. James thought that Being or existence was comprised of discrete, individual beings and their actual or potential relationships with other beings. James felt we live in a fundamentally pluralistic universe; from this intuition, he drew important conclusions about human beings and their relations. In fact, I am not sure it was not the other way around. He may well have reasoned from the relationships among human beings to his metaphysical conclusions. I believe any thoughtful teacher could reason from social relations within her or his own classes to the mightiest of metaphysical conclusions. The mystery of life is in the daily details. One result of thinking we live in a pluralistic universe is that it teaches the value of inclusion and openness to difference, alterity, and otherness. A pluralistic universe *is* a diverse universe. Such a metaphysic militates against totalizing and totalitarian ideals of exclusion and dogmatism.

A pluralistic metaphysics does not offer "foundations" for educational thinking; rather, it exposes the dangers of assuming ultimate foundations, absolute standards, and indubitable norms. Instead, it demands intelligent action to create morally acceptable connections that are esthetically harmonious. Joy, and sorrow, accompanies any deep commitment to a living ideal of practice. To miss the joy and sorrow is to miss all; it is a failure of understanding. To miss the joy and sorrow in multicultural education is to miseducate. Until students laugh and cry in the classroom, the issues of educational diversity have been evaded.

CHAPTER 3

William James's Prophetic Grasp
of the Failures
# of Academic Professionalism

Bruce Wilshire

NEARLY 100 YEARS AGO, William James was ahead of most of us. In "The Ph.D. Octopus" (1903/1987) he foresaw the existential crisis into which the professionalization of disciplines and the segmentation and bureaucratization of the university were leading us:

> America is . . . rapidly drifting towards a state of things in which no man of science or letters will be accounted respectable unless some kind of badge or diploma is stamped upon him, and in which bare personality will be a mark of outcast estate. It seems to me high time to rouse ourselves to consciousness, and to cast a critical eye upon this decidedly grotesque tendency. Other nations suffer terribly from the Mandarin disease. Are we doomed to suffer like the rest? (p. 69)

What happens to our sense of ourselves—our cemented sense of our significance and worth—when to establish our identity we must display a certificate stamped by institutions? Particularly by ones to which we have never wholeheartedly bonded. James fears that our identity will crumble, in spite of all the shiny facades erected around it.

James's voice intermixes with other prophetic ones: Kierkegaard's— that lampooning of learned professors who "build a mansion of world-historical thought but live in a shack out back"; Nietzsche's—

The proficiency of our finest scholars, their heedless industry, their heads smoking day and night, their very craftsmanship: how often the real meaning of all this lies in the desire to keep something hidden from oneself!

Dostoevsky's—

Ah . . . nowadays everything's all mixed up . . . we don't have any especially sacred traditions in our educated society; it's as if somebody patched something together the best he could out of books . . . or extracted it out of the ancient chronicles. But those would be the scholars, and they're all blockheads . . .

And we cannot leave Dostoevsky without hearing the peevish and spiteful voice of The Underground Man who complains of his inability to become, to *be*, anything—even an insect.[1] Finally, let us hear for a moment that balked and despairing but persevering giant, Max Weber (1946), who details "the iron cage of bureaucracy" (see section VIII, "Bureaucracy").

What is it that all these voices lament? It is simply stated but difficult to unpack the meaning of it: To be, we must be validated by the universe that evolved us and holds us. When our place within the universe is no longer guaranteed by ages-old religions, or by settled modes of ethical thought, the vacuum draws into itself untested institutions, turned obsessively within themselves, to stamp us with a putative identity. Lost, one might say, is our ability to *vow* to be this or that, a vow coordinated with the wheeling universe itself.

Joseph, chief of the Nez Perce people—
From where the sun now stands, I will fight no
more forever. (See Howard & McGrath, 1964, p. 282)

James detected that sore, that wound, that all our science and quasi-science and technology and methodology and scientific linguistics and semantics can conceal but cannot heal: the inability to be firm, centered, and confident in our inherently expansive and ecstatic being.

———————

Let us focus on that academic field that some might expect to pursue the question of being—philosophy. Aristotle declared that it is this question that has always been, and will always be, asked. But enlightened "scientific" thinkers, authorized now by a national professional association, seem to know better. Only a few philosophers have raised it in this century, e.g., James in *Some Problems of Philosophy: A Beginning of an Introduction to Philosophy*, Heidegger in many places, and, implicitly, Dewey and the later Wittgenstein.

Most of the rest just assume that the question of being is too vague or abstract. It must be replaced with specific questions that can be handled by specific methodologies. Lacking a centered sense of themselves as vital members of the whole, they fail to see that Aristotle's question applied to our times might allow a coordinated view, which, gathering things together, would encourage *coherence and concreteness.*

Whereas in Aristotle's vision quantity and quality are essential aspects of the ground of being, in the scientist-philosophers from the 17th century on they fly apart. When universities were professionalized in the last decades of the last century, they were partitioned and constituted along the lines of dualisms or polar oppositions (see Wilshire, 1990, esp. pp. 37ff). These are eccentric bifurcations in which one side or the other is given precedence as a result of whatever wind of doctrine or individual whim is blowing at the moment: subjective/objective—which matched qualitative/quantitative—and self/other, individual/group, mind/matter, rational/irrational, present/past, male/female, and so on. Professors live embedded in these mental-institutional structures. No fiddling with managerial arrangements in the university pulls them out of this trance.

I have just concluded teaching a course called "Philosophy in Literature." Both students majoring in philosophy and those in English complained of their experience in the university over several years: Each field was obsessed with the technical apparatus and glossary of terms distinctive to it. Subject matter of the greatest human concern was peripheralized or eclipsed by the shiny tools that ought to have revealed it. The students' experience fell to pieces.

This must happen when an organic sense of the whole falls away, leaving the quantitative and the qualitative disconnected, and when inquirers lose a sense of their own centers as existing beings. Individuation cannot be a vital matter of responsibly placing and conducting ourselves as whole living things in the world but must be decided by externals: the current methodologies of professional-academic disciplines that define and individuate themselves nationally and internationally in the information business, and by which young professionals must be certified if they would advance in the business. For a prime example, anthropologists arrive uninvited in the front yards of indigenous peoples and expect them to submit themselves as objects for scientific investigation. The researchers assume superior knowledge and a kind of divine right—indeed, obligation—to understand these others.

Very recently certain anthropologists have exhibited greater sensitivity to their research "subjects." But even if culturally disruptive "trade goods"—gifts to elicit information from informants—are discontinued, the very act of studying and objectifying cultures is alienating for them (and probably, ultimately, alienating also for the Westerners doing the studying). However, given the ever-encroaching commercial interests of North Atlantic culture, there is little even the best intentioned anthropologists can do to protect indigenous peoples.

Across academia, it is assumed that all issues are questions that we can formulate in some specialized vocabulary or other, and that the only responsible way to get "the big picture" is to add up the results from each field. But the summing somehow never takes place. The possibility of other questions, perhaps better questions, is concealed, and the concealment concealed.

When this kind of presumption reigns in the field of *philosophy*, the results are particularly fatuous and absurd. A kind of scientism pervades the most seemingly various philosophical coteries. This is the view (unsupportable by science) that only science can know, or some conceptual activities somehow associated with science or appearing sharp and precise and "scientific" (see Wilshire, 1998). But science at any time cannot even know that it is asking all the right questions. And when it presumes hegemony, it just assumes that art, religion, "literary" history, common sense, and everyday intuition cannot know essential aspects of reality. This is fanaticism and dogmatism every bit as rank and brash as any religious organization ever exhibited, and, indeed, without the religion's cover story about the ultimate mystery of things.

Professional philosophers today commonly assume that logical positivism, with its uncritical reliance upon the science of the day, is dead. This is self-congratulatory delusion, the fruit of a scientistic faith in progress. For example, the positivistic opposition between the emotive and the cognitive informs at a subterranean level much of the crossover work of philosophers and cognitive scientists. Take Steven Pinker's (1997) *How the Mind Works*. He advances interesting ideas about understanding the human mind in terms of "reverse engineering": We see that adaptations to environments have been achieved, and define our task as explaining the means by which these have come about. And certain computer models of information processing are provided that have some value.

But Pinker finds music making—universal and fundamental in all cultures—to be anomalous (see Pinker, 1997, pp. 534–537). I believe music is a primal adaptation. When normal body-selves respond to the "outer" environment, or take initiatives with respect to it, the body resounds fittingly within itself. Music is feed-out-feed-back that conducts, confirms, orients body-self, and underwrites its identity through time. It has done this from time immemorial. Pinker's dualistic talk about "the mind" renders him incapable of grasping how music is primarily adaptive, a motor of evolution: He generates a pseudoproblem of identity. As thinkers, we

are not left fully engaged with our bodies, not fully engaged with our capacities for ecstatic life. This furthers contemporary alienation and disinte-
gration of identity. How ironical for an evolutionary approach to self! Despite some interesting science, the overall effect of Pinker's work is scientism.

What this means is that there must be something basically wrong or
missing in his view. James (1899/1958) could have told him what it is:
"To miss the joy is to miss all" (p. 155). Pinker's work exhibits the "haunt-
ing unreality of 'realistic' books." The "fusion of reality and ideal novelty"
excites and empowers us, and does so because we are organisms that, to
be vital, must celebrate our being. On this level we are not all that different from chimpanzees who feel a storm coming on, resonate to it, and do
their marvelous rain dance in which, apparently, they celebrate the bare
fact of just being in a universe of such power.

The rhythms, melodies, harmonies, phrasings of our music are part and
parcel of this celebration of bodily and personal being. Only thinkers lost in
scientism and the information business could fail to see it, or glimpsing it,
find it anomalous. They have read too much in *Mind* perhaps and not lived
enough in mindful and grateful celebration of life. Dostoevsky defined the
modern human as "the ungrateful animal," and Heidegger tried to cultivate *denken als danken*, thinking as thanking. But they no more than James
are "mainstream philosophers" today. What passes as education is not the
educing (*educare*) of our needs, yearnings, and questionings as beings who
must develop ourselves or rot in boredom—or spin out of orbit in eccentric-
ity. But it is rather instruction in data and the methods for amassing more:
instruction, *instruere*, structuring-into. Such has a place, of course, but without a vital sense of the organic whole, we do not know what that place is.

Or take the old positivist cut dividing "doing philosophy" and "doing
the history of philosophy." The latter has a place within "scientific" philosophy, for it is construed as the scientific study of the past: scholarly antiquari-
anism with its apparatus of relevant languages and literature searches, and
so on. This cut is still commonly made, and historians in the field of philosophy stand firm for the degree of respectability still possible for them.

For William James this division is artificial and stultifying. All meaning and truth are a species of goodness, and this is the "fruitful building
out" of the past into the present and future. Meaning making and truth
are essential features of being vitally alive and centered, of fully being, and
philosophy is meant to nurture and feed us ecstatic body-minds.

———————

Professionalized philosophy has done exactly what James said it would
do in 1903: It distends and dissociates us from our moral and psychical
centers as persons. Endless ill-formed and fruitless debates, for example,

over "determinism or freedom," have sapped human energies and burdened library shelves. James responds to the existential crisis that is upon us. If we would grasp the question of freedom—as many of our undergraduates want us and need us to do, afflicted as they frequently are with addictions and despair—it cannot be within some concocted framework that passes as scientific detachment and objectivity. That way we have already gone out of touch with our immediate experience of ourselves. We must pose the question in a way that does not beg it against freedom. In his *Talks to Teachers* ("The Will"), he argues in the fitting way: Logically and scientifically speaking—really scientifically speaking—to *wait* for evidence for *freedom* is nonsensical. *If* we are free, the first act of freedom should be freely to believe in free will!

This is the heart of what Ralph Barton Perry (1938/1979) happily meant in his title, *In the Spirit of William James*. It's thinking charged with the spirit of adventure that refuses to be trapped in isms or in hypostatized abstractions or noun phrases like "the mind." That refuses to get caught in a verbalism like "the mind turning in upon itself." That escapes the self-deception of an act of reflection and analysis unaware of itself that mistakes its artifacts for "building blocks of knowledge and life." I mean putative "sense data," images, sensations that act like a screen or veil that divides us from the world that formed us over millions of years.

James's (1912) notion of pure or neutral experience is no mere academic-intellectual exercise but a vital stage of learning, knowing, and being—education. In locating a level of experience antedating, and more fundamental than, the very distinctions between self and other, subject and object, mind and matter, James is opening a way for those of European origin to rejoin the rest of the human race—and to do so without jettisoning (assuming we could) the actual glories of actual science and marvelous technology.

I mean his pure experience or direct realism (Hilary Putnam's phrase) reintroduces us to the oldest forms of religious and healing orientation within the world. Take creatures steeped in regenerative appearance and power, say, snakes or bears or eagles. James is saying the *numerically identical creature* that walks, slithers, or flies right there also figures directly in the careers of each of us knowing and feeling beings, particularly if we are open to it—if we have placed faith and trust in the healing powers of the universe that formed us.

Education today must be ecological. This is not because it is fashionable to be this, but because it is physically and spiritually necessary for our lives. In 1998 a marvelous book appeared. Edited and introduced by

Frederique Apffel-Marglin, it is titled *The Spirit of Regeneration: Andean Culture Confronting Western Notions of Development*. It offers articles by Peruvian intellectuals who are returning to their Andean roots after discovering the limitations—or worse—of Western notions of development: sweeping formulas of agribusiness and international trade that ride roughshod over the local knowledge of growing, nurturing, and living that has funded itself over 10,000 years in the Andes. There is a web of life, of concrete coherence, in which everything converses with and nourishes everything else: greatly various gods, goddesses, animals, climatic regions and altitudes, seasons, stars, the sun and moon—or the color, taste, texture of soils and the 2000 plus species of potato that the people nourish and that nourish the people and that outnumber the pestilences or climatic anomalies that might strike any particular species. Talk of Clifford Geertz's (1983) *Local Knowledge*! These Peruvian intellectuals are deprofessionalizing themselves.

I am inspired by this. Along with Ivan Illich, for another example, I think we must both deprofessionalize and deschool ourselves if we would break out of a mindless secular catechism.

Before making any proposals for restructuring the university, we should be sure that the heart of James's vision is securely in place. Otherwise, the status quo perpetuates itself furtively, that is, the managing mania, what Mary Daly calls methodolatry. James's is the vision of human life as freedom, of human life as ecstatic.

In that impossible book which somehow did get written, *Varieties of Religious Experience*, James (1902/1985) wonders what we contact in religious or mystical experience. He thinks that on its "hither side" it is our own subconscious minds (whatever that means exactly). On its "farther side"? He can only say that it is "the more." That is all that can be honestly described. To attempt to follow the flow of our feeling into this "more," into its depths and shadowy surroundings, is to be free. It cannot be followed in our everyday mode of awareness for it does not present itself as an action-oriented movement. It is a kind of abandonment, a way of being, and a "choice" that would encompass all choice.

James's student, William Ernest Hocking, asserted that the original sin is the failure of awareness. The language is not too strong. The failure of awareness cannot be attacked by individuals, no matter how sharp and sincere and responsible they might be. A lack of awareness cannot be remedied on command: When awareness is lacking, we cannot know just what is missing, just what must be achieved by just what means and struggles.

We face the essential finitude of human being—how we conceal the fact of concealment itself, and how we typically overlook the very possibility of our self-deceptions and our lacks.

Like Socrates, James stings us into wakefulness with respect to our lacks and our mind games. He italicizes situations in which we cannot escape choice, in which opportunities will never come again, and in which not to choose is to choose. The ultimate forced option is, will we choose to wake up? But, again, it is not a choice to achieve an end by such and such means. It must be a kind of strange choice to be trusting and vulnerable, to be open to the unexpectable, to be open to the inarticulable nothingness of nonbeing that is possible for us at any moment, to be open to death. Only thus can we be open to fuller awareness and to life.

James suggests that we exist in profound self-deception, and without a sense of this, all talk of education is "syllabub, flattery, and spongecake," as he says somewhere. The world is meaningful, his philosophy of pure experience teaches us, because it is experienceable in various ways. But as meaningful, as experienced and experienceable by me, the world has always had me in it! How can I *not* be?

The good teacher and learner is always prodding us out of this deadening self-deception, this dribbling out and wasting of our lives. The prodding cannot be direct, for then we, the prodded, raise our defenses and fearfully block the dilation of consciousness into "the more." "The more" holds the dim and dreaded real possibility (focal at some moments) that we are incredibly fragile and ephemeral, existing for a few moments within the vast ongoing universe that spawned us, generation after generation, over millions of years—existing for a few moments and then gone.

James (1899/1958) sidles up beside us and nudges us toward awareness. His "On a Certain Blindness in Human Beings" is mainly stories—by R. L. Stephenson, W. H. Hudson, Walt Whitman, and others. As if only stories, not our desiccating Cartesian epistemologies, could put us in touch with what most needs to be known, ourselves. But in his own gnomic—better, shamanic—voice, James (1899/1958) sometimes meets us:

> When your ordinary Brooklynite or New Yorker, leading a life replete with too much luxury, or tired and careworn about his personal affairs, crosses the ferry or goes up Broadway, his fancy does not "soar away into the sunset" as did Whitman's, nor does he inwardly realize at all the indisputable fact that this world never did anywhere or at any time contain more of essential divinity, or of eternal meaning, than is embodied in the field of vision over which his eyes so carelessly pass. There is life; and there, a step away, is death. (pp. 162–163)

To acknowledge death, to acknowledge it in one's body, is to be freed to the preciousness of each moment of life. If we are aware, just to be is joyous. "For to miss the joy is to miss all. In the joy of the actors lies the sense of any action" (op. cit.). James draws from Stephenson: "His life from without may seem but a rude mound of mud: there will be some golden chamber at the heart of it, in which he dwells delighted (p. 155)."

Any proposals to reorganize the university not predicated on the principle that "to miss the joy is to miss all" perpetuate "the iron cage of bureaucracy," business as usual: finding tenure track jobs for bright young Ph.D. students, the unreeling of technical expertise to lure approval from authorities in the professional association, all the ephemeral pleasures of the engineering mentality that has lost touch with poetical and musical sensibility and real, troubling, human concerns.

Professional attitudes are incarnated in, and controlled by, national academic associations, for example, the American Philosophical Association. It is a rigid pecking order that controls nearly all the prestigious jobs (in an ever-shrinking pool) and nearly all grant money, because referees for all occasions are picked from the top of the hierarchy. Those outside it are invisible. It is not too much to say they are untouchable. Each academic field, from English to physics, has its own professional association and is pretty well defined by it.

The academic world is segmented into bureaus. This stifles creativity, even minimal general education. A graduate student properly professionalized in philosophy, say, will tend nearly always to miss the philosophical content in both the literary and scientific domains (although given the ruling "analytic" philosophy, which fancies itself to be scientific, there is slightly less chance of missing philosophical content and issues in the sciences).

It is hard for generally informed citizens to believe, but it is true: Figures whom they themselves may recognize to be philosophers may not be recognized to be such by the best and the brightest Ph.D. products of the best and the brightest philosophy departments. I mean household names like R. W. Emerson and even William James, not to mention "merely literary" figures such as Dostoevsky or Tolstoy or Melville, or "religious figures" like Kierkegaard, or "sociologists" such as Max Weber. Preening, shameless, unabashed parochialism parading as clarity, science, and enlightenment presents a nearly incredible spectacle. Everyone suffers, most obviously students who hunger and thirst after ecstatic connectedness and the creation of meaning. Dominant analytic philosophers betray the trust that the public places in them.

"To miss the joy is to miss all." By joy, I mean specifically the moral-ecstatic energy of the creation of meaning across received boundaries. To leave out of account this missing joy as one tries to reconstruct the university is to be caught up in flailings and fumblings and exhaustions that miss the central point, the heart of education itself: the creative elic-iting and forming of self. It is idolatry shrouded in good intentions—methodolatry.

We should not proceed further without mentioning a cautionary his-torical fact. When the American Philosophical Association was being or-ganized in 1901, an invitation to join (and probably to be elected presi-dent) was issued to James. He replied that he expected little to come from professionalizing what should be the patient conversation between trusted friends and colleagues. "Count me out," he replied curtly. Very soon, how-ever, two younger philosophers—John Dewey and Josiah Royce—were elected president. James promptly changed his mind about joining, and was elected president.

Well, well, what does this prove? What we should know and remem-ber all along: human all too human. There is no underestimating human vanity, or the fear of being unrecognized and erased and deprived of power to resist a world in which we dimly but really apprehend ourselves to exist precariously every moment. Not even a famous Harvard professor from a famous family is immune. James was particularly prone to jealousy re-garding accomplished younger men, as his ambivalent attitude toward his brother, the novelist and dramatist Henry Jr., amply attests. I think this is more than gossip. Consult Leon Edel's (1976) biography of Henry. A strand through three volumes traces the brothers' relationship.

————————

I will sketch some steps we might take to reorganize the university to bring it closer to what the public thinks it is already, an educational insti-tution. Each step presupposes a new attitude toward the university. The birthright of all humans should be the opportunity to develop each's ca-pacities to the utmost, to experience the joy of having these capacities touched, educed, and drawn out (*educare*). Just by virtue of being human, everyone has a stake in the university, an idea beautifully elaborated in Henry Rosovsky's (1991) *The University: An Owner's Manual*. From the most frightened freshman to the most exalted dean, everyone's voice must con-tribute to the drama of what we are to make of ourselves.

Once the first seeds of a new attitude and its new expectations sprout, perhaps the first "structural" move should be to eliminate the philosophy department. All fields, pursued to their conceptual foundations, involve philosophical assumptions and commitments, however implicit. This was the original rationale for the Doctor of Philosophy degree itself: Anyone who does any creative work in the foundations of any received discipline should receive the ultimate recognition of intellectual distinction. And in fact, some of the most important intellectual work in recent centuries has been done by people who would not be employed in philosophy departments: Darwin, Freud, Jung, Einstein, Bohr, Pauli, Heisenberg, Mann, and Borges, for example. And, especially more recently, a group of women has emerged, including Elizabeth Cady Stanton, Jane Ellen Harrison, Willa Cather, Marija Gimbutas, Julia Kristeva, Luce Irigary, Toni Morrison, and Leslie Marmon Silko.

To eliminate philosophy departments would not entail dismissing the members of the department. They should be left free to associate themselves with whatever departments are closest to their interests and accomplishments, and they would, presumably, associate themselves with members whose interests are closest to theirs.

I also suggest that each member of the university, tenured and untenured, be required to deliver a presentation every 5 years to the intellectual community of the university at large. Inevitably, in speaking across departmental lines, thinkers would dwell on assumptions and issues relevant to all fields, that is, on philosophical matters.

In the end, we should proceed to a completely decompartmentalized and deprofessionalized university with all deliberate speed. That is, to a *university* that lives up to the literal meaning of the name: that which has a center and turns around it—the creation of meaning, the discovery and husbanding of truth, and the development of persons. All that would remain would be a very few general fields, defined in greatly overlapping terms, and headed by universal minds who appear now and again in the strangest places. Consider Isaiah Berlin, Albert Einstein, James Conant, E. O. Wilson, Susanne Langer, or William James himself.

The present situation has reduced itself to absurdity. Yes, there is overlap between philosophy departments and cognitive science departments, say. But this itself is eccentric and produces grossly incomplete views of "mind," such as Steven Pinker's. Beyond this is the patently absurd: Fairly recently the Leiter Report appeared, ranking analytic philosophy departments. In itself it might be considered trivial, the work of a recent Ph.D. from Michigan State, a one-man gang, so to say. But nothing exists merely in itself, the Leiter Report has had considerable impact—given the vanity and fear of human beings—and it is symptomatic of a larger reality, laughable though some might think it. Each year it ranks departments contending for the top spots. In detailed footnotes, the analytic "stars" are tracked from school to school as they fly to ever-brighter lights, or as rumors circulate that they might be contemplating a move. Or, perhaps they might not move, as a spouse might not be moveable, or they might retire, and so forth. The report reminds one of gossip columnists peddling news of Hollywood stars, or of how the moves, pranks, and peccadilloes of royalty were watched intensely and reported at the turn of the century—and still are. A frothy article by Christopher Shea (1999) details the controversy that has finally arisen over the report. My opinion of the report is rendered exactly by Shea: "A fatuous piece of bullshit."

The report includes the judgment that the best training in nonanalytic approaches to philosophy (so-called Continental thought) is, nevertheless, obtained in the best analytic departments. Nonanalytic approaches are lumped under the heading "Continental." This apparently exhaustive set of alternatives completely occludes the whole tradition of American philosophy—a third alternative. Fatuous in the extreme, the report has had impact. Nothing better indicates, I think, the lack of confidence in one's own judgment, particularly analytic philosophers' lack of centeredness in their own situated, bodily and feelingful existence, and, concomitantly, their inability to ground their evaluations in intellectual history.

But it is not only their failure but also that of university personnel in positions of power. How can deans, for example, allocating funds and professorial positions to their colleges, and themselves trained in the "best" multiversities today, be expected to know what is happening in the various professional-academic "worlds"? Evaluations, however, must be made, and they will be—within whatever flimsy and fatuous frameworks for ranking are available, and however incredibly short is the time given them to evaluate.

The slightest knowledge of intellectual history, and the barest confidence in one's own judgment, shows that the most creative advances in knowledge and appreciation occur not in "mainstream" departments but in the foggy overlap areas between disciplines, or in areas that have not yet been mapped out and given a name, but in which individuals exercise their intuition, invention, perseverance.

It is time that the iron cage of academic bureaucracy be dismantled. The progress of knowledge itself requires it. Even more obviously, students' hunger for meaning, and the whole society's call for integration and council, are too urgent to allow dawdling. Emerson (1982) prophesied this would be increasingly the case,

> The state of society is one in which the members have suffered amputation from the trunk, and strut about so many walking monsters—a good finger, a neck, stomach, an elbow, but never a man. (p. 84)

William James is closer to us than is Emerson. It is his warnings—as a man of science, of common sense, and of wide and humane learning—that we should most directly heed.

———————

I have written centrally about the degeneration of academic philosophy in the university. But this is a bell-wether discipline: Mandarinism and vitiation here reflect hyperspecialization, frivolousness, and flaccidness across the culture. A necessary condition for recovery is to place as much stress on rebuilding education and educators as was placed on rebuilding Japan and Germany after World War II, or now on spending billions to bail out nations that have collapsed economically. We should send a vast Peace Corps into the public schools, reward persons with compassionate hearts and good minds and the toughness of Green Berets, and give master teachers their economic and social due. We should pay the tired, weary, and demoralized—tired, weary, and demoralized for good reason—to retire early. The present situation is an insult to us all.

I agree with Jim Garrison:

> What I found in education was a world of wonderfully dedicated kindergarten through twelfth grade teachers controlled by bureaucracy, downtrodden by dead but dominant versions of technocratically applied positivism, . . . and scape-goated for their efforts in ameliorating social ills.[2]

———————

The notion of "social ills" should be unpacked. Both William James and John Dewey knew that science and technology must inevitably develop, but that there was much more required for a fulfilled life than they could supply. Despite all our interventions, inventions, conventions we still belong to Nature. Despite all our clever turnings of attention and employment of technological "fixes," the vast matrix of our lives is involuntary. As things are going, the mal-coordination of the voluntary and the involuntary only increases.

In their somewhat different styles, both James and Dewey see that for thought to be effective it must be both pragmatic and primal. The tragic feature of Dewey's thought is that he knew that modern life had introduced dissociations on the subconscious level of minding, but his deployment of critical thought penetrates to this level only sporadically. Art can do some important knitting together here, Dewey saw. Bodywork of the Alexander variety, say, can do some more. But Dewey could not supply a wholly viable alternative to ages-old myth and ritual, could not suture together science, technology, and "individual fate lore," could not reintegrate Father Sky and Mother Earth, as Black Elk would have put it.[3] Dewey (1891/1969) quotes Mathew Arnold on contemporary persons as

> Wandering between two worlds, one dead,
> The other powerless to be born. (p. 114)

Perhaps the old world is not as dead as Dewey and Arnold thought, and perhaps the Socratic job of midwifery to the new world that Dewey calls for should take this question into consideration.

James's tragedy is several-faceted. He saw that belief—indeed, belief beyond presently available evidence, over-belief—is essential for a sound and coherent life. But he himself had great difficulty believing. It took a tremendous effort of will to sustain himself in "the strenuous life," particularly as his life ebbed out of him in sickness and advancing age. Some of us understand this only too well.

A reader of this essay complained that it "goes way beyond what is supported by James." Since some—who probably are not well acquainted with James—might agree, I will add a few final words.

No. I imagine that if James could see what has happened to "education" at the end of this century, he would denounce it more eloquently and damningly than I ever could. This is how he responded in 1901 to the invitation to join the fledgling American Philosophical Association:

> I don't foresee much good from a philosophical society. Philosophy discussion proper only succeeds between intimates who have learned how to converse by months of weary trial and failure. The philosopher is a beast dwelling in his individual burrow. Count me *out*. (Cited in Wilshire, 1990, pp. 106–107)

True, as I've noted, James joined the American Philosophical Association and was elected president in 1905. But his better self is evident in his initial refusal. He knew from long experience with the likes of Charles Peirce and Josiah Royce that philosophers best converse with intimates through months of weary trial and failure. This is so because we grope for meaning, and we must be able to trust others to patiently show where we are going wrong and to help us to go right. How would James react to the greatly impersonal and rushed atmosphere of philosophy today? I think he would be appalled.

There is a profound difficulty here for professionalized thought of all kinds. Professionalization sets up a vast machinery of evaluation of submitted work. It seems self-evident today that work should be "blind reviewed," and by more than one person.

But probably not everyone judged to be competent will detect very creative work the first time through it. Probably two or three readers will not give it a "publish" (for most editors of the "best" publications it seems obvious that one black ball in the urn is like a profaning fly in the ointment—"we publish only the best!").

Built into most of our academic institutions today is an ever more stupefying conservatism. It was evident to Emerson (1982) before James was born. In *The American Scholar*, he wrote:

> [The scholar] must relinquish display and immediate fame [and in creating and discovering endure] the self-accusation . . . the frequent uncertainty and loss of time . . . the state of virtual hostility in which he seems to stand to society, especially to educated society. (pp. 95–96)

To use a distinction made famous by Thomas Kuhn, academia on all levels tends to reward competent but conventional thought and tends to discourage revolutionary thought—what we desperately need to survive as individuals and as a species.

All this is hard to stomach for academics who, for the most part, have been rewarded for competent but conventional work. But if we want change, we will have to bite the bullet, maybe swallow it. I will close with the most notorious case of discrimination against regenerative and revolutionary thought I know of: the persecution and exclusion of C. S. Peirce, probably the most brilliant mind (along with Jefferson) that the United States has produced. Good biographies have finally appeared to the point at which only a few of the most salient facts need be recounted: the vengeful pursuit of Peirce over 40 years by the president of Harvard, Charles Eliot, his betrayal by the now nearly forgotten astronomer Simon Newcomb (who, among other things, scuttled Peirce's application for a desperately needed Smithsonian fellowship), his dismissal as assistant professor at Johns Hopkins on vague grounds of impropriety.

I conclude with lines from the obituary of Peirce by Joseph Jastrow, ninth president of the American Psychological Association:

> It cannot but remain a sad reflection upon the organization of our academic interest that we find it difficult, or make it so, to provide places for exceptional men within the academic fold. Politically as educationally, we prefer the safe men to the brilliant men, and exact a versatile mediocrity of qualities that make the individual organizable. . . . Certainly it remains true for all times that no more effective stimulus to promising young minds can be found than to give them the opportunity of contact with master minds in action. The service that a small group of such men can perform is too fine, too imponderable, to be measured; and likewise too intangible to impress its

value upon the judgment of those with whom these issues commonly lie. (Cited in K. L. Ketner, 1998, p. 29)

Most educational institutions today focus on organizing the individual. Standardized tests typify this: They lend an aura of objectivity and reliability to cloak a profound anxiety about what's truly important for knowers to know and to be. The discipline that should epitomize unfettered and unabashed mind—philosophy—has become self-absorbed (just what James and Max Weber said would happen): inhibited, crabbed, and professionalized practically beyond belief. "Analytic philosophers" in "the best" institutions shut themselves off from the history of philosophy (even in the West), also from profoundly philosophical ecological and educational debates raging around us currently. They shut themselves up in self-congratulatory coteries that convince themselves that they can decisively rank individuals and departments. The musty smell is plain to everyone except the occupants of the closets. Never before has William James's thought and example been more needed. His work throws open windows and doors. We see where we are truly at home: in the unknown.

NOTES

1. These quotations from Kierkegaard, Nietzsche, and Dostoevsky are respectively from *Journals*, "Schopenhauer as Educator" (*Untimely Meditations*), *Crime and Punishment*, and, of course, *The Underground Man*. I trust that the reader will pardon me for failing to be scrupulous in annotation, here and below—particularly in an article with this bent!

2. Personal communication.

3. See Dewey's *The Problems of Men* (1946a, 1946b, 1946c), especially the articles on William James (where Dewey uses the phrase "individual fate lore") and the Introduction. The Introduction to *The Problems of Men* is found in the critical edition; see John Dewey (1946/1989), pp. 154ff. Dewey contrasts "the secular" to "the theological" and "the supernatural." But there is a meaning of "religion" that falls into neither camp, and it is just this meaning that is relevant for understanding the Native American, Black Elk, as well as Thoreau, Emerson, and James. See Dewey (1937/1987). I thank John McDermott for help in finding my way in the critical editions of James and Dewey.

CHAPTER 4

Pluralism and Professional Practice: William James and Our Era

Ron Podeschi

THERE ARE PARALLELS between the first decade of the 20th cen-tury,when James was completing his life's work before his death in 1910, and the new century that is now being launched. Of striking significance in both eras are dramatic changes in technology with their powerful consequences in the worlds of work and education. We are now in the midst of globalization through communication revolutions, instead of the earlier burgeoning of U.S. industrialization through transportation breakthroughs. Nonetheless we still have the same problem that William James confronted: *how to enhance creative individuality in the face of societal forces that push us toward narrow standardization and mechanical objectivity.* This problem now hits home for us in education with a brand of pro-fessionalization that pushes for technical expertise and methodological consensus, threatening a pluralism of ideas and ideals.

The connection between this problem of epistemological parochialism and James's philosophical importance grew for me in the 1970s when pro-fessional attention turned to behavioral objectives, computerized test scores, and statistical analyses (Podeschi, 1976). In the 1960s and 1970s, as Porter (1995) explains, the massive influx of quantitative criteria for public deci-sions was not only a response to the political ethos, it also reflected the sta-tistical paradigm employed in force by the "weaker" disciplines such as the social sciences and education. By the 1980s school reform movement, some of us were calling for teacher education to be unchained from the narrow set of assumptions underlying the so-called knowledge base (e.g., defining "teaching" by achievement test scores)—assumptions that escalate parochialism and debase pluralism (e.g., Podeschi, 1987).

At present, such mechanical objectivity inside educational institutions continues to be perpetuated as pressures mount from the outside. Instead of concern with the philosophical implications of professional practice, there is a preoccupation with rules and calculation as "a defense against meddlesome outsiders and a strategy for controlling far-flung or untrustworthy subordinates" (Porter, 1995, p. 194). In response to this current syndrome, some critics dismiss the whole idea of professional communities as oppressive. To me, such a response is too simplistic. In this chapter, through exploring James's philosophy, I shall probe a question that needs attention in contemporary professional life: *why, and how to, enhance pluralism while at the same time maintaining viable professional communities?*

TENSIONS IN "THE JUNGLE OF EXPERIENCE"

James understood that there are inevitable tensions in reaching for both the ideals of community and the ideals of pluralism. Instead of depending upon abstract dichotomies, he faced the inevitability of making difficult moral decisions in what he called "the jungle of experience" with all its complexity and ambiguity.

If James were here in our era, he would be wary of current discourse in education that files "community" away as an "oppressive modernist construction," and at the same time he would be rejecting those prevailing notions of "community" that overweight consensus and stability (Abowitz, 1997). In addition, while rejecting universal notions of the individual as unchanging, James would also be rejecting simplistic characterizations when analyzing pluralism. He now would be emphasizing the contextual fluidity of individual experience, not overgeneralizing about cultural differences.

In spite of seeing existential tensions in "the jungle of experience," James did have a tempered optimism for human possibilities. However, Jamesian faith in the possibility of progress was always moderated by the complex realities of human experience. In this regard, Gale (1999) contends that

> The best way to characterize the philosophy of William James is to say it is deeply rooted in the blues. It is the soulful expression of someone who has "paid his dues," someone who, like old wagon wheels, has been through it all. . . . James is very much in the Nietzschean and Wittgensteinian mold. . . .

> The deep difference between James and Dewey is that Dewey couldn't sing
> the blues if his life depended on it. (p. 1)

Although not singing the blues in this chapter, I shall be pointing to
tensions and dilemmas in professional practice that reflect my own experiences in recent decades. Also reflected in my analysis will be my own
presuppositions. As James well knew, each of us has our own place to
stand—whether as practicing educator or interpreter of William James.

As a doctoral student in the early 1960s, I studied European continental
philosophy (e.g., Merleau-Ponty) and its parallels to James as an existential phenomenologist. Later in that turbulent decade, after my first years
of work at a small college and increasingly facing ongoing dilemmas in
institutional life, I found myself growing closer to James as an existential
pragmatist. At one point, while standing up for two colleagues being fired
for anti–Vietnam War activities, I resigned in protest. College administra-
tors, calling for "community stability," had pushed any pluralism of ideas
and ideals into a danger zone. During that time of turmoil, James reminded
me that faith in rational processes has its limits in "the jungle of experience." There is a time to take a stand rather than carrying on any more
discussion. James remained close to me as I then made my way in a large
state university. Through early experiences there, a quote from an 1899
letter of his became a fixture on my office wall.

> I am against bigness and greatness in all their forms, and for the invisible
> molecular moral forces that work from individual to individual, stealing in
> through the crannies of the world like so many soft rootlets, or like the cap-
> illary oozing of water, and rendering the hardest monuments of man's pride,
> if you give them time. (See Cotkin, 1990, pp. 174–175)

COMMUNITY, TRADITION, AND OPENNESS

What best suited James's personality, philosophy, and politics in his era,
as Cotkin (1990) points out, was a stance against "bigness—whether in
military might, philosophical systems, scientific certitude or government
bureaucracies" (p. 174). This stance was rooted in James's belief in an idea
of community inherently tied to valuing tradition. For him, the integration between community and tradition was the way to counteract the
negative effects of societal changes. Individual freedom needs the support
of community with roots in traditions in order to guard the *will* of the
individual against domination by large organizations—and especially by
large-scale technology that can "chain the individual to the iron of abstrac-
tion" (p. 174).

James's idea of tradition is the kind of perspective that is seen in Dewey: historical truths tested through time and experience. However, James brings the idea into a deeper level of subjective reality than Dewey, into a deeper level of *feeling*: the bare impressions as they are lived in concrete experience. In this immediacy of life, there is *prereflective* meaning for the individual (Gale, 1999).

The lack of respect for the subjective realities of others was the underlying reason that James fought so hard against what he saw as U.S. imperialism in the Philippines. And for him, there was a positive by-product to the pragmatic truth of respect: Those who respect others' subjective realities are then opened to new influences, new possibilities. According to Cotkin (1990), "James saw openness to diversity and acceptance of individualism as the American birthmarks of this natural ideal of community and tradition" (p. 167). (I want to replace "individualism" with "individuality" in this characterization, and will posit later a distinction between these two terms, a distinction important to understanding James's philosophy.)

James's emphasis on diversity is rooted in both philosophical description and prescription. His bedrock of "radical empiricism"—which posits that even the tying together of individual experiences is itself a subjective experience—*describes* pluralism as the permanent form of the world. His epistemology inherently follows, as he posits in *Talks to Teachers* (1899/1958).

> The truth is too great for any one actual mind, even though that mind be dubbed "the Absolute," to know the whole of it. The facts and worths of life need many cognizers to take them in. There is no point of view absolutely public and universal. Private and incommunicable perceptions always remain over, and the worst of it is that those who look for them never know where. (p. 19)

At the same time, James was *prescribing* pluralism. As Putnam (1997) explains, "he legitimizes a plurality of world-views each of which balances in one way or another our needs for the explanatory and unifying power of classifications, for appreciation of the multiplicity of particulars in all their diversity, and for making sense of our practical impulses" (p. 283). James did believe that if we are genuinely aware that our knowledge is limited, we shall value diversity and be prepared to learn from others— even open to having our own point of view changed.

James now would even appreciate the diversity of current interpretations of his work. He might even appreciate the irony of the annotated bibliography of publications about his work and the field of psychology that includes a section entitled, "Psychologists' Rejection of James as a Psychologist" (Taylor, 1996). However, James would be concerned with the polarizing labels applied to him at times, for example, opposing labels as "the exemplar of the modern spirit" and "the postmodernist in absentia" (Cotkin, 1990, p. 2).

MODERNISM, POSTMODERNISM, AND OTHER DICHOTOMIES

James would reject today's simplistic dichotomy created between an optimistic "modernism" with emphasis on objectivity *and* a skeptical "postmodernism" with emphasis on subjectivity. Rather than seeing James either as a modernist or a postmodernist, I place James on a continuum, utilizing Rosenau's (1992) distinction between "skeptical postmodernists" and "affirmative postmodernists." And I classify James as an "affirmative postmodernist" with emphases on indeterminacy, diversity, and complexity.

James (as postmodernists do) questioned rigid boundaries between science and humanities, theory and fiction, reality and image. He viewed social science as process oriented, and as involving compromises and inconsistency. Personal experience, emotions, even the mystical were on the table for exploration.

At the same time, the tendencies of "skeptical postmodernists" point to what James did *not* do: reject theory and theoretical perspectives; believe in the play of words more than concepts of truth and reason; resist concepts of self-identity, free will, personal responsibility, and moral judgment; and see fragmentation and meaninglessness in human life.

On the other hand, certain characteristics of "affirmative postmodernists" fit James well: valuing of descriptive social science that enhances reason; viewing of truth as personal and community-specific, but not arbitrary; and confronting problems by making normative choices rather than retreating into nihilism.

Objectivity and Subjectivity

For James, there is not a dichotomy between "feeling" subjectivity and "rational" objectivity. Indeed, he pointed to the need to integrate the two. Whereas abstract objectivity without direct "knowledge by acquaintance" is artificial, subjectivity dominated by feelings and without "knowledge about" becomes narrow and provincial (Wild, 1969, p. 70). James perceived inevitable tensions in living out the needed balance between these two dimensions of knowledge, and would now concur with Porter (1995) that objectivity reached through professional consensus can be a prerequisite for basic knowledge and justice, "but an excess of it crushes individual subjects, demeans minority cultures, devalues artistic creativity, and discredits genuine democratic participation" (p. 3).

James is "modern" in that he seeks recurring patterns in human life, and also in that his epistemology values rationality and evaluative criteria. On the other hand, as Seigfried (1990) points out, he was a critic of "the charade of scientific neutrality . . . sociological talk about general laws, statistical averages" (p. 113). In *The Principles of Psychology*, James agonizes over the eventual awareness that empirical psychology cannot escape from being metaphysical in the sense that underlying presuppositions are always there to be examined "even though they should be excluded by his own empirical program of research . . . such assumptions establish themselves in 'our very descriptions of the phenomenal facts' and cannot be left unquestioned" (Edie, 1970, p. 497). However, this kind of "postmodern" awareness never had him relinquish rational thought and objectivity. As Seigfried (1990) explains, it is the living acts of reasoning that leads to his "reconstruction of rationality— a pragmatic rationality. This knowledge is no chimera, but the experimental basis for the claims we make as to how we relate to the world" (p. 250).

In the current "science wars," he would side with the mediating position that Rorty (1999) takes: It is better to let go of both "objective reality" and "social reconstruction." Rorty, as James would, posits that useful work, in whatever field, does not need philosophical correctness or categorical certainty. Each side is seen as having strengths that should be modeled: The community of "objective" scientists is willing to listen to arguments, think through the issues, and to examine the evidence; the "social constructionists" point out that such analyses are framed by contextual assumptions, with many classifications about human beings (e.g., "race") being more harmful than not.

Optimism and Anguish

Putnam (1997) contends that James was a child of his times—when belief in social progress was even stronger in the United States than in our era. Although the naivete of American mainstream faith in individual as well as social progress is far from erased, it has received jolts during the 20th century. It should be pointed out, however, that James, living life on both sides of the Atlantic Ocean, rejected the belief that individual and collective pasts can be overcome by purely human initiative—a belief long viewed as naively American by European observers (Evans, 1976). His vision was never that of a romantic humanist who believes self-fulfilling personhood needs only release from institutional influences. Indeed, James's optimism was tempered even with tragic dimensions. For him, there is no escape from the human uncertainties of risk, sacrifice, and pain.

James in his times surely does not fit the superficial label given to him by authors of *Habits of the Heart* (Bellah, Madsen, Sullivan, Swidler, & Tipton, 1985), who characterize James as "only a sophisticated example of the widespread combination of popular psychology and vaguely spiritual religiosity that Americans from Mary Baker Eddy to Norman Vincent Peale have offered as the key to happiness and health" (p. 120). Ironically, James would agree with *Habits'* negative assessment of the current culture of bureaucratic individualism: a merger of *utilitarian individualism* with its prototype of the manager valuing technical efficiency and *expressive individualism* with its prototype of the therapist valuing personal fulfillment. He knew that such a culture would lead to a loss of personal commitment as well to a dichotomy between ethical ends and technical means. James also knew that it takes ethical courage to go upstream against the force of institutional currents such as mechanical objectivity.

THE SELF, AGENCY, AND AMBIGUITY

My framing James as an existential pragmatist, who sees tension rather than dichotomy, needs to extend to the question of his philosophy of "self." Any perspective concerning community and pluralism will inevitably need to confront assumptions underlying a concept of the individual. This is especially true of James, who carried core elements of "humanism," a label he used himself for his philosophy (Gale, 1999). Humanism, although varying through historical permutations, is characterized by four core elements: the idea of a self; a self capable of growth and virtuous action; a self that has responsibility for what one becomes; and a self that is responsible for social progress (Pearson & Podeschi, 1999).

James's humanistic ethics, which permeate the whole of his writings, highlight a striving *will* toward free and responsible action that leads to good consequences for others as well as for one's self. There is a unified continuity in the self that "involves a real belonging to a real Owner, to a pure spiritual entity of some kind" (James, 1890/1950, p. 337). A Jamesian concept of self within "the jungle of experience," however, is complex, and this complexity needs to be explored as a base for more fully understanding the perspectives being explored in this chapter.

The Fluidity of Our *Selves*

For James, as Edie (1970) explains, the "self" is just another object in the ongoing stream of consciousness of our individual worlds. Rather than a stable entity, this self as object is on the move, experienced differently as our contexts change. But experienced by whom? According to James, this "empirical me" is experienced by the "I"—a feeling of personal sameness, of an identity, of an "inner self."

This "I" actually experiences a diversity of "empirical me's." This diversity is found within, and between, categories that James (1890/1950) sees ranging from the "bodily," to the "social," to the "spiritual." Because of the many selves, the "I" is at times confronted by confusion and conflict. So there are dilemmas in choosing one's self, portrayed by James in his own dramatic style:

> Not that I would not, if I could, be both handsome and fat and well dressed, and a great athlete, and make a million a year, be a wit, a bon-vivant, and a lady-killer, as well as a philosopher; a philanthropist, statesman, warrior, and African explorer as well as a "tone-poet" and saint. But the thing is simply impossible. (p. 309)

Compared to this quote of James, your and my thoughts about our own conflicting selves would probably be more modest, and feel more real to us: for example, the conflict between our self as a professional and as a parent; or the conflict between our "academic" self and that of our "hometown" self—the one that comes to life when we return to the background contexts in which we grew up. Even within professional contexts, our "me's" might conflict with one another: for example, the theoretical self at the university and that "practical" self immersed in the day-to-day complexities of school or community life. Sarason (1996) gets to this implicitly when he concludes that the university critic who goes into schools is like a traveler going to foreign lands.

James (1890/1950) not only emphasized that the "me" is fluid, but that there is a distinction between the "actual" self and the "potential" self. He declared "the potential social self" as the most interesting because of its connection to our moral conduct. It is particularly interesting because of the persistent paradoxes present within our social settings. In any given situation, this "ideal self" finds itself competing with other possible "ideal selves" being influenced by other "social judges."

Moral Choice and Progress

Moral choice for James, with its possibility of progress, comes through the social contexts in which a real choice cannot be avoided—when there are potentially significant consequences (Barrett, 1978). Moral behavior, whether personal or professional, is characterized more than anything by the individual's long-range intentions—"his more imperative goods." What actually happens in the daily detail of life depends upon the strength of the ethical *intentionality* by us as individuals, not some generalized human nature (James, 1891/1971, 1896/1956). However, the "ideal self" that is carried within us during choice and action falls short within the social realities of our nonideal worlds. In "the jungle of experience," the individual faces vines of ambiguity and dilemma, sometimes inducing a need for clarity—sometimes even for prayer.

James (1891/1971) highlighted a distinction between "strenuous" and "easy-going" moods, pointing to potential tensions between intentions toward ethical ideals and ones that shrink from discomfort. The strenuous mood "needs the wilder passions to arouse it, the big fears, loves, and indignations; or else the deeply penetrating appeal of some one of the higher fidelities, like justice, truth, or freedom" (p. 306). He would now agree with MacIntyre (1981) that, whereas *external* goods (e.g., approval, status) tend to induce caution, goods *internal* to a professional community (e.g., equity, excellence) have a higher dimension that may well induce institutional risk for the individual. James (1891/1971) described it as "the contrast between the ethics of infinite and mysterious obligation from on high, and those of prudence and the satisfaction of merely finite need" (p. 307).

James saw human beings as having the potential to meet the high challenge of intrinsic values that are tied to traditions—a potential that can be tapped in order to gain the necessary independence from institutional conventions of extrinsic values. At the same time, he would have concurred with Lasch (1986) that there needs to be continual questioning of community traditions so that "community" does not become cover for conformity.

James and Individualism

In his era, James's view of self and agency did have its critics. For example, Santayana viewed him as having a "moralistic view of history," arguing that his traditions were only "a salad of illusions" (Cotkin, 1990, p. 167). And W. E. B. DuBois, who called James his favorite Harvard professor, concluded that he promoted a "New England ethic of life as a series of conscious moral judgments . . . [not seeing] that slavery was a matter of income more than morals" (Posnock, 1997, p. 328).

Nor is James's "moral individualism" without current critics. For example, James's stance against big organizations and large-scale solutions is seen not only as weak in historical analysis but as rooted in his self-imposed political impotence that induces a therapeutic moral critique (Posnock, 1997). And Cornell West views James's philosophy as one of those lacking involvement with down-to-earth political and social realities, "treating people simply as believers and language users with particular small problems to solve in a piecemeal way . . . [not] as objects or imposers of large scale domination" (see Cormier, 1997, p. 351).

James did have concerns about economic individualism, but he did not have the confidence in large-scale transformation that Dewey did, being skeptical of what he saw as utopian zest. In addition, James smelled paternalism in what he viewed as the tendency of such efforts to look at the downtrodden as soft and squeamish rather than as individuals with moral strength. Although he was aware of societal forces upon the individual, James's philosophy centers on individual efforts to resist these forces, not on structural analysis and change.

There are various characteristics in defining individualism (Pearson & Podeschi, 1999). James does not fall into the metaphysical domain of individualism in which the self exists apart from any social arrangement, that is, independent from society. Nor does he believe in an individualism in which the individual person and his or her rights and needs take precedence over all collectives, spanning all moral and political decision making. However, there is a territory of individualism that James is near: the characteristic of emphasizing individual intentions and acts.

Individuality and the Intentional Self

James's primary concept of the self should be seen as paralleling "individuality" more than "individualism." Individuality, not individualism, is the opposite of conformity and defines individuals not only by the uniqueness of their own development but also by how they are uniquely embedded in a particular social fabric. This concept of individuality flows in and out of James's philosophical heart. As Wild (1969) explains James, there is dynamism as well as ambiguity in the process of self-development. "The self that I am at present is not the same as I was yesterday, or a year ago. There is real diversity. . . . But there is also something more. It cannot be separated from the objects with which it is concerned, their fringes, and therefore, the whole world in which it lives" (pp. 102, 105). Individuality, then, is generated in the midst of the particulars of one's life-world, the site where the core self is in a continuing building process.

We need to remember that James's multiple "me's," while embedded in a multiplicity of "oughts," need integration by the "I." This "I," or "inner self—a field of consciousness fringed with subconscious possibilities—is the primer of an individuality played out within social worlds" (Seigfried, 1990, p. 362). For James, individuality and personal identity are more deeply rooted in *feelings* than in conceptual thought—"the darker, blinder strata of character" (Gale, 1999, p. 222). Even the spiritual self has an inner nucleus that is sparked by bodily feelings, bringing warmth and intimacy to our present action (Wild, 1969, p. 100).

For James, this inner subjective being is the active and emotional source of experience (Edie, 1970, p. 512). Although the consciousness of this "I" cannot be separated from its life-world, nor brought to full reflection, there is a *pre-reflective knowing* that allows for moral freedom. Knowing and willing are not separated. Attending to something is an act of volition as well as an act of knowing, since one's attention could be elsewhere (Edie, 1970, p. 521). As Wilshire (1971) emphasizes, "the secret of freedom is the secret of control of mental effort. . . . The self requires consciousness of self, and this consciousness requires conscience—a keeping of promises to oneself" (pp. xxvii, xxxiv).

The "Self" and Cultural Assumptions

Of course, assumptions underlying a concept of the self may be seen as *cultural* as well as *philosophical*. Although James understood that there are cultural influences on the social self, it is questionable whether he had much understanding how different cultures influence concepts such as "motivation" and "freedom." Some cultures, for example, emphasize individualization and autonomy. Other cultures conceptualize "motivation" and "freedom" more in terms of social embeddedness and dependency. The Jamesian view of the self may be thought of as an integration of both of these concepts.

Cultural influences also affect whether, and how, an "inner self" is perceived. Hoffman (1998) points out that the inner-person domain of the self is neglected in current educational discourse that focuses only on outside influences—a focus that overlooks the variety of cultural ways of defining the self. "Identity" can be more than a "product of resistance to dominant perspectives and values" (p. 330)—a statement with which James would have agreed. He perceived the "I" as a consciousness that has a certain freedom from one's social influences. In addition, he would have agreed with Hoffman's perspective that individual identities in any cultural context are not fixed but need to be seen as complex, sometimes contradictory, and frequently filled with tensions. Even the "potential" or "ideal" self is in dynamic fluidity between our "me's" and our "I."

It was James's understanding of the self as in process that leads him to the recognition of the crux of human fallibility: the limitations of individual knowing. Because of this recognition—although believing deeply in questioning the ideas of others—he had little tolerance for the intolerant. This does not mean, however, that James's own ideal self, personally or philosophically, was immune from societal influences. James surely did not have the benefit of our contemporary perspectives about the influences of race, class, and gender.

For example, Townsend (1996) argues that James was particularly blind to his own gendered self, one caught in the Harvard ethos of "ideal manhood." But in spite of seeing James as blind to his own class bias as well as to his gendered self, Townsend states that his great strength was in understanding the role of openness and empathy in recognizing limitations of the human self—including one's own limitations. For James, human relationships should include tolerance and respect of others' ideal selves—the assumptions that makes others' lives significant to them. And this process of openness then needs to include a willingness to bring new insights from others into play with our own ideal self.

Whatever the ideal self each of us carries into our own "jungle" of professional practice, vines of ambiguity and dilemma await us. We now turn to this context of work, seeking perspectives from actual experience as well as from Jamesian thought.

DYNAMICS AND DILEMMAS OF PROFESSIONAL PRACTICE

James's faith in progress in the daily detail of professional life is centered in the potential of inner selves rather than in institutional processes. If he were in the current culture of bureaucratic individualism, he might be saying what he did a century ago in "The Ph.D. Octopus": "The institutionalizing on a large scale of any natural combination of need and motive always tends to run into technicality and to develop a tyrannical Machine with unforeseen powers of exclusion and corruption" (James, 1903/1971, p. 344).

Resistance, Community, and Courage

For James, individuals put the ethical act into high gear when they are prepared to break institutional rules that have grown too narrow for the situation. When he expresses faith in "breaking rules" and in "forces stealing in through crannies of the world," he sounds like those postmodernists who see unpredictable opportunities for exploiting the complexity and contradictions of lived experience, even in the most oppressive institutions. These postmodernists view normalization in any social practice as having to rub against particular situations, and that "spaces" in the daily routines can be promising possibilities of agency. However, other postmodernists question the real impact of such individual action, pointing out that such "resistance" may actually play into participants' own oppression by creating an "illusion of freedom"—an illusion that only enmeshes them deeper into the workings of, and control by, dominant power (Schutz, 2000). From this latter perspective of diffuse power quietly muzzling efforts of those who resist, James would appear naïve.

Nevertheless, James would not now give up the possibility of a viable professional community, and would concur with MacIntyre (1981) that collective work leading to professional excellence is rooted in a shared background of traditions—even while the shared ideas and ideals need continuous questioning and debate. In addition, professional practice, while needing institutional standards and specialized skills, should be rooted in the depth of ethical selves that will withstand the corrupting power of institutions. This will take not only courage but also tolerance for ambiguity.

Dilemmas are inevitable for James. Because our ethical selves play out in nonideal worlds, there will be conflicts to face in institutional life. As an example, virtues required to keep the intrinsic goods alive in a professional community might get in the way of individuals' achieving extrinsic goods, such as status and promotion. And as Soltis (1987) emphasizes, such extrinsic goods are not irrelevant or bad. They are often necessary in order to participate in the judgments needed for achieving the intrinsic goods. Naivete about how extrinsic goods work in institutions can play havoc with how ideals actually survive. At the same time, the process of striving necessary for recognition and status might make individuals neglect what is being eaten away out of their ideal selves.

There is a tricky tightrope to be walked *between* having the necessary courage to support professional ideals *and* not being naïve about consequences on the professional self in the institutional arena. In our era, we might have more awareness of how outside forces influence institutional life than James did in his era (Abowitz, 1997). Nevertheless, James can remind us of an important distinction: using status to resist an institutional mindset *versus* using status to avoid real choices. As Hatch (2000) points out (after personally going through the politics of reforming a college of education), there is a vital difference *between* resistance that is rooted in free acts *and* "bad faith" when individuals have freedom to act but avoid responsibility.

Dilemmas are made more complex when one's own allegiance to professional ideals points in different directions. James knew that ends-in-view can be in conflict with one another in the realities of lived experience, just as he knew that there are tensions between conflicting selves within the individual. Facing risk with courage is made even more difficult when the "I" is faced with confusing ambiguity caused by competing intrinsic values.

For example, I shall never forget my torn allegiance when confronted by the principal of a central city high school where I was intensively involved as a teacher educator of undergraduates. My class meetings were held each week at the school after my university students had participated in classrooms and experienced the dynamics of the school. The principal pushed me to take sides between the polarized members of his faculty as he tried to implement curricular change. In defense of my academic freedom as a teacher, and in defense of my students who worked with a range of faculty, I refused to take sides. However, at the same time, I felt philosophical affinity with the principal's goals.

Another example, more common in institutional life, occurs when the need to exploit complexity and contradictions runs against grains of honesty and trust with colleagues. Resisting bureaucratic processes in order to accomplish a worthwhile goal might diminish professional relationships, which in turn might harm other worthwhile goals in the future.

Collaboration and Diversity

Openness and trust with colleagues are also important in a deeper way. Tacit understandings among participants are vital where there is a pluralism of ideas and ideals. As Porter (1995) explains, professional communities need to be small and informal in order for deliberation, interpretation, and negotiation to proceed with vitality. Such processes entail trust, openness, and subjectivity—which, in turn, create responsibility. In contrast, large-scale institutional processes, supporting and supported by mechanical objectivity, often breed anonymity without personal responsibility.

James was not naïve about personal subjectivity in community life. A focus on individual preference might create tensions with community stability. There may be too much emphasis on uniqueness in a collaborative project when more commonality is needed for effectiveness—just as there may be too much consensus at a time when differing voices are needed (Schutz, 1999).

I experienced dilemmas in balancing consensus and diversity throughout much of my interdepartmental work in teacher education programs. On the one hand, I could understand why colleagues pushed for a consensus that would generate guidelines and standards for faculty as well as for students. These efforts can lead to a clearer sense of mission needed for program integrity. On the other hand, I found such efforts tended to mute differing voices of students as well as of faculty. The loss of participation by those who raise red flags can lead to the demise of the dialectical process that is needed for program openness and fluidity.

In our era, when there is increasing need for large-scale collective action in defending against threatening outside political forces, James now would have to face another dilemma. Using the power of mainstream professional organizations as needed defense may unintentionally promote narrow standardization and mechanical objectivity. Think, for example, of the need of a credentialing agency in order to protect a professional community from harmful state budget cuts, while this same agency is promoting practices that are antithetical to creative individuality.

Protecting the needs of a professional community can also bring another dilemma to the surface when faced with an equally important need of protecting the pluralism that comes from alternative communities outside mainstream educational institutions. Weiss (1995) warns that a focus limited to professional communities can suppress pluralism by neglecting a wide range of communities that are crisscrossed with dimensions of race/ethnicity, class, and gender.

Schutz (2000) points to the myriad of fundamentally different ways of resisting, ways that are rooted in the varied assumptions of particular communities. For example, my own experience in working with minority communities points to some groups that resist through direct conflict, whereas others resist through maintaining a quiet independence while collaborating with mainstream institutions. Such cultural patterns might be in contrast to assumptions of well-meaning professionals, who, in reaching out to a minority community, may be unknowingly imposing their own assumptions about change.

However, awareness of alternative communities and their assumptions does not dissolve professional dilemmas. My most painful experience was facing a conflict in my university liaison role in working with a Southeast Asian refugee community. Members of that community became polarized among themselves concerning the university dismissal of a Southeast Asian advisor of students. My being able to understand intellectually the conflicting assumptions involved did not dissolve the professional tensions created by my having to stand up one way or the other. Whereas I had been a mediator between the community and the university for over a decade, my professional role in this particular situation could not avoid a real choice with significant consequences—nor the inevitable conflicts that would result.

CONCLUSION

My interpretation of William James in this chapter has emphasized the inevitable tensions between creative individuality *and* professional community, subjective feelings *and* objective rationality, freedom of choice *and* social embeddedness, an ideal self *and* fluidity of the self, courageous resistance *and* collaborative consensus, optimistic progress *and* anguishing realities. For James, "having a place to stand" *and* doing professional practice with openness to new possibilities is not a contradiction but does create existential dilemmas in the "jungle of experience." This parallels the tension that Gale (1999) highlights in James: the "becoming" of growth and action for the future *versus* the "being" of the present. "To be human is to accept the unresolvable tension between wanting to be both at the same time" (pp. 332–332).

My own intellectual and experiential "places to stand," including those in this chapter, cannot escape the contextual influences in my life any more than James could escape those of his life. Even my stating this reflects the *contextualist* approach I take in analyzing James, an approach that views philosophy of education and its implications within sociohistorical contexts. "The validity of a contextualist positioning of the philosopher and philosophy within the crucible of society, culture, and politics must reside in how well this perspective leads us forward by bringing forth new insight and understanding" (Cotkin, 1990, p. 3).

However, understanding what one believes, why one believes it—and even understanding the limitations of those beliefs—do not dissolve either the dilemmas in doing philosophy of education or the tensions of putting ideas and ideals into professional practice. James would have agreed with Nozick (1981) not only that our own priorities are unequal in our hierarchy of beliefs but also that our beliefs are incompatible with other of our beliefs, and that not one of our beliefs is completely adequate by itself.

What James offers us is encouragement that this kind of self-knowledge can help mediate the tensions within our self as well as within our life-worlds. In addition, James encourages us to face what for me is the ultimate dilemma: having an authentic place to stand, whatever the issue, and at the same time realizing that it is *our* position, not *the* position. In the case of this chapter's discussion of James's philosophy, it is *my* portrayal, not *the* portrayal. Openness to others and to new possibilities means having to confront the inevitable bedrock of our own philosophical-cultural assumptions. At the same time, each of us needs to stand, act, reflect—and write—all in "good faith." This is what James asks us to do with the pieces of freedom that are ours.

Acknowledgments. I want to express gratitude to Aaron Schutz, University of Wisconsin-Milwaukee, as well as to my coeditors and the Teachers College Press staff, for the helpful suggestions in developing this chapter.

CHAPTER 5

James's Metaphysics of Experience and Religious Education

SIEBREN MIEDEMA

I N THIS CHAPTER I present William James's view of experience as his primal metaphysical concept and show some of its implications for religious education. I rely, in part, on Lamberth's (1997, 1999) reconstruction of James's metaphysics of experience in terms of a radically empiricist worldview (*Weltanschauung*). This integrated interpretation of James's work helps prevent us from characterizing his religious writings as dealing only with the subjective and privatized domain of personal experience so that we can see some implications for the public domain.

By way of contrast, Richard Rorty (1997) has recently claimed the following:

> The underlying strategy of James's utilitarian/pragmatist philosophy of religion is to *privatize* religion. This privatization allows him to construe the supposed tension between science and religion as the illusion of opposition between cooperative endeavors and private projects. . . . A suitably privatized form of religious belief might dictate neither one's scientific beliefs nor anybody's moral choices save one's own. That form of belief would be able to gratify a need without threatening to thwart any needs of any others and would thus meet the utilitarian test. (p. 85)

Rorty's claim is in line with the sharp distinction he makes between the public and private sides of our lives. Rorty thinks our responsibilities to others constitute only the public side of our lives that often competes with our private attempts at self-creation. Further, he does not think public motives always have priority over private motives (Rorty, 1989). In Rorty's liberal utopia, according to one critic, there is:

> a rigid distinction between a rich, autonomous private sphere that will enable elite "ironists" like himself to create freely the selves they wish—even if this be a cruel, anti-democratic self—and a lean, egalitarian, "democratic" public life confined to the task of preventing cruelty (including that of elite ironists). (Westbrook, 1991, p. 541)

The first part of this chapter is devoted to questioning Rorty's characterization of James's philosophy of religion as privatized. In the second part, I take Rorty's characterization as a starting point for an in-depth analysis of the diverse positions religion has taken in society since the 19th century. I also analyze what this has meant for the form and content of religious education in public schools. The results of this analysis are summarized as the *differentiation* thesis and the *deprivatization* of religion argument. The latter argument, which reflects my own position, points to the transformative force that religious education can exert for both public and private schools. Finally, in a third section of this chapter I relate the reconstruction of James's view of religion undertaken in the first part to my analysis in the second part. At this point, we will be able to see what Jamesian insights into religious experience mean for religious education understood as a catalyst in the dynamic formation of personal identity. Such a conclusion will show the relevance of James's metaphysics of experience for the challenges faced by religious education at the beginning of the 21st century.

WILLIAM JAMES'S CENTER OF VISION

In an earlier publication on James and religious experience, I contend that the recent turn to experience in theology (e.g., Gelphi, 1994) calls for special attention to the legacy of pragmatism. This is especially so for those seeking nonfoundationalist, naturalistic alternatives to transcendentalist and revelationist positions (Miedema, 1996).

In spite of my positive evaluation of James at the time, I was left with two unresolved issues. The first, springing from reading James's (1902/ 1982) *The Varieties of Religious Experience* as well as secondary literature (e.g., Bird, 1986; Vanden Burgt, 1981), had to do with James's focus on *personal* experience as the heart of the religious domain. For James, religion has to do with practical, living affairs that include such aspects as conversations with the unseen, voices and visions, responses to prayer, changes of the heart, deliverances from fear, inflowings of help, as well as assurances of support (James, 1907/1975). I could understand James giving primacy to personal experience over religious institutions, traditions, and creeds. Nevertheless, because I was not inclined to interpret James's view as a subjectivist or privatized position, it was unclear to me how his emphasis on the personal should be read.

The second issue relates to James's labeling himself in the Postscript of *Varieties* as a "piecemeal supernaturalist." There he proposes a way of understanding the workings of divinity in human life as a relationship between the ideal and real worlds. James sought to respond to the split between the conventional natural scientific view, which eliminates religious phenomena from the world, and conventional religious views, which place everything truly real in a separate realm beyond the physical. He was also contrasting his position to that of the refined or universalistic supernaturalists. These include the Kantians, who presuppose a separation between the ideal world as the realm of God, and the real world as the realm of human existence and experience. In contrast, James's (1902/1982) approach "admits miracles and providential leadings, and finds no intellectual difficulty in mixing the ideal and the real worlds together by interpolating influences from the ideal region among the forces that causally determine the real world's details" (pp. 520–521). For me, though, the pressing question still was how to combine the phenomenological approach used in the greater part of James's book with this much smaller, and in my opinion very unclear, epistemological/ontological approach at the end of *Varieties*.

So I was searching for a Jamesian reconstruction that would help me to grasp his central vision in such a way that I could deal with these two issues. In my odyssey, I found Levinson's (1981) book on James and religion, which, although helpful, did not fully satisfy my intellectual hunger. Finally, it was the Harvard philosopher of religion, David Lamberth (1999), who provided me with a comprehensive reconstruction of James's philosophical and religious worldview. I also discovered that from his interpretation, James offers, at least heuristically, some philosophical insights useful for the current debate over privatization versus deprivatization in religious education.

Lamberth (1999) claims that James's ideas—first labeled by James as both "radical pluralism" and "pluralistic empiricism" before ending with "radical empiricism"—constitute a single center of vision, his metaphysics of experience. He dates the origin of this view to 1885 when James began to explore a monistic metaphysics not contaminated with the mind/body dualism. Lamberth argues that James's Hibbert Lectures on metaphysics that James delivered at Oxford in 1908, later published as *A Pluralistic Universe* (James, 1909/1947) along with the posthumously published collected *Essays in Radical Empiricism* (James, 1912/1947) form the basis of James's mature philosophical vision. Based on a reconstruction of this work, Lamberth is able to show that James's views about religion are thoroughly involved in his philosophical *Weltanschauung*. That is why he offers, in contrast to the familiar psychological reading of *Varieties*, a philosophical reading that makes clear the central involvement of his views on religion with his philosophical program.

In particular, Lamberth (1999) demonstrates that the concept of experience is the core metaphysical term in James's radically empiricist worldview. For example, just a year after the publication of *Varieties*, James (1987) wrote that he wanted to

> admit the concrete data of experience in their full completeness. The only fully concrete data are, however, the successive moments of our several histories, taken with their subjective personal aspect, as well as their "objective" deliverance or "content." After the analogy of these moments of experiences must all complete reality be conceived . . . [leading] to the assumption of a collectivism of personal lives . . . variously cognitive of each other, variously connotative and impulsive, genuinely evolving and changing by effort and trial, and by their interaction and cumulative achievements making up the world. (pp. 544–545)

This passage is notable because in contrast to *Varieties* it characterizes the subjective elements of experience as only one aspect, and, indeed, emphasizes the objective aspect (see Lamberth, 1999, p. 13).

James (1897/1979) explains his doctrine of radical empiricism thus:

> I say "empiricism," because it is contented to regard its most assured conclusions concerning matters of fact as hypotheses liable to modification in the course of future experience and I say "radical" because it treats the doctrine of monism itself as an hypothesis . . . it does not dogmatically affirm monism as something with which all experience has got to square. (p. 5)

Therefore, James's metaphysics of experience is a hypothesis about matters of fact, that is, conclusions and ideas about things, which can be met in the course of experience. It is also a hypothesis about the presuppositions of monism itself, that is, the fundamental and organizing questions or meta-ideas (see Lamberth, 1999, p. 11).

In his most sophisticated definition of the methodological postulate of radical empiricism, James (1909/1975) asserts that "things [be] definable in terms drawn from experience" (p. 6). This formulation points to the heart of James's methodological concern. Those elements are excluded that transcend experience in principle rather than by circumstance, for example, transcendent entities such as God, the all-knower, the soul, the transcendental ego, the absolute Truth. Elements that underlie experience while nonetheless not appearing within experience. At the same time it leaves the door open to include everything that occurs within or at the level of experience (see Lamberth, 1999, p. 17).

Connected with radical empiricism's methodological postulate is its factual thesis: "*The relations that connect experiences must themselves be experienced relations, and any kind of relation experienced must be accounted as 'real' as anything else in the system*" (James, 1912/1947, p. 42). The impact of this postulate is that, according to James, conjunctive as well as disjunctive relations between things are in principle equally important. In other words, the differences and boundaries separating things from one another are no more real than the relationships connecting them. Knowing or cognition is also a relation that emerges within experience. There is no need for an additional force unifying the discontinuous into an integrated world, such as an individual ego, spirit, God, the rationalists' all-knower or the empiricists' aggregating mind or soul (see Lamberth, 1999, pp. 18–19; emphasis in original).

Beside the methodological postulate and the factual thesis, James's metaphysics of pure experience contains another dimension, one by which he wants to overcome the dualistic structure of thought and thing, mind and matter, subject and object so predominant in Western philosophies. Experience, James (1912/1947) believes, has "*no such inner duplicity; and the separation of it into consciousness and content comes, not by way of subtraction, but by way of addition*" (p. 9; emphasis added). This view implies that the separation of thought and thing thought about is not an ontological/ metaphysical given. Instead, it is an analytical distinction added to a state of initial wholeness. In this metaphysics, which James also characterized as a mosaic philosophy, "there is no bedding; it is as if the pieces clung together by their edges, the transitions experienced between them forming their cement" (p. 86). In other words, distinctions between thought and thing or subject and object emerge from within experience rather than being preexistent. However, from what do they emerge?

James's (1912/1947) metaphysical thesis starts with the following supposition:

> There is only one primal stuff or material in the world, a stuff of which everything is composed, and if we call that stuff pure experience, then knowing can easily be explained as a particular sort of relation towards one another into which portions of pure experience may enter. The relation itself is a part of pure experience; one of its terms becomes the subject or bearer of the knowledge, the knower, the other becomes the object known. (p. 4)

James makes this point more nuanced by stating that "there is no *general* stuff of which experience is made. There are as many stuffs as there are 'natures' in the thing experienced"(p. 26). Therefore, his metaphysical conception of pure experience leaves open the possibility for extreme variation in content or nature for the various "experiences" that are subsumed under it. Here James distinguishes between an experience (perceptual or conceptual) in the first-order or the modality of direct acquaintance, and a second-order reference to that experience, that is, experience in the modality of knowledge about. This implies that both pure experience and direct acquaintance involve concepts or conceptual experiences. Therefore, the distinction is not radically conceptual versus aconceptual but, conceptually speaking, a matter of degree (see Lamberth, 1999, pp. 38–39). There is also a difference in the degree of concreteness between the first and the second type of knowing. The first type is more concrete than the second one, but the difference is a relative one.

Every kind of experience enters into James's conception as in some sense real: "The world of pure experience taken as a whole includes illusions, imaginary objects, dreams, falsehoods, ambiguous experiences, future and past experiences and persons—virtually anything that does not pretend to transcend experience" (Lamberth, 1999, p. 42). However, as James asserts, "real" and "true" are practical judgments we make about pure experiences and the conceptions (and propositions) we connect with them respectively. These are judgments based on the functionality of the relations we construct among or attribute to the experience.

NEW LIGHT ON THE *VARIETIES*

Based on this reconstruction of James's metaphysics of experience, I now come back to *Varieties*, and to the two questions I formulated above. In composing the *Varieties*, James had initially intended to write a series of psychological lectures to be followed by a series of metaphysical lectures (Lamberth, 1999). Although the final publication was more factual than philosophical, it was not "all facts and no philosophy," as James (1920/ 1926) characterized in a letter to Schiller (vol. II, p. 165). Especially in the chapters "Philosophy," "Conclusions," and "Postscript," James gives attention to a philosophical hypothesis about the described phenomena of religion that is fully consistent with his radically empiricist worldview outlined earlier.

James's emphasis in *Varieties* on feeling to the detriment of thought and understanding has led many to characterize his view on religion to be merely subjectivist. Nevertheless, this emphasis is understandable when one recognizes that he is primarily engaged in a criticism of rationalism. Philosophically, however, James (1920/1926) seeks "to treat thought and feeling as of the same order as a matter of course, making distinctions between and among them on a case-relative, practical basis" (vol. II, p. 111). James's psychological perspective also leads him to focus on the experience of the individual, but this is consistent with his metaphysical thesis of pure experience and does not, contrary to Rorty, imply any privatization of the religious domain whatsoever. On the contrary, the goal of James's (1902/1982) philosophy, as he explicitly states in several places in the last part of *Varieties*, is to redeem religion from unwholesome privacy and to give public status and universal right to its deliverances (see pp. 432, 453, 507).

Following from his methodological postulate, which admits all experience as real, religious states are states of mind researchable by psychology as a science. James's definition of religion as "*the feelings, acts, and experiences of individual men in their solitude, so far as they apprehend themselves to stand in relation to whatever they may consider the divine*" (p. 31; emphasis in original) is consistent with his factual thesis. From his metaphysical as well as methodological view, James can grant what psychology and religion both implicitly grant. It is the view that relations among the basic elements admitted are factual and real, as real as anything else in the system.

Instead of accepting Rorty's line of thought of a separation of science (the public) and religion (the private), we should, in my opinion, follow Lamberth's (1999) suggestion to read James's preference for a crasser or piecemeal supernaturalism "as an attempt at a metaphysically pluralistic accommodation of both science and religion, retaining the empirical facts and successes of each, while renegotiating the mutually exclusive grounds of their apparently contradictory presuppositions" (p. 128).

Both Lamberth and Cornel West point to another fundamental difference between Rorty and James. Where Rorty is interpreting James's position as radically antirealist and so identical with his own position emphasizing the sufficiency of language for constituting and understanding the word, these two authors characterize James as a "minimal realist" (see Lamberth, 1999, p. 215; West, 1993, p. 91). James's nonreductionist, holistic realism is "a new path in philosophy between forms of idealism and empiricism, seeking a *via media* in epistemology, ethics, and politics . . . [recasting and deemphasizing] realism and truth, rather than rejecting them, focusing instead on lived [or pure] experience, processes of knowledge, and human sociality and context" (Lamberth, 1999, pp. 214–215).

THE DIFFERENTIATION THESIS

In this section I now want to return to Rorty's characterization of the privatization of religion and take this as a starting point for an in-depth analysis of the diverse positions religion has taken since the 19th century to the present. In one move, I will also analyze what this has meant for the form and the content of religious education in state schools.

Since the 19th century the role and function of institutions in society have been analyzed based on a set of arguments that has been characterized as the *differentiation* thesis. In this view stress is laid on

> the differentiation of the economy from the household and the emergence of the nation-state.... While many other systems (e.g. art, law, mass media) are also viewed as developing relatively differentiated forms ... the economy and nation-state, with their large-scale, bureaucratic forms of organization, are generally seen as setting the terms of modern life. (Osmer, 1999, p. 280)

The differentiation thesis also included a view on the role and function of religion in society. The relative autonomy of all societal subsystems, according to this view, resulted in a new role for religion. Religion lost the integrative function in society it had earlier in history and became just one system among many other systems—a system primarily located in the private sphere for the benefit of individuals, families, and groups. The public role of religion was largely viewed as indirect, an expression of the moral commitments of individual members as they participated in other social spheres. Religion no longer played a privileged and normative determining role (let alone in the form of church dogma) within other societal spheres.

This view on the role of religion in society had its impact on the role of religion in state schools as well. From the differentiation perspective, the public school was positioned as a function of the nation-state, that is, supplying education for all students regardless of their sex, race, social background, and religion. That would allow public schools to fulfill an integrative function in society by educating all future citizens. In The Netherlands, for example, the founding of the New Kingdom in 1813 implied the separation between state and church. Although the elementary state schools were still Protestant schools with prayer, singing of psalms, and story telling about Jesus as the example par excellence of morality, there was no place any more for the teaching of Protestant confessions of faith. The teaching of church dogma was seen as a task of the different religious denominations themselves. The state school should serve national unity by emphasizing moral education and virtues sustaining humanness. The strict regulations brought into force in 1830 only endorsed the ruling educational policy with respect to the relation between state school and the religious denominations (cf. Miedema & De Ruyter, 1999). From 1830 state schools have turned more and more in the direction of some form of neutrality regarding religion (cf. De Ruyter & Miedema, 2000).

In the United States the teaching of religion in public schools became problematic in the 19th century as well (cf. Osmer, 1999). Before that time, beliefs and moral principles of Protestant Christianity and even catechism were part of the curriculum of the public schools. The turn was initiated by the public education movement and resulted in the constitutional principle of the disestablishment of religion from public schools. Religions and religious teaching were removed from the explicit curriculum. In consequence of a series of court decisions in the 20th century, the still existing truncated forms of religious expression and teaching (e.g., morning devotions with a time of prayer and the study of the stories from the Bible) were characterized as illegal.

The relative autonomy of the state school, its autonomous relationship to religious institutions, and the impossibility of any form of substantial religious education (only cognitive information on various religions is provided) are reinforced by the secularization argument. The argument runs as follows: The secularization process has led to the situation where a majority of parents do not have any binding with religion whatsoever and do not want their children to be socialized into a religion via religious education in school (Dronkers, 1996). The decline of the religion thesis, reinforced by a view paralleling the work of Weber, Durkheim, and Habermas, "religion's beliefs and practices are viewed as the outdated vestige of premodern, traditional forms of life that are superseded as science and other forms of modern rationality gain greater influence in society" (Osmer, 1999, p. 281).

DEPRIVATIZATION OF RELIGION

Recent research in the sociology of religion and practical theology has undercut the view that religion has lost its societal function, and that religious education should not be part of state schools at all as in the United States, or that it should be only in the form of one school subject among others as in The Netherlands. These recent findings make it clear that the differentiation thesis (different institutions perform different functions) as well as the secularization thesis (modern societies are increasingly secular) leave considerable room for interpretation and negotiation (cf. Osmer, 1999; Ziebertz, 1995).

The emergence of global systems of communication, transportation, and economic exchange has created a new situation in which individual systems are no longer bound together because economic decisions affecting the whole world are being made outside of one political order. The global economy is providing an all-pervasive system affecting all the other systems. Because of this development, differentiation can no longer be adequately conceptualized in terms of the development of a more complex division of labor within nation state. Consequently, the aims of public schools for creating a viable national identity and for preparing young people for participation in the national economy are no longer sufficient.

Education in state schools should take the consequences of globalization seriously by preparing students for their encounters with "cultural others." This also means preparing them for encounters with "religious others," because recent empirical research shows that the impact of religion in political, economical and cultural areas is enormous. This phenomenon has been characterized by Casanova as the *deprivatization of religion* in modern life (cf. Osmer, 1999). Contrary to the claim of the differentiation thesis that religion has lost its integrative function for society as a whole, and become a system primarily located in the private sphere on the level of individuals and families, the deprivatization view puts religion back in the public domain, even on a global scale. This insight challenges state schools to answer the question as to how they are going to prepare students for their encounters with people who are adherents of other belief systems, and to share in other religious practices. The same questions need answering by religiously affiliated schools, and especially by the closed, segregated variants of these schools. Do they, because of their specific arrangements, foster or hinder the preparation of students for dialogue with adherents of other religions?

Doubts about the secularization thesis provide an additional reason for posing the question above. The thesis that religion is in decline in modern societies often defines religion as socialization into and membership in a particular religious community or church. However, in the present postmodern context, there is an astonishingly high endorsement of religiosity in general. The content of this religiosity is predominantly undetermined, is no longer exclusively institutionally centered, and is very often far more individual-centered. The secularization thesis of the decline of religion is indeed valid for the process of church-bound religious socialization, at least in Europe, but this is only one of the forms of religiosity that can be found in present societies and may be embodied by students attending state schools. So the secularization thesis should at least be complemented with, if not replaced by, the *plurality of religiosity thesis* (cf. Ziebertz, 1995).

RELIGION AS A TRANSFORMATIVE RESOURCE

Recasting the differentiation thesis, both Schweitzer (1999) and Osmer (1999) point to the important role *civil society* can play in the healthy functioning of democratic cultures. In an interpretation of the Habermasian distinction between system and lifeworld, they define civil society as "a sphere of social interaction between economy and state composed above all of the intimate sphere (especially the family), the sphere of associations (especially voluntary associations), social movements, and forms of public communication" (Osmer, 1999, p. 85; cited in Schweitzer, 1999, p. 305). Civil society, according to Osmer, is located between the state and the economy, including but transcending the private sphere. Religion is an important *mediating structure*, in this view, located in civil society between the public and private spheres.

This view is fully in line with my own conclusion based on an earlier analysis of Habermas's dichotomy of system (characterized by strategic-instrumental action and material reproduction, embodied by economy and state) and lifeworld (characterized by communicative action orientated to mutual understanding and embodied by culture, society, and personality). In my analysis, I attempted to locate the school within this dichotomy. In my view, the school as a pedagogical institution has a place on the seam between system and lifeworld, that is, schools are remarkable mediating institutions, characterized by their functions of distributing cultural traditions and renewing personalities. From the pedagogical aim of communicative competence, schools also anticipate a person's need to act communicatively. Within a critical social theory, whose core is the theory of communicative action, the school also produces social, cultural, and religious meaning (cf. Miedema, 1994).

Schools—including their religious domains, practices, and experiences—can indeed be interpreted as *transformative resources* for both the public and the private spheres, fostering attitudes, insights, and experiences in students in both religiously affiliated and state schools related to religious issues that might free them from the fixation of patterns of conventional ritual behavior, dogmatic belief propositions, and from stigmatizing other cultural and religious ideas, habits, and practices. Such schools can also foster students with insights that make them aware of the possible corrosive effects of the global marketplace, media, and transportation, all of which disrupt local and global communities. Therefore, education (including religious education) has the possibility of reacting to the colonization of the lifeworld (via media money and power) not just defensively but also offensively. It may help students to develop and establish a critical, systemic, and normative perspective on the dangers of processes of colonization. Here the ideas of "another world," that is, a more humane world, subject to the criteria of understanding, solidarity, and justice can be practiced and tested in action (cf. Miedema, 1994).

The view expressed here is, in my opinion, fully in line with Strike's (1999) plea for an ethic for strangers—an ethic that can mitigate the dividing line between the sphere of the personal and associational, that is, the community and the world of strangers (the society). Strike argues for a strategy that denies that fellow citizens are strangers. Taking full account of our diversity, we should not forget that we are also members of a larger inclusive community. According to Strike (1999), these fellow citizens are

> people with whom we are connected as members of a common polity whom we must enter in dialogue in order to make mutually satisfactory arrangements for our common good. . . . The other may continue to be a member of another religion, another linguistic group, or another culture. . . . But those strangers who are fellow citizens are people for whom I am responsible and whom I must engage in deliberations about our common fate. (p. 9)

In a pluralistic society, the polity is a place where strangers meet as citizens. The polity constitutes a different kind of community between "Gesellschaft" and "Gemeinschaft." For schools, the relevant question is in what way they help to construct the "commons" in the polity (see Strike, 1999, pp. 10, 19).

The connotation of the aim of education in general, and of religious education in particular, is important here. In my view, the aim of schools should explicitly be directed at the development of the whole person. For that reason, substantial religious education ought to be an integral part of the curriculum of every school. Religious education should not be conceptualized exclusively in cognitive terms. Schools that organize separate activities in which only objective information about a religious worldview, or about different religious worldviews under the label of religious education, do not offer the optimal conditions for active and dynamic personal identity formation processes (cf. Wardekker & Miedema, in press).

Knowledge should be functionally related to the religious experiences of the students. In religious education, the gaining of religious experiences and a religious attitude should not be fully separated from the gaining of other experiences and attitudes. Schools should be open to the potential religious qualities of all kinds of experiences. Every artificial distinction between the religious and other domains of experience should be precluded. Explicit presentation and representation of a rich and plural array of religious material in the form of religious frames of reference, models, practices, rituals, and narratives is a necessary prerequisite for making the individuation on the basis of socialization possible.

Presentations and representations are not intended to be transmitted by the teachers and internalized by the students in their presented or represented form but rather offered as possible identity-forming transformative material for the students. Characteristics for this should include openness, a nondogmatic attitude, self-directedness, and all possible room for students' own development. Contrary to an institution for the transmission of knowledge, the school should function as a community of diverse religious practices (cf. Wardekker & Miedema, in press). This is where students can learn to view one another as citizens of an embryonic society, "who are responsible for one another and who must pursue their common ends through dialogue and cooperation" (Strike, 1999, p. 19).

Personal identity formation in religious education can also be supported, but at the same time a critical-evaluative attitude should be stimulated in the students. Unquestioning acceptance, or full identification with the view of the teachers, is not the criterion for successful identity formation. Growth of the potentiality of an active and critical reconstruction of different and differing perspectives (ideals, norms, values, knowledge, and narratives) is the goal. These practices and processes in school may result in the growing capacity of the students to integrate these perspectives into their own personalities, to the ongoing organization and reorganization of perspectives, that is, the reconstruction of self. Stimulating the process of identity formation of students as part of the process of coping with diverse perspectives of others, and integrating these in their own actions, is the aim.

CONCLUDING REMARKS

In this section, I relate James's metaphysics of experience to the role, form, and content of religion in society and to religious education in schools at the beginning of the 21st century. I relate his vision in at least a heuristic way to five issues:

1. Although James was paying a lot of attention to the religious experience of the individual, his view does not imply a privatization of religion. He did not advocate an exclusive focus on privacy, or a societal po-

sitioning of the religious domain in only the private sphere of church and family. His plea is, rather, to give public status and universal right to religion's deliverances. I take his radically empiricist view as being complementary with the *deprivatization* of religion, defended by sociologists of religion and practical theologians. For this reason, religion and religious experience should have their legitimate place in public as well as private schools.

2. Religion should not be opposed to science. Religion and religious experience are normal states of mind as well as the human condition at large and, hence, should be treated like other states of mind. Thus religion in schools should be part of the regular, integrative curriculum and not be left out or limited to purely cognitive treatment. I interpret James's holistic view as being fully in line with my definition of the primary aim of education as directed to the development of the whole person, that is, that all domains of human potentiality and ability—be they cognitive, creative, moral, religious, expressive, or the like—should be taken into account.

3. James's radically empiricist vision is a pluralistic view that clearly follows from his metaphysical thesis of pure experience, as when he states that "there are many stuffs as there are 'natures' in the thing experiences" (James, 1912/1947, p. 26). In my view, he is fully in accord with the plurality of religiosity thesis referred to above. This thesis emphasizes that religiosity is no longer exclusively institutionally centered but very often individually centered. As we saw earlier, James gave primacy to personal religious experience over the institutional side of religion, which he characterizes as a secondary phenomenon. Nevertheless, this is not to say that he thought institutions do not have meaning or impact. Levinson (1981) points to the fact that James takes a far more balanced position regarding the relation between the individual and social life in his essay on the one and the many, such as when James (1907/1975) wrote, "Human systems [i.e., institutions] evolving in consequence of human needs . . . [can] keep human energy framing as time goes on (pp. 78–76).

4. I see a parallel between my claim that schools can function as transformative resources for both the public and the private sphere with respect to the religious domain and the answer James gives in his lectures to Cambridge teachers to the question, what makes a life significant? There James (1899/1958) states that "the thing of deepest—or, at any rate, of comparatively deepest—significance in life does seem to be its character of *progress*, or that strange union of reality with ideal novelty which it continues from one moment to another to present" (p. 187). The actualization of novelty or the starting off of a transformative process presupposes the efforts of individuals and groups to strive for the realization and

maintenance of these ideals or remote goals. For James the core function of religion and religious experiences is precisely the support of these efforts, which he characterizes as the strenuous mood of living. For James (1897/1979) the strenuous mood is characterized by the willingness to fight for and rigorously pursue basic life goals or ideals, including those that are far off in the horizon or have no guarantee of success:

> The capacity for the strenuous mood lies so deep down among our natural human possibilities that even if there were no metaphysical or traditional grounds for believing in God, men would postulate one simply as a pretext for living hard, and getting out of the game of existence its keenest possibilities of zest. . . . Every sort of energy and endurance, of courage and capacity for handling life's evils, is set free in those who have religious faith. For this reason the strenuous type of character will . . . always outwear the easy-going type, and religion will drive irreligious to the wall. (p. 161)

It is James's view, according to West (1989), that "religion generates human heroic energies and facilitates personal struggle in the world" (p. 66). It is precisely here that the transformative power of religion is located.

5. For James the universe is still in the making. Therefore, individuals are cocreators of the world in partnership with God—a God who is not an abstract or remote transcendental entity but who (and that is his hypothesis) can be met "in the course of experience," as "the beyond in the midst" (Miedema, 1995, p. 61) or as "transcendency-in-immanency" (Van Peursen, 1994, p. 125). This view is a challenge for all those religious educators who want to provide optimal conditions for active, dynamic, and experiential processes of forming the religious personal identity of students in school. We need educators who are open to the potential religious qualities of all kind of experiences, and who are willing to create opportunities so that students have the possibility to meet God or "the beyond in the midst" in the course of these experiences.

CHAPTER 6

James's Story of the Squirrel and the Pragmatic Method

CLEO CHERRYHOLMES

PRAGMATISM IS STRAIGHTFORWARD and complex. Its contributions to education are direct and open as well as indirect and multifaceted. William James began the third of his Lowell Lectures with a
story about a dispute that arose during a camping trip. This story provides
an opportunity to explore major pragmatist tenets and to demonstrate how
pragmatism contributes to educational thought and practice.

William James delivered the Lowell Lectures in Boston at the Lowell
Institute in November and December 1906 and gave them a second time
in New York at Columbia University in January 1907 (James, 1907/1981,
p. 3). "What Pragmatism Means" was the second lecture in the series in
which he provided an account of pragmatism as a school of thought and
as a "method." He began this lecture with the story of a quarrel, which
developed during a camping trip, about a squirrel, a tree, and an observer.
Here is the story as James told it at the beginning of the lecture.

> Some years ago, being with a camping party in the mountains, I returned
> from a solitary ramble to find every one engaged in a ferocious metaphysical
> dispute. The *corpus* of the dispute was a squirrel—a live squirrel supposed to
> be clinging to one side of a tree-trunk; while over against the tree's opposite
> side a human being was imagined to stand. This human witness tries to get
> sight of the squirrel by moving rapidly round the tree, but no matter how
> fast he goes, the squirrel moves as fast in the opposite direction, and always

keeps the tree between himself and the man, so that never a glimpse of him is caught. The resultant metaphysical problem now is this: *Does the man go around the squirrel or not?* He goes round the tree, sure enough, and the squirrel is on the tree; but does he go round the squirrel? . . . Everyone had taken sides, and was obstinate; and the numbers of both sides were even. Each side, when I appeared, appealed to me to make it a majority. Mindful of the scholastic adage that whenever you meet a contradiction you must make a distinction, I immediately sought and found one, as follows: "Which party is right," I said, "depends on what you *practically mean* by 'going round' the squirrel. If you mean passing from the north of him to the east, then to the south, then to the west, and then to the north of him again, obviously the man does go round him, for he occupies these successive positions. But if on the contrary you mean being first in front of him, then on the right of him, then behind him, then on his left, and finally in front again, it is quite as obvious that the man fails to go round him, for by the compensating movements the squirrel makes, he keeps his belly turned towards the man all the time, and his back turned away. Make the distinction and there is no occasion for any further dispute. You are both right and both wrong according as you conceive the verb 'to go round' in one practical fashion or the other." (p. 25)

James reported that most of his camping friends accepted his solution, although one or two called it a "shuffling evasion, saying they wanted no quibbling or scholastic hair-splitting" (p. 25). They wanted an answer to the question of the man going around the squirrel in terms of "just plain honest English 'round'" (p. 25).

James (1907/1981) began his lecture with this story, he said, because, "it is a peculiarly simple example of . . . *the pragmatic method*" (p. 25). This is his summary of its lesson.

> The pragmatic method . . . is to try to interpret each notion by tracing its respective practical consequences. What difference would it practically make to any one if this notion rather than that notion were true. (p. 26)

The pragmatic method is here used to resolve a dispute. The dispute is whether a person circling a tree with a squirrel also circling the tree in such a way that the tree remains between them goes around the squirrel or not. The person surely goes around the tree. But does the person go around the squirrel? There was one question and two contradictory answers. At stake in this dispute was the meaning of "go round." Those on each side in the argument assumed that the concept of "go round" was univocal, universal, and had an essence. The disagreement was between their different views on the univocality, universality, and essential meaning of "go round." If alternative meanings of "go round" had been available, there may have been no disagreement in the first place.

James called the question *"Does the man go round the squirrel or not?"* a "metaphysical problem." Metaphysical refers, according to *The New Shorter Oxford English Dictionary* (Brown, 1993), as "1c Not empirically verifiable. 2a Immaterial, incorporeal, supersensible; supernatural. 4 Based on abstract general reasoning or *a priori* principles" (p. 1756). The argument was metaphysical because it was about the meaning of "go round" determined by abstract general reasoning. Abstract general arguments are often put forward in order to determine an essential meaning where essence refers to, also from *The New Shorter Oxford English Dictionary*, "3 The intrinsic nature or character of something; that which makes it what it is; the attributes, constituents, etc., that something must have for it not to be something else and that serve to characterize it" (p. 852). The dispute was metaphysical because it moved beyond what could be practically decided—not that we can ever escape metaphysics, but there are different degrees of reliance on or independence from, as you wish, context and purpose in arriving at meanings. A troublesome problem with arguments about abstract meanings is that if we were to stumble upon the essential meaning of a word or concept, how could we possibly know? Because essences lie beyond context, purpose, and observation, they can be debated and argued endlessly.

James eliminated the metaphysical dispute by locating the single question of what "go round" means into two contexts that bypassed the need to determine a univocal meaning or essence. James's two questions avoided the metaphysical meaning of "go round" by specifying what it *practically means* to "go round the squirrel."

1. Does *go round* "mean passing from the north of him to the east, then to the south, then to the west, and then to the north of him again?"

2. Does *go round* "mean being first in front of him, then on the right of him, then behind him, then on his left, and finally in front again?"

These two interpretations of what it means to "go round the squirrel" position the concept of "go round the squirrel" in the contexts of compass directions and body positions. The contextualizations that came with James's two questions ended the confusion that had accompanied the earlier attempt to determine a universal meaning of "go round."

There is a broad parallel between the pragmatic method that James illustrates with the story of the squirrel and Peirce's pragmatic maxim where pragmatism was first formally stated. Here is Peirce on the maxim that he offered as a way to clarify the meaning of intellectual concepts.

> The method prescribed in the [pragmatic] maxim is to trace out in the imagi-
> nation the conceivable practical consequences—that is, the consequences for
> deliberate, self-controlled conduct—of the affirmation or denial of the con-
> cept; and the assertion of the maxim is that herein lies the *whole* of the pur-
> port of the word, the *entire* concept. (Peirce, 1905/1984, p. 493)

The mechanics of James's story and Peirce's maxim may seem, at first
glance, to be different because one deals with solving an argument and
the other with establishing the meaning of a concept. But, as the above
reading of James's story illustrates, James's pragmatic method resolved the
dispute by turning the argument from one about essence into one about
the clarification of meaning(s) in terms of consequences; that is, what are
the consequences of asking one question instead of another? Peirce (1905/
1984) also located meaning in context when he wrote that meaning is
found in "trac[ing] out in the imagination the conceivable practical consequences—that is, the consequences for deliberate, self-controlled conduct" (p. 494). Deliberate, self-controlled conduct does not exist outside
of context and purpose. Peirce's appeal to the "conceivable practical consequences" constrains the meaning of concepts by what one can imagine
in the context of action. Peirce's maxim, as does James's method, rejects
a search for univocal and universal meanings.

This leads to another reading of James's resolution to the argument.
Neither James's pragmatic method nor Peirce's maxim are about consequences in some abstract sense or random search for the simple reason
that if one explored all of the consequences of a concept or question, inquiry could proceed indefinitely. Such a search would only be limited by
our lack of imagination, time, and other resources. Conceptions are explored in terms of desire, in terms of where you wish to go, in terms of
what you can imagine from where you are. James's two questions can be
thought of as asking the disputants, what do you want to know? about
what do you wish to inquire? where do you want to take this inquiry?
Do you want to argue about the abstract meaning of "go round," about
whether the observer goes to the north, east . . . of the squirrel, or about
whether the observer goes to the front, right . . . of the squirrel? The pragmatic method is about the meaning of consequences in context and not
about some abstract meaning of consequences, an oxymoron for sure.

James used the story in large part to demonstrate an intellectual characteristic of the pragmatic method. The pragmatic method itself becomes
operational only in context—an instance of applying the pragmatic method
to itself—and not all contexts are equally congenial to such inquiry and
action. After specifying what text pragmatic inquiry will investigate—say,
the question of "go round"—the question becomes one of how the inves-

tigation will proceed. Social tolerance and inclusiveness open up the search. The story about the camping trip is silent on these issues, but elements of both are to be found. Recall that the dispute was initially among an even-numbered group of campers equally divided on each side of the question. James returned. James was invited into debate. Initially James was invited to vote, each side hoping that he would swing the decision in their favor. So the group invited and included a new party to the discussion. He, seemingly, was highly respected and therefore little tolerance was required to invite him to decide the question—by casting the deciding vote. But it was an exercise of inclusiveness and tolerance nonetheless. The point of their invitation was, at the outset, to win an argument. Nevertheless, the effect of their invitation was to admit to the conversation a new point of view, one that settled the disagreement not by voting but by providing a new way of reading the consequences of what they were asking. Pluralistic inclusiveness and tolerance, in this case including a new party and a new view, undermined the initial univocal conceptualization of the issue. The pragmatic method thrives when basking in inclusiveness and tolerance where those who are "other" are invited to join attempts to imagine an increasingly broader, more productive, and more esthetically satisfying set of consequences.

There are additional political implications of the story. James's pragmatic method that "interpret[s] each notion by tracing its respective practical consequences" and Peirce's maxim that "trace[s] out in the imagination . . . conceivable practical consequences" have been interpreted as intellectually and politically conservative. Louis Menand (1997) put it like this:

> Pragmatism is an account of the way people think [about consequences]. This may not seem like a terribly useful thing to have. After all, if pragmatism's account of the way people think is accurate, then we are already thinking the way pragmatists tell us we are. . . . It is as though someone were to offer us an account of the way our hair grows with the promise of having it will give us nicer hair. (p. xi)

Ernesto Laclau (1996) made a similar point with respect to pragmatism and the study of history.

> If pragmatic redescription is all there has been in history—and I do not back down from this conclusion—Rorty [and other pragmatists have] . . . to show in what way not only Dewey, James or Wittgenstein have been engaged in pragmatic games, but also all kind of metaphysicians and dogmatic politicians who claimed to be doing exactly the opposite. Pragmatism becomes . . . something like an intellectual horizon allowing us to describe all currents of thought and all events in history. (p. 61)

The charge contained in these two quotations is that we are and always have been pragmatists. If we have always been pragmatists, what added value does pragmatism bring to our thought and lives? Here is a response that comes from both James and Peirce. In James and Peirce's view, meanings of concepts are constructed by the questions we ask, the concepts we explore, and the imagination we bring to them. We construct pragmatic meanings of concepts and actions when texts are generated about the consequences of affirming them or acting on them. Everyone, however, seems to be conceptualizing consequences all the time. On this reading, pragmatism can turn out to be intellectually and politically conservative. After outlining this problem in more detail, I will show how James's story of the squirrel suggests a resolution to it.

James's pragmatic method and Peirce's maxim can be read simply as *describing* how we think and act—this is the nature of the Menand and Laclau criticisms. When read this way, pragmatism may well be guilty as charged. But an auxiliary assumption must be added if James's pragmatic method and Peirce's maxim are to be read solely for purposes of description. Here is a combination of James and Peirce plus such an assumption.

> (James's pragmatic method and Peirce's maxim) The pragmatic method locates meaning in our conceptions of consequences because it, "interpret[s] each notion by tracing its respective practical consequences," (James) and "trace[s] out in the imagination . . . conceivable practical consequences" (Peirce).
>
> *Assumption 1:* Individuals think and act in ways that are constrained by what they can imagine, how they can exercise their imagination, and what conceptions they have learned to value.

This reading of "tracing consequences" asserts that individuals think and act by choosing among what they can imagine, and that what can be imagined is shaped by one's experiences, history, and situation. Beliefs and actions represent a confluence of what can be imagined, what understandings individuals can bring to themselves and their situation, and what they can desire. Following this line of argument, a descriptive pragmatism moves back and forth from the texts (individual thoughts and actions) that one can write to contexts (situations) that one can describe. This hermeneutic movement reflects how an individual has learned to think of herself or himself and conceptualize the world. The downside of this descriptive construal of the pragmatic method is that it is oriented to the status quo, and the texts that can be written about the present are constrained by conceptions from the past.

The pragmatic method can be read also as a guide to experimentation that simultaneously is contiguous with and other to description. This requires a second auxiliary assumption.

Assumption 2: The ability to imagine more rather than fewer consequences generates a larger set of outcomes that, in turn, increases the possibility that more rather than fewer satisfying experiments can be conducted with the world.

This assumption is about criticism and learning, criticism of past beliefs and present views of the world and learning to move beyond established orthodoxies, institutions, and practices. On this reading, the pragmatic method of James and Peirce's maxim is prelude to Dewey's view of pragmatism as active engagement with the world. The more extensive the consequences that can be imagined, the more thoughtful and judicious one can be in deciding what to believe and how to act.

Reading the pragmatic method as experimental interaction with the world is intimately, and profoundly, connected to curriculum. Curriculum, as I think of it, is what students have an opportunity to learn. Students learn at least some of what they have an opportunity to learn; this, in turn, shapes what they can imagine, and the meaning, in the pragmatic sense, they can bring to their lives. Curriculum, then, is a contest over what can be imagined and what experiments with the world can be designed and completed. Curriculum can be deadly and stultifying if it focuses too intently on descriptions of the past, because description, by itself, need not promote and can limit what can be imagined. Curricular tolerance and inclusiveness operate to produce variety in encountering the world. This is one lesson of inviting James to join the discussion around the campfire. He suggested an alternative way to conceptualize the dispute.

Whatever else education produces it generates, at least some of the time, multiple descriptions, interpretations, criticisms, explanations, theories, and understandings of ourselves and the world. Different conceptions have different consequences and different consequences lead to still more conceptions and on and on. The larger our set of imagined conceptions as well as the imagined consequences of each conception the more freedom we have to engage and experiment with the world. By moving away from an essentialist view of "go round," James provided alternative interpretations of the dispute that produced a resolution. This is the effect of education writ small, the production of alternatives in our experiments with the world. The pragmatic method operates by pushing to enlarge what can be imagined and articulated and then testing as well as contesting what will be admitted to the center of our web of beliefs.

Education is a pragmatic exercise. Education and curriculum, what students have an opportunity to learn, enlarge the scope of our imagination and, hence, our possibilities. What opportunities we provide students to learn are subject to never ending debate because the debate is about how we should live our lives and shape our society. These debates are about what belongs in the center of our web of beliefs and how far we should exercise our imagination in challenging accepted beliefs. In a pluralistic society, different populations believe different things and tolerance, a *desideratum* of the pragmatic method, is required to avoid slipping into violent exchanges. This is one lesson of James's appeal to avoid seeking a unitary and essential meaning of "go round" that triggered the dispute in the first place. Pragmatism and education are necessarily political and entwined with the effects and exercise of power as we cope with our inability to articulate essential meanings in providing students opportunities to learn.

CHAPTER 7

A Feminist Re/examination
of William James as
a Qualified Relativist

BARBARA THAYER-BACON

I COME TO William James's work as someone who has had to warm up to James; I started as an outsider. I began on unfriendly terms with James because the first book of his I read was *Talks to Teachers on Psychology: And to Students on Some of Life's Ideals* (1899/1958). As a teacher, and a woman, I was offended by James's patronizing tone as he advised them/us "merely *as teachers*" not to worry (our pretty little heads) about science, and in particular, psychology, for we are overworked already and do not need to add more burdens and develop a bad conscience (pp. 26–27). I struggled with James's focus on students as individuals only, for I view students as individuals-in-relation-with-others. I found James's war metaphors alarming, as he described "the mind of your own enemy, the pupil, is working away from you keenly and eagerly as is the mind of the commander of the other side from the scientific general" (p. 25) and as he described how to find in a struggle with nature the same heroism and strength that war brings out in men, due to war's intensity and dangers. I strongly disagreed with James's description of the role of a teacher, which sounded more like an animal trainer than an educator to me: "You should regard your professional task as if it consisted chiefly and essentially in *training the pupil to behavior*; taking behavior, not in the narrow sense of his manners, but in the very widest possible sense, as including every sort of fit reaction on the circumstances into which he may find himself brought by the vicissitudes of life" (p. 36).

I teach James in my philosophy of education classes because of the significant role he played in American education and psychology, and I work hard to present him fairly and generously, with care, prior to any judgment of his work. This effort and my students' warm responses to much of his advice have caused me to give James a more serious look. And other pragmatists whose work I am in sympathy with, particularly John Dewey (1916/1966, 1929/1960) and Charlene Haddock Seigfried (1978, 1990, 1996), have convinced me as well to give James another chance. I am very grateful that I have re/examined James's ideas; for in doing so I have found an important associate. I have found someone else who struggled to describe how it is we know in holistic terms, relying on a unitary logic and a relational ontology.

My theory of relational (e)pistemology (ways of knowing) is based on the assumption that we are social beings who are embedded and embodied. We are born already members of a community, situated within a particular time and setting and experiencing the world in unique ways. A relational (e)pistemology is not based on an assumption of absolutism, that universal Truth exists and we, as knowers, can know that Truth, contrary to traditional epistemological theories. This is why I place parentheses around the "e" in epistemology in describing my own theory, to clarify, and distinguish it from traditional epistemological theories. Although James places his emphasis on human beings as individuals rather than as social beings, in contrast to a relational approach, still, his radical empiricism and pluralism are based on an assumption of contextuality that we share in common. In this chapter, I explore James's radical empiricism and pluralism, comparing his concept of truths to my *qualified* relativistic perspective, which I distinguish from a *naïve* relativistic position. Naïve relativism relies on a view of reality as a function of human belief and truth as a function of human practice with the logical result that nothing can be proven right or wrong therefore anything goes. Qualified relativism agrees that nothing can be proven absolutely right or wrong but suggests that we can arrive at truths to guide us that are qualified by as much evidence as we can socially muster to settle our doubts and satisfactorily end our inquiry. I argue that James, who was often accused of naïve relativism, actually represents a more qualified relativistic perspective. James offers sound advice on how to avoid the charge of relativism by dissolving the relativist/absolutist duality.

In exchange for the sound advice James offers feminists, feminists have advice to offer James on another important way we can avoid a charge of naïve relativism as well as absolutism, weak or strong (Siegel, 1987), by embracing a view of human beings as social beings. Our own individual fallible perspectives preclude us from claiming a God's-eye view of Truth. However, if we embrace a transactional view of individuals-in-relation-with-others (individuals affect and are connected to others and others are affected and connected to individuals), we have the grounds to insist on the need for others to be involved in the social negotiating process that inquiry must go through, and thus the means to challenge our own/each other's fallible perspectives. We have the grounds to argue for a democratic, pluralistic model of education. Let's begin by exploring James's epistemology, his theory of how it is we come to know.

JAMES'S TRUTHS

Pragmatist scholars such as Seigfried (1990) and West (1989) classify William James as a classical American Pragmatist, yet he certainly held views that differed from his fellow pragmatists, in particular C. S. Peirce. James often compared his views to those of Peirce, and considered his own arguments as contributing to Peirce's views, yet Peirce went to great length to disassociate his own views from those of his friend, James. There are reasons for this disassociation, and these reasons not only help us distinguish James from Peirce but also point to James's unique contribution to pragmatism (some of my discussion of James's work is derived from Chapter 2 of Thayer-Bacon, 2000).

For example, it is well known that James credits Peirce as being the father of pragmatism. However, Peirce (1905/1958) later renamed his own view "pragmaticism" in order to distinguish his ideas from what he judged was James's more relativistic approach. For Peirce, human beings are fallible, limited, contextual beings who cannot trust their ideas or our experiences to lead them to certain Truth. Thus Peirce and his theory of fallibilism bring previous philosophers' assumptions of a God's-eye view of Truth into question. Peirce suggests that because all of us are fallible individuals, we need to work with others, as a scientific community of rational inquirers, to help further our knowledge and understanding. Peirce does not describe "others," nonexperts, as needing to be necessarily included in the discussion, for not everyone has the background knowledge necessary to do the investigating. He wants philosophy to act like science and cooperate, repeat, and test our observations. Peirce (1905/1958) wants philosophy to use severe but fair examination, and use suitable technical nomenclature (single definitions that are universally accepted), where a rationally false step is rarely taken (pp. 184–185).

Peirce's pragmatism is not a theory of Truth but of meaning. Peirce postulates Truth to be something we are emerging toward, in the future. Each generation of scholars works to understand what is Truth as much as they can, and they pass that understanding on to the next generation, who continues the work, and so on. Peirce (1878/1958) states, "True opinion must be the one which they would ultimately come to" (pp. 133–134). He suggests that Truth is what we get at the end of inquiry, at the end of time. It is Peirce's belief that there will be a final, permanent set of beliefs that are True, for there is a resistant reality of material objects that exists external to us and independent of our sense experiences.

Peirce (1878/1958) is clear that reality is not dependent on what any of us individually believes; however, he adds that reality does depend on the real fact that investigation that is continued long enough will lead us to reality. In other words, in answer to possible concerns that his description of reality makes reality dependent on thoughts, Peirce says that reality is independent of what you or I may think about it as people who are finite, though reality is not necessarily independent of thought in general. In the end, our investigations will lead us all to the same conclusions. Peirce's postulation of an independent, objective reality is how he escapes relativism. However, his suggestion that we cannot be sure we have a final understanding of this reality opens the possibility of a more relativised view.

Peirce has been criticized for embracing what seemed to others to be a deterministic stance, that in the end we will all agree on a final opinion of reality, yet for him "ultimate agreement" is simply meant to function as an ideal that should direct us, for "of course, such ultimate agreement never comes" (West, 1989, p. 51). Thus Peirce embraces a doctrine of absolute chance, for there are infinite possibilities for making connections, interactions, and significations of reality. Peirce (1893/1960) writes:

> We cannot be quite sure that the community ever will settle down to an unalterable conclusion upon any given question. Even if they do so for the most part, we have no reason to think that unanimity will be quite complete, nor can we rationally presume any overwhelming *consensus* of opinion will be reached upon every question. All that we are entitled to assume is in the form of a *hope* that such conclusions may be substantially reached concerning the particular questions with which our inquiries are busied. (p. 420)

Peirce's idea of Truth as an emerging absolute, which demands of us endless investigating changes in the hands of other pragmatists, such as James. In James's (1909/1975) hands, Truth becomes truths, which are relative to an individual's situation or context. James followed Peirce's radical lead of incorporating contingency and revision into a theory of truth, yet he unties his theory of truth from Peirce's view of the evolutionary process of inquiry toward Truth and his assumption that Truths are objectively real.

With Peirce James postulates Truth at the end of time but knows that this is just a belief. For James, "To say something is true is to say that it is satisfactory" (Seigfried, 1990, p. 314). In *Pragmatism*, James (1907/1975) italicizes the following definition of truth: *"True ideas are those that we can assimilate, validate, corroborate and verify. False ideas are those that we cannot"* (p. 97). Truth grows and expands in James's hands, and takes on a changing, relational quality. Truth means that ideas (which are themselves just parts of our experience) become true insofar as they help us get into satisfactory relation with other parts of our experience. "The pragmatist, therefore, does not ask with what true ideas agree but what concrete difference in actual life an idea's being true will make" (Seigfried, 1990, pp. 293–294). James (1907/1975) said:

> Truths emerge from facts; but they dip forward into facts again and add to them; which facts again create or reveal new truth (the word is indifferent) and so on indefinitely. The "facts" themselves meanwhile are not *true*. They simply *are*. Truth is the function of the beliefs that start and terminate among them. (p. 108)

Or, put another way: "Truth is only our subjective relation to realities" (p. 89).

Seigfried (1990) argues that James's appeal to the concrete situation does not make him "an unbridled relativist" as others portray him (p. 304). In James's own time, he was criticized for emphasizing the subjective side of truth and ignoring the objective side. James went to great length to refute rationalism and to show that "the rationalist belief in rigor and finality is a chimera." As Seigfried points out: "There is no loss in substituting tentative for absolute standards if absolute standards are impossible" (p. 298). "The charge of subjectivism can be sustained only by clinging to the dogmatic view of reality characteristic of rationalism, which was already refuted by him [James]" (p. 311). James (1907/1975) responded to what he called slanderous criticisms of relativism by asking:

> Pent in, as the pragmatist more than any one else sees himself to be, between the whole body of funded truths squeezed from the past and the coercions of the world of sense around him, who so well as he feels the immense pressure of objective control under which our minds perform their operations? (pp. 111–112)

We call "knowledge" or "truth" what we can assert to the best of our abilities, based on our best efforts to consider all options and solve all doubts so that we can say that what we assert is warranted by our best evidence, based on our best criteria. Or, as James put it, until we are satisfied. James's pragmatic view is not a form of vulgar relativism (also called strong relativism, radical relativism, or the view from everywhere), as he is often accused of, nor is his view as absolute as Peirce's qualified universal view. What James presents is a qualified relativistic view that aims to dissolve the absolute/relative distinction. I use the term "qualified relativism" in an effort to bring absolutism and relativism together, not to reify their separation. However, James's view is vulnerable to criticism because he embraces an individualistic model for knowers rather than a more social model, like that described by Dewey. While James argues for the sacredness of individuality, Dewey (1916/1966) argues for a transactional relationship between individuals and others, and for the importance of inquiring within democratic communities. I will come back to this point in the Conclusion.

Let me say at this point, I use the term *"qualified relativism"* in an effort to distinguish this perspective from vulgar relativism (the view that there is no right or wrong answer, anything goes). Unfortunately, most scholars do not make such a distinction but rather describe relativism in glossed over or extreme terms. Relativism is described as the view from everywhere, and absolutism is described as the view from nowhere. What I describe could be called the view from somewhere. It is different from Peirce's nonvulgar absolutist view, in the same way that James's view differs from Peirce's. I suggest that the difference lies in our logic and ontology, for Peirce remains clearly within the traditional Enlightenment paradigm, even as he describes inquirers in nonvulgar absolutist terms and he proposes an ontology that is based on three basic categories. Peirce still wants to use logic to lead us to the Answer, which he believes in the end will be the same, agreed-upon Answer for all of us. A qualified relativist does not believe we can count on logic to lead us to the Answer, for logic itself is historically influenced and not infallible. Also, a qualified relativist does not believe that in the end there will be one Answer upon which we all agree. Peirce's desire to defend pragmatism against charges of relativism is based on an acceptance of a binary absolutism/relativism distinction which James worked hard to dissolve. What a qualified relativist proposes is nothing less than a transformation of the Enlightenment paradigm by dissolving the binary logic supporting that paradigm.

It is ironic that Peirce's pragmatic method and his concept of fallibilism are what first inspired James to question distinctions between subject/

object, knower/known, and relativism/absolutism. Peirce's ontological realism caused him to strive to separate himself from his fellow pragmatist. Perhaps we can better understand the difference between nonvulgar absolutism (Siegel, 1987) and qualified relativism if we further explore the ontological differences between Peirce and James. Their ontological views affect their epistemological theories, and vice versa. Their beliefs about what sort of world this is will determine how they see it and act within it (what they know), and how they perceive and act will determine their beliefs about the world. We will find that James offers us clear guidelines for distinguishing nonvulgar absolutism from qualified relativism. James shows us how the absolutist/relativist distinction dissolves with his theory of radical empiricism and pluralism. I return to James to examine further his ontological differences from Peirce and how these differences affect their concepts of truth(s). In the next section, I explore James's radical empiricism and in the following section, I will consider James's radical pluralism.

JAMES'S RADICAL EMPIRICISM

James does not maintain the same position as his friend Peirce in terms of an ontology that is based on three basic categories. He also does not embrace a dualistic ontology; rather he strives to describe a unifying one. Because James was accused in his own lifetime of being too subjective, and too relativistic, he addresses head-on the topic of binary logic in his debates with rationalists about his theory of truths. James defends his epistemological theory with the help of a complementary ontological theory, which he calls *radical empiricism*.

In *The Meaning of Truth*, James (1909/1975) defines radical empiricism thus:

> Radical empiricism consists first of a postulate, next of a statement of fact, and finally of a generalized conclusion. The postulate is that the only things that shall be debatable among philosophers shall be things definable in terms of experience. The statement of fact is that the relations between things, conjunctive as well as disjunctive, are just as much matters of direct particular experience, neither more so nor less so, than the things themselves. The generalized conclusion is that therefore the parts of experience hold together from next to next by relations that are themselves parts of experience. (pp. 6–7)

In James's (1912/1976) final work, *Essays in Radical Empiricism*, which was published posthumously, he described his radical empiricism this way:

There is, I mean, no aboriginal stuff or quality of being, contrasted with that of which material objects are made, out of which our thoughts of them are made; but there is a function in experience which thoughts perform, and for the performance of which this quality of being is invoked. That function is *knowing*. (p. 4)

Thus we find James describes a relational ontology that begins as a unity, not as separate entities. James (1912/1976) calls his unity "primal stuff" or "pure experience," the *thatness* of being. With his radical empiricism, knowing is therefore easily explained as "a particular sort of relation towards one another into which portions of pure experience may enter" (p. 4). There is only one primal stuff or material in the world, a stuff of which everything is composed. James's radical empiricism moves to get rid of dualisms in reality. For him, experience has no inner duplicity. Experience just is, in its pure *thatness*. Experience is subjective *and* objective, it is private *and* public, it is internal *and* external, it is thought *and* thing. What we do with pure experience, when we categorize and separate it and create lines of order for it, is by way of addition, not subtraction to pure experience (pp. 6–7).

Experience can serve different functions, and may be of different kinds. When it is taken in different contexts, in different associations, it plays different parts. Thus in a binary logic experience is forced to be either absolute or relativistic, either universal or particular. However, with James's radical empiricism we understand that it is not contradictory to say that experience is both absolute and relative, it is both particular and universal. This tremendous insight James brings to pragmatism is an offering that scholars are still exploring, as I am here in this chapter. James does not present a pragmatic realism as Peirce does (McCarthy, 1997).

James (1912/1976) explains why he calls his ontology "radical empiricism." Rationalism, as the opposite of empiricism, starts with the one, a unified whole, but cannot address particulars, the many. Empiricism starts with particulars, the many, but cannot unify them into a whole. James's description starts with the parts, what he calls pure facts, which is why he calls it "empiricism." It's "radical" because the *"relations that connect experiences must themselves be experienced relations, and any kind of relation experienced must be accounted as 'real' as anything else in the system"* (p. 22, emphasis in original). James thought that empiricism overemphasizes the bare *with-itness* between parts, the disconnection, and rationality tends to ignore how parts are disconnected, whereas radical empiricism emphasizes both the unity and disconnection between parts. The radical empiricist argues that the relation of continuity is a *whatness* just as empirically real as the whatness of separation and discontinuity.

James (1912/1976) tells us he emphasizes the relation of continuity in his discussions because conjunctive experiences have been discredited by empiricists and rationalists and disjunctivity has been overemphasized. Knowers are separated from the known, subjects from objects, and treated as absolutely discontinuous. James reminds us, we add to pure experience, by differentiating and distinguishing, but we always start with "sensible realities" that come to life "in the tissue of experience." Knowledge "is *made*; and made by relations that unroll themselves in time" (p. 29, emphasis in original). Or, put another way: "The instant field of the present is always experience in its 'pure' state, plain unqualified actuality, a simple *that*, as yet undifferentiated into thing and thought, and only virtually classified as objective fact or as someone's opinion about fact" (pp. 36–37, emphasis in original).

The charge of relativism is something James and I can only be guilty of if one assumes there is a distinction between relativism and absolutism. Then absolutism represents what is universally true, and relativism represents what is individually true. However, this false distinction between relativism and absolutism is based on the assumption that knowers are divorced from what is known, that the world exists independently of us and what sense we make of it. This distinction is shown to be false by James's radical empiricism. We find that when the dualism between knowers and the known (subjects/objects) collapses, so does the dualism between relativism and absolutism. What I describe as a qualified relativist position, one based on a pluralistic, fallibilistic perspective and a relational ontology, is the best position I argue any of us are justified to take. Even nonvulgar absolutist positions require a leap of faith that cannot be warranted by our reasoning abilities, as fallible, embedded and embodied social beings.

James tells us his philosophy "harmonizes best with a radical pluralism," so I would like to turn now to an exploration of just what he means by "radical pluralism," and see how his pluralism compares to the pluralism to which feminists refer. Contrary to Peirce's community of scholars, feminists argue the need to include outsiders (others) in any testing of "truths," as women have historically been categorized as the Other (feminist standpoint epistemology). They find support for this position with Dewey, but what about James? Given that James argues for radical empiricism from within an individualistic perspective, maybe his radical pluralism further protects him from charges of relativism, since he does not turn to a social democratic model for support. I turn to James's radical pluralism to help us further understand his qualified relativistic view.

JAMES'S RADICAL PLURALISM

In *A Pluralistic Universe,* James (1909/1977) argues that the world we experience is more than we can describe. James declares, "Concrete reality and experience are richer, more dynamic, and thicker than can possibly be expressed by our concepts" (cited in Bernstein's Introduction, p. xiv). James describes reality as genuinely continuous and active. "Reality is not a closed system; it is ontologically open" (cited in Bernstein's Introduction, p. xvi). He describes our theories as incomplete, open, and imperfect. He shows how conceptual knowledge is very valuable, but it stays on the surface of things. Conceptual knowledge is like a fishing net that we use to capture our experiences. It helps us catch knowledge about things, while the rest of our experiences fall through the holes of the net. Conceptual knowledge cannot catch up all that exists. For James, "What really *exists* is not things made but things in the making" (p. 117, emphasis in original). "Reality, life, experience, concreteness, immediacy, use what word you will, exceeds our logic, overflows and surrounds it" (p. 96). Reality is nonrational; it is where things *happen.*

James shows over and over again how philosophy is guilty of "vicious intellectualism" owing to its reliance on the use of concepts as if they are absolute when they are unable to penetrate and capture the flux and depth of concrete reality and experience. It's not that certain concepts are limiting, but that all concepts are. Vicious intellectualism is when we treat a name as if it includes all that the name points to, as if the name stands for reality. James criticizes various forms of vicious intellectualism: absolute idealism and atomistic empiricism, for example. Empiricism explains wholes by parts (each-form), and rationalism explains parts by wholes (all-form).

James suggests there are degrees in rationality; there are tighter weaves of netting used to catch up concepts. He describes the universe as loosely connected. Rather than taking either side of the each/all debate (relativism or absolutism), James (1909/1977) suggests we embrace the notion of *some.* "Radical empiricism and pluralism stand out for the legitimacy of the notion of *some*: Each part of the world is in some ways connected, in some other ways not connected with its other parts, and the ways can be discriminated, for many of them are obvious, and their differences are obvious to view" (pp. 40–41, emphasis in original). With James, the classical absolutism/relativism dualism collapses, as does monism and even atomistic pluralism. James does not solve the absolutism versus relativism problem; he dissolves it.

James (1909/1977) discusses the work of Henri Bergson, a French philosopher who was first a mathematician before becoming a philosopher. He tells us Bergson is who made him bold, for Bergson criticizes intellectualism. Bergson helped James understand that Plato began vicious intellectualism by teaching us "that what a thing really is, is told to us by its *definition*" (p. 99). Plato thought that a definition could stand for reality. James argues that first we have immediate experience, his radical empiricism, the mere *thatness* of experiences. Then we frame our experiences; we name them, with concepts. However, our immediate experiences always overflow concepts and logic, conjunctions and disjunctions. "Concepts are only man-made extracts from the temporal flux" (p. 99). So we find that first concepts become a method, then a habit, and finally a tyranny. "Concepts, first employed to make things intelligible, are clung to even when they make them unintelligible" (p. 99).

Since Plato and Aristotle, we have valued fixities over change, concepts over immediate experiences. Bergson inverts Plato and moves away from concepts toward perceptions. As James describes this inversion, he contrasts theoretical or scientific knowledge to speculative knowledge (Bergson's perceptions). Theoretical or scientific knowledge is knowledge *about* things. It touches on the outer surface of reality and can only name the surface as a spectator. Speculative knowledge is a passive and receptive listening, an intuitive sympathy, a dive back into the flux itself to *know* reality, in terms of direct acquaintance. Concepts negate the inwardness of reality. Because concepts fix things into place, they help us avoid context. "When we conceptualize we cut out and fix, and exclude everything but what we have fixed. A concept means *that-and-no-other*" (James, 1909/ 1977, p. 113, emphasis in original). Logic makes static cuts at life trying to hold it in place, and "real life laughs at logic's veto" (p. 115).

To sum up James's (1909/1977) argument:

> Our intellectual handling of [life] is a retrospective patchwork, a postmortem dissection, and can follow any order we find most expedient. We can make the thing seem self-contradictory whenever we wish to. But place yourself at the point of view of the thing's interior *doing*, and all these back-looking and conflicting conceptions lie harmoniously in your hand. . . . What really *exists* is not things made but things in the making. (p. 117)

Thus we find that James's (1909/1977) doctrine of pluralism means "that nothing real is absolutely simple, that every smallest bit of experience is a *multum in pravo* plurally related, that each relation is one aspect, character, or function, way of its being taken, or way of its taking something else; and that a bit of reality when actively engaged in one of these relations is not *by that very fact* engaged in all the other relations simultaneously" (p. 145, emphasis in original). Whenever we try to describe our experiences, "something always escapes." Logic will always fail to reach completely adequate conclusions, for it always omits something. Absolutism insists everything is present to *everything* else, but James has proved that with our concepts, "things are 'with' one another in many ways, but nothing includes everything or dominates over everything" (p. 145).

Again, we find that the difference between Peirce and James highlights James's unique contribution to pragmatism. Peirce clung to absolutism, even though a nonvulgar absolutism, thus undermining his own fallibilism with his ontological realism. James dissolves the absolute/relativist dichotomy with his theory of radical empiricism and pluralism. For James, the universe is unfinished and everything cannot be present to everything else.

How does James compare to feminists who consider themselves qualified relativists? Certainly his argument for the limitations and tyrannical use of man-made concepts is one that is very helpful to feminists, as they make the case that concepts have fixed the world in ways that exclude them, and that concepts are in need of constant critique and revision. They agree with James that concepts need to be treated with humility and responsibility. James's idea of sympathetic acquaintance, of passive and receptive listening, is also in harmony with work feminists are doing to describe women's ways of knowing and caring reasoning (Belenky et al., 1986; Gilligan, 1982; Keller, 1983, 1985; Noddings, 1984; Ruddick, 1989; Thayer-Bacon, 1993, 1997, 2000a, 2000b).

However, one weakness James has is his clinging to an individual model. Although he argues for pluralism in terms of experiences that are fluid and in flux, that are many, he does not consistently address pluralism in terms of the diversity of human beings within his epistemological theory. Although James powerfully makes the case for the limitations of concepts and logic and our use of them to fix our experiences, he does not take up Peirce's fallibilism and expand upon it, as Dewey does, to include the limitations of human beings, in general, due to their own situatedness. James makes a strong argument and is successful at avoiding the charges of relativism, but feminists have much to offer that helps make James's case even stronger. Let us step outside of James's worldview and look at the issue of qualified relativism from a feminist perspective.

FEMINISTS AS QUALIFIED RELATIVISTS

Feminists who argue as qualified relativists stress that the construction of knowledge is social, interactive, flexible, and ongoing. Qualified relativists describe knowers as socially embedded and embodied inquirers who are limited in their knowing by their environment, which includes their experiences with the world around them and each other, and their human capacities. Because people are social beings formed in relationships, those relationships will cause people to be formed certain ways and not others and will limit the possibilities of knowing. As Jane Flax (1983) points out, "the boundaries of knowledge are our experiences and our human abilities" (p. 249). Qualified relativists argue that Euro-western philosophy *and* science are both embedded within layers of contextuality that influence and limit philosophers' *and* scientists' theories and experiments continually.

Qualified relativists embrace Peirce's fallibilism, James's truths as satisfactory relations, and Dewey's warranted assertability. Qualified relativists "assume . . . that knowledge is the product of human beings. Thinking is a form of human activity that cannot be treated in isolation from other forms of human activity including the forms of human activity which in turn shape the humans who think. Consequently, philosophies will inevitably bear the imprint of the social relations out of which they and their creators arose" (Flax, 1983, p. 248). They argue that our ontological and epistemological premises are like a net of beliefs woven together that become partially self-validating and that are greatly affected by our contextuality.

Qualified relativists find that criteria for choosing ideas or judging concepts are fallible, as criteria are human constructions, and therefore subject to change and improvement. As Sandra Harding (1993) describes, "the grounds for knowledge are fully saturated with history and social life rather than abstracted from it" (p. 57). Or, as Lorraine Code (1991) asserts: "Theories that transcend the specificities of gendered and otherwise situated subjectivites are impotent to come to terms with the politics of knowledge" (p. 315). Feminists describe the criteria we use to help us settle our doubts similarly to the classic pragmatists, yet without the bias toward science that Peirce, James, and Dewey tend to express. They place an emphasis on the social negotiating process that inquiry must go through, to help us reach satisfactory (though usually temporary and tentative) conclusions. We continue to inquire, and we try to support our understandings with as much "evidence" as we can socially construct, qualified by the best criteria upon which we can agree. A qualified relativist grounds her claims "in experiences and practices, in the efficacy of dialogical negotiation and of action" (Code, 1993, p. 39).

The roots of American Pragmatism developed at the same time that science was gaining in status in the Euro-western world, and the value and status of scientific thinking is assumed by Peirce, James, and Dewey in their work. However, we find in James's radical pluralism a criticism of philosophy and science (theoretical or scientific knowledge) as being just knowledge *about* things, which only touches the outer surface of reality. Thus James offers support for feminist arguments that science itself is embedded in values that cause scientists to describe the world in certain ways and not others.

Yet James does not overall offer feminists support for their position that knowers are social rather than solitary, individuals. James holds a democratic respect for the sacredness of individuality and believes there is no point of view absolutely public and universal. For James (1907/1975), pragmatism is a reconciler and mediator; it is a way of testing probable truth. Pragmatism's only test is "what works best in the way of leading us, what fits every part of life best and combines with the collectivity of experience's demands, nothing being omitted" (p. 522). Feminists agree that there is no view from everywhere, but they do not wish to embrace a view from nowhere either. Qualified relativists insist of acknowledging our own particularities and situatedness, which we learn to recognize through our social interactions with others not like us.

Because James embraced individual values, and a "live and let live" attitude, he never had to place his own sexist views under scrutiny. Thus his individualism made it possible for him to avoid confronting his own limitations, which were harmful and had exclusionary results for women (Seigfried, 1996). James's "live and let live" attitude allowed him to maintain his romantic notion of women as Other and not have his sexist stereotypes challenged and criticized by others. James's insistence on individualism allowed him to continue to embrace patriarchal values, which is why it is difficult to call him a friend of feminism, although we can call him an associate, as I did in my opening.

Because James insists on maintaining an individual perspective, he loses opportunities for recommending how we can gain understanding of our own contextualities and further avoid charges of relativism. However, another pragmatist and friend of James's, John Dewey, offers feminists a transactional model that helps us further avoid these charges. Dewey describes individuals as selves-in-relation-with-others. For Dewey, dynamic changes take place with the self and others owing to their interactions with each other, and all are affected by this relational process. With Mead (1934), Dewey recognizes that individuals start out as members of communities. However, Dewey distinguishes his views from Mead's when he goes on to describe how social groups affect individuals *and* individuals affect social groups, whereas Mead's focus tends to remain on the social influence on individuals. In *Democracy and Education*, Dewey (1916/1966) offers a description of a democratic community that recognizes the interactive, interdependent qualities of individuals-in-relation-to-others.

James's individualism places him at risk of not having to address his own limitations, whereas Dewey's transactional model insists on placing one's views in continual critique with others' perspectives. We can understand how the two philosophers differ by comparing James's and Dewey's views to feminist standpoint epistemologists, such as Sandra Harding. Harding's feminist standpoint epistemology is a project of authorizing the speech of marginalized subjects. In "Rethinking Standpoint Epistemology: What Is 'Strong Objectivity'?," Harding (1993) presents the position that subjects who are not members of the community have views to offer, as outsiders, that will help members of the community become more aware of their own biases and prejudices. People from other cultures can help us better understand our own culture. (And reading books, etc., written in earlier times helps us understand past views in relation to our current cultural views). So, for example, interviewing women and asking for their perspectives may help women and men see the world from other angles; or talking to women from oppressed, third world nations will help women from first world nations see the assumptions they make about life as a woman.

Harding's (1993) method is to draw from the margins, "from marginalized lives," and to "take everyday life as problematic" (p. 50). She "sets the relationship between knowledge and politics at the center of [her] account" (p. 56). Her perspective emphasizes the social influence communities have on knowledge production. As she so aptly describes this social context, subjects/agents are not individuals, they are "multiple, heterogeneous and contradictory or incoherent, not unitary, homogeneous, and coherent as they are for empiricist epistemology" (p. 65). Please note that although Harding argues, like Mead (1934), that we are each influenced by the community (or communities) we are born into, it is important to consider the level this effect has on the individual or the community. Dewey's (1916/1966) transactional model helps feminists avoid excessive social determinism and individualism, with his argument that social context is interrelational and transactional, a dialectical relationship that is not just one-way.

Although Harding (1993) presents feminist standpoint epistemology as relying on a logic that refuses to treat its subjects of knowledge as if they are general and universally True, she goes on to make the claim that some perspectives are more revealing than others. When she does so, she is in trouble, for she falls into the same trap for which she has criticized other theorists. Harding recommends that looking from the margins helps people see the dominant culture and its assumptions of superiority. The question that other feminists have asked, particularly third world nonwestern feminists, is, why do you assume that marginalized perspectives have more agency than perspectives within the dominant culture (Bar On, 1993; Narayan, 1989)? "Although the claim to epistemic privilege as a tool may seem to be a claim of the oppressed, due to some of its history, it nonetheless reveals itself also as a master's tool" (Bar On, 1993, p. 97). If it is wrong for men to assume they understand and can speak for women, isn't it also wrong for (white, middle-class, heterosexual) women to assume they can speak for women who are poor, women who are black, women who are lesbians? "There are no tools that can replace it [the notion of epistemic privilege], nor are any needed, because when the oppressed feel a need to authorize speech, they are acting on feelings that are a function of their oppression. Speech needs to be authorized only when silence is the rule" (Bar On, 1993, p. 97).

Contrary to James's individualism, feminists as qualified relativists argue along similar lines to Dewey's (1916/1966) concept of a democratic community. They agree with Dewey that the more other voices are included in the conversation, the more each of us can trust that we have considered all available information and can hope to make a sound judgment. Public schools are a place where diverse children can come together and begin to learn more about their own limitations through their interactions with others not like them. That anyone can hope to arrive at a judgment that is a consensus/integration of other voices is probably not possible. It is likely not even desirable. Not all of us are going to agree on the rightness of judgments made by individuals or communities. However, discussion of the ideas is something inquirers can strive for. A transactional model of individuals as social beings who are in relation to each other helps us further avoid charges of relativism, and still enables us to embrace a qualified relativist position.

CONCLUSION

I have argued that, depending on one's own ontological leanings, it is possible to find support for absolutism as well as relativism in classic pragmatism. Peirce represents a nonvulgar absolutist perspective with his pragmatist realism, and James represents a qualified relativist perspective with his radical empiricism and pluralism. However, to make absolutism/relativism one's focus for argumentation is really to miss the tremendous insight that pragmatism has to offer, which is a way to dissolve this dualism. Although James (and Dewey) spent significant energy in his own lifetime trying to clarify this point, it seems to be one that continually resurfaces, for the desire for a separate Reality and transcendental Truth runs long and deep in Euro-western philosophical traditions.

I hope that my exploration of James's epistemology and metaphysics has helped shed light on what distinguishes James, and my, qualified relativism from Peirce's pragmatic realism. James and I agree that truths or knowledge are what we can assert to the best of our abilities, based on our best efforts to consider all options and solve all doubts so that we can say that what we assert is warranted by our best evidence, based on our best criteria. James and I also embrace a relational ontology that begins as a unity, the mere thatness of pure experience, and describes pure experience as always overflowing our concepts and logic. I also hope that by comparing and contrasting James's views to Peirce's the reader has gained a greater appreciation of James's unique contributions to pragmatism. James offers us a way out of dualistic thinking, by embracing a concept of experience as an unanalyzable totality. Our analysis is what we add to pure experience. Experience can take on many shapes and forms, depending on its functions. We understand experience in terms of its relations.

However, we have also found where James differs from feminists, for James applied his relational ontology mainly to criticisms concerning concepts but not concerning social relationships. I have recommended that James's relational ontology needs to be expanded to include social relationships. I have suggested that Dewey and social feminists both argue for a relational ontology on the grounds of social relations. Their work has much to offer James in helping to extend his arguments against individual relativism, just as James has much to offer feminists by extending their arguments against conceptual relativism. Feminists offer educators support for the affirmation of cultural diversity and the need to include others, outsider views, in the inquiring process. Including others helps us reach beyond our own limitations. Yet feminists also warn educators to be careful not to privilege particular outsider views, for all views are limited and partial. Like James, feminists offer educators a description of our world as pluralistic in terms of believing in the impossibility of attaining knowledge that is universal, that there will be one set of final answers, one Form of Truth at the end of time.

In the last section I argued that a claim to know can only be assured through interaction with others, and that assurance is tenuous, open to further revision. I did not offer there a theory of Truth, nor did I offer a theory of relative truths. I suggested truths, warranted assertions, are what we can qualify by all the evidence and critique we can muster, as embedded and embodied social beings in conversation with each other. As teachers and students, we must negotiate with each other in order to come to an agreement of what is, and then pass our efforts on to the next generation for them to debate and discuss further. I suggested that individuals can/do make individual contributions to knowledge, but they do not do so as isolated individuals, they are always already community members. We can avoid charges of social determinism and/or naïve relativism by placing our emphasis on the social negotiating process that we must go through, to help us settle our doubts and satisfactorily end our inquiry.

CHAPTER 8

From Radical Empiricism to Radical Constructivism, or William James Meets Ernst von Glasersfeld

D. C. PHILLIPS

EARLY IN MY academic career I was asked by my dean to organize a debate, to be open to the campus-wide community, on the future of private, nongovernmental schooling; he was particularly insistent that a well-known Marxist theorist with strong views on the topic be invited to participate, and my task was to invite an "opponent" and to sweat over the details. All this I did. But the day before the widely publicized event, the anti-Marxist phoned to inform me that he was ill. Desperately I solicited names of a last-minute replacement from my colleagues—"who had strong feelings on private schools and was a lively speaker?" At last I found a name, and the person agreed, despite the shortness of time. To my horror I discovered, just before the debate opened, that he, too, was a Marxist! Clearly I had bungled my first public test. I need not have worried; as soon as the introductions were done, the speakers went for each other's throats in a manner that was quite astonishing. I learned an important lesson: Just because individuals accept the same philosophical or political "ism," it does not follow that they will agree. And conversely, just because they accept different "isms," it does not follow that they will disagree over issues of practice or policy. The devil, as usual, is in the details of the respective positions.

I dredge up this piece of ancient history to alert readers to a key issue that surfaces in the following discussion. Though the two are separated by a century, there is nonetheless a great deal that unites the philosophical commitments of the men named in my title, the great co-founder of late-19th and early-20th-century classic pragmatism (and self-styled "radical empiricist") William James, and the currently heavily cited founder of late-20th-century "radical constructivism" (a major position influencing contemporary thought about school curriculum and teaching especially in science and mathematics), Ernst von Glasersfeld. And yet, despite the great similarities in the philosophical positions that they have endorsed, there are important differences in emphasis. How can this be? Whose emphases stand up better to critical scrutiny? But to complicate matters further, there seem to be major similarities in the educational practices that they would endorse. Does radical empiricism, then, collapse into radical constructivism? Or perhaps vice-versa? Is James really a late-20th-century intellect, or is von Glasersfeld a late-19th-century one? What, I sometimes have wondered, would they have said to each other if they had met on the same podium?

Before launching into this daunting agenda, I need to attend to two preliminary matters. First, it is appropriate to make a brief comment about the men themselves. I have met neither, though of course I wish I had. Although there are aspects of the thought of each with which I disagree (more, perhaps, in the case of my contemporary than in the case of James), I find their writings attractive: They produce (or produced) lively, clear prose; and they are straightforward about the positions they endorse and the implications that they see as following from these. Their own personalities seem to infuse their work; and both are, simply, *interesting*. (James's biography is quite well known; von Glasersfeld (1995) has an autobiographical sketch in his major book.) Finally, von Glasersfeld greatly appreciates William James, and his recent book has a number of very positive references to the famous pragmatist—all to passages and aspects of James's writings that I, too, admire. One cannot help liking a person who has the same philosophical heroes.

Second, it might be as well at the outset to indicate something of the close resemblance between the two men, apart from their mutual use of the term "radical." Consider the following two passages, which seem to impart a strikingly similar message but which nevertheless mask some important but fairly subtle differences that will emerge more clearly later. The first comes from von Glasersfeld (1995):

> From the constructivist perspective, knowledge does not constitute a "picture" of the world. It does not represent the world at all—it comprises action

schemes, concepts, and thoughts. And it distinguishes the ones that are considered advantageous from those that are not. In other words, it pertains to the ways and means the cognizing subject has conceptually evolved to fit into the world as he or she experiences it. It follows that what we ordinarily call "facts" are not elements of an observer-independent world but elements of an observer's experience. (p. 114)

Compare this with the following extract from *Essays in Radical Empiricism*, a collection of essays that was published in book form in 1912, several years after James's death. Here James (1912/1966) explains why it is that the unbroken stream of a person's experience, which initially has "no inner duplicity," eventually gets filled with "ever more abounding conceptual distinctions":

> The naturalist answer is that the environment kills as well as sustains us, and that the tendency of raw experience to extinguish the experient himself is lessened just in the degree in which elements in it that have a practical bearing on life are analyzed out of the continuum and verbally fixed and coupled together, so that we know what is in the wind for us and get ready to react in time. Had pure experience, the naturalist says, been always perfectly healthy, there would never have arisen the necessity of isolating or verbalizing any of its terms. (pp. 96–97)

In short, because the environment is just as likely to harm us as to nurture us, we need to crystalize out of our experience some "advantageous" concepts and regularities that will allow us to deal with it successfully.

In both passages we can detect some key—and interrelated—themes: (1) the evolutionary or biological function of thought; (2) the fact that ideas are human constructs that serve (or that we hope serve) to foster survival in a sometimes inhospitable or "unhealthy" environment; and (3) the fact that the basic reality for humans is experience—it is this that is aboriginal and from which our knowledge is filtered out. Because of these similarities, because they share many of the same concerns (although, clearly, James's philosophical horizon is much broader than von Glasersfeld's and encompasses issues of ethics and religion that the latter does not address), I shall write as if the two of them are contemporaries. More than this, I shall treat them as if they are in the same family—although, when family disagreements come to the fore, my own view is that von Glasersfeld would have been wise to capitulate to his older brother.

It is time to turn to the similarities that were listed above—similarities that will turn out to mask some significant differences of emphasis. Because these are interrelated, they will be discussed together, but the two men at the focus of our attention will be taken separately.

JAMES AND THE THINKING ORGANISM AS ACTOR

James was one of the earliest to recognize the psychological implications of evolutionary theory, and he was (to use Newton's well-known expression) one of the giants upon whose shoulders John Dewey stood; there are passages in the latter's *School and Society* (notably in Chapter IV, "The Psychology of Elementary Education") that are very close indeed to James's words in his preceding psychological writings. James was not, of course, the first to see the relevance of evolutionary thought—Herbert Spencer "beat the gun" and wrote a book on evolutionary psychology a few years before the appearance of Darwin's book in 1859. After a short period of initial admiration of it, James came to disagree with the line that Spencer took, and his first publication in 1878 (James, 1878/1992, pp. 893–909) was in fact a critique of the predecessor's work (of which, more later; for a recent discussion of this aspect of Spencer and James, see Godfrey-Smith, 1996). But it is interesting to note in passing that Ernst von Glasersfeld (1995) refers to James's critique of Spencer as "a brilliant essay, in which he pits Darwin's precise notion of selection against Spencer's hollow sociological assumptions" (p. 42). Despite their mutual antipathy toward Herbert Spencer and their admiration of Darwin, there are, as we shall see, some significant differences between the pragmatist and the radical constructivist.

James's core evolutionary line of thought is set out very straightforwardly in the short and readable book, *Talks to Teachers on Psychology* (1899/ 1915), that was based upon the extremely popular lectures he gave in the years immediately following the publication of his two-volume (and now classic work) *The Principles of Psychology* in 1890. He argued that the theory of evolution had effected a transformation in our view of the function of thought, moving the focus from the "rational function" where the "classical tradition in philosophy had placed it," to the role it plays in prompting us to "useful conduct." James (1899/1915) wrote:

> Man, we now have reason to believe, has been evolved from infra-human ancestors, in whom pure reason hardly existed, if at all, and whose mind, so far as it can have had any function, would appear to have been an organ for adapting their movements to the impressions received from the environment, so as to escape the better from destruction. (pp. 726–727)

A paragraph later he added:

> I shall ask you now . . . to adopt with me, in this course of lectures, the biological conception, as thus expressed, and to lay your own emphasis on the

fact that man, whatever else he may be, is primarily a practical being, whose mind is given him to aid in adapting to this world's life. (p. 727)

The role of education, he asserts, is to "supervise" the process by which students acquire "numerous and perfect" reactions to the "impressions" that they are receiving from the environment (ch. 6). These various passages seem to paint a picture of the human capacity to think as somewhat passive—they make it appear as if cognition only aids us in adapting to an "external" environment that is, in a sense, "given" to us or that forces itself upon our attention. But this was far from James's intent, and it is here that the 1878 essay on Spencer is vitally important as a corrective.

JAMES, MIND, AND THE REAL WORLD

Although James placed a great deal of emphasis on experience, and even elevates it to the primary metaphysical category in his later work (see, e.g., the essay "A World of Pure Experience" in his *Essays in Radical Empiricism,* 1912/1996, ch. 2), he was—from his earliest through his later writings— in some sense of that much abused term a *realist* about the external world. The world as we initially experience it may indeed be "a blooming buzzing Confusion" (to use his oft-quoted expression), but it is a real world, nevertheless. We gradually learn how to make sense of it, and we even help to shape it—for, crucially, the human mind is *part* of the world, and it can affect and to some degree shape that world via the actions that it directs, the concepts that it builds, and so forth. That is the message conveyed in a powerful passage in James's (1878/1992) essay on Spencer, a passage that von Glasersfeld does not sufficiently appreciate:

> I, for my part, cannot escape the consideration, forced upon me at every turn, that the knower is not simply a mirror floating with no foot-hold anywhere, and passively reflecting an order that he comes upon and finds simply existing. The knower is an actor, and co-efficient of the truth on one side, whilst on the other he registers the truth which he helps to create. Mental interests, hypotheses, postulates, so far as they are bases for human action—action which to a great extent transforms the world—help to *make* the truth which they declare. In other words, there belongs to mind, from its birth upward, a spontaneity, a vote. It is in the game, and not a mere looker-on. (p. 908)

This passage seems to be the source of the label "the spectator theory of knowledge" that John Dewey used for the position that he, too, derided—

and the attacks on which were not only the core of his epistemology but an important springboard for much of his educational theory as well (see Dewey, 1929/1960, and also the lengthy discussion in Kulp, 1992); Dewey stressed that our actions, guided by our ideas, can bring into existence an environment that had been envisioned in advance. The same passage might also have been the inspiration behind the title of Richard Rorty's (1979) famous attack on mind as a "mirror of nature."

In essence James was objecting here to what Peter Godfrey-Smith (1996) has recently called the "externalism" in Spencer's position. In Spencer's account, the "causal arrow" went from the external environment to the mind of the organism; mind evolved to effect "adjustments" of the "inner" to the "outer," a view that makes mind, in an important respect, a rather passive adaptive faculty that *reacts* but that does not *initiate*. James (1878/1992) wrote that a "brain which functions so as to [only] insure survival may, therefore, be called intelligent in no other sense than a tooth, a limb, or a stomach" (p. 905). According to James's view, however, mind is active, it initiates, it can bring about changes in the environment that would not otherwise exist. The intelligent cognizing organism will not be concerned to act just so as to foster survival in a hostile environment; it will be "teleological" in the sense that it will operate according to desires, values, and ideals:

> In other words, we are fated to be, *a priori,* teleologists whether we will or no. Interests which we bring with us, and simply posit or take our stand upon, are the very flour out of which our mental dough is kneaded. The organism of thought, from the vague dawn of discomfort or ease in the polyp to the intellectual joy of Laplace among his formulas, is teleological through and through. (p. 904)

This position might also be "externalist" in Godfrey-Smith's terminology, but it is a far cry from Spencer's brand of externalism.

James, then, sees mind or intelligence—and the cognizing organism—as part of the world, interacting with it and influencing it while being influenced by it. This is a view that, as numerous later commentators have noted and built upon, is an attempt to breach the chasm that traditional epistemologies open up between inner and outer—between mind and world, which are usually conceived as inhabiting different realms, thereby creating the problem of how it is that one can interact with (or know) the other.

As mentioned earlier, this view that mind is "in the game" was incorporated, near the end of his life, into James's metaphysics of pure experience (published in book form in 1912) according to which "there is only one primal stuff or material in the world, a stuff of which everything is composed . . . pure experience" (James, 1912/1996, p. 4). The epistemological point of this emerges in the following passage:

> The first great pitfall from which such a radical standing by experience will save us is an artificial conception of the *relations between knower and known.* Throughout the history of philosophy the subject and its object have been treated as absolutely discontinuous entities; and thereupon the presence of the latter to the former, or the "apprehension" by the former of the latter, has assumed a paradoxical character which all sorts of theories had to be invented to overcome. (p. 52, emphasis in original)

It seems fair to remark that the view that mind was both an *agent* in the world and (thereby) an *inhabitant* of the same world as the things about which it may want to gain knowledge—a view that James held from his first writings until his last—sprang initially from his common sense and his work as an evolutionary-oriented psychologist, and also from his nascent philosophical musings. Later, in *Essays in Radical Empiricism*, he defended this position—or undergirded it—with a subtle metaphysical theory.

JAMES'S MATURE METAPHYSICS

The details of James's mature position are worked out in some detail in the essays collected in the 1912 book and raise difficult questions which, mercifully, are not on the agenda for discussion here. The three points that will be relevant when we turn to a comparison with Ernst von Glasersfeld are as follows. First, as discussed above, James continued to place the knower in the real world, and not in a separate realm; he removed the chasm between inner and outer, between knower and the known. He does this in 1912 by situating them both within the "flux of experience" (see Ellen Kappy Suckiel's "Introduction" to James, 1912/1996). Second, as pointed out earlier, it is fair to count James as a realist; indeed, in 1912 he occasionally uses the expression "natural realism" to describe his own position. But clearly the 1878 essay on Spencer is replete with realist language; and it is worth noting, too, what he says near the end of this piece: "The only objective criterion of reality is coerciveness, in the long run, over thought" (James, 1878/1992, p. 908). Reality is what we constantly knock up against; it is (to use a non-Jamesian term) a constraint. All this, of course, fits well with the "biological conception of mind" that he advocated in *Talks to Teachers*; there is indeed something real, something coercive, about an environment that is out to kill us unless we are smart enough to foresee the threats and take evasive countermeasures! Third, it follows from the facts that (according to the James of 1912) mind and nature are aspects of "pure experience," and that parts or aspects of pure experience can come into relationships with other parts, that we can have direct contact with objects in nature. To use the example to which he constantly returns in *Essays in Radical Empiricism*, we can directly perceive the object known to Harvard folk as Memorial Hall (a real object if ever there was one). As a famous later Harvard philosopher expresses it, "James contended that there is nothing at all wrong with the commonsense idea that . . . we directly perceive external things—people, trees, buildings, and the rest" (Putnam, 1990, p. 230). But although this view was defended with some subtlety in 1912, essentially the same position can be found in his work from almost two decades earlier. Thus in *Psychology: The Briefer Course* (1892)—which was a one-volume version of his great two-volume *Principles*—he defended, a page before his classic reference to the experience of the baby as being a "blooming buzzing Confusion," the commonsense view that:

> Every thing or quality felt is felt in outer space. It is impossible to conceive a brightness or a color otherwise than as extended and outside the mind. Sounds also appear in space. Contacts are against the body's surface; and pains always occupy some organ. An opinion which has had much currency in psychology is that sensible qualities are first apprehended as *in the mind itself*, and then "projected" from it, or "extradicted", by a secondary intellectual or super-sensational mental act. There is no ground whatever for this opinion. (James, 1892/1992, p. 23, emphasis in original)

This passage is a nice segue into the work of Ernst von Glasersfeld, who actually advocates the "groundless" position to which James refers!

ERNST VON GLASERSFELD AND THE CONSTRUCTION OF "REALITY"

The sources of von Glasersfeld's "radical constructivist" philosophy are clear; he himself acknowledges the classic empiricists Locke and Berkeley, the early-18th-century constructivist philosopher Giambattista Vico, and also Kant and Piaget (the latter, of course, having himself been influenced by Kant and Darwin). Furthermore, von Glasersfeld (1990) came to think of himself as a "post-epistemological" thinker (p. 19). There are grounds, however, to think that there is nothing "post" about him at all— his thought is firmly entrenched in the mainstream epistemological tradition; some commentators have seen him as a contemporary (and therefore out-of-date) classic empiricist, and this is closer to the mark (see, e.g., Matthews, 1994, ch. 7). But the most accurate accounting of him is that he is swimming in the strong skeptical current that has been flowing through Western epistemology since its beginning; indeed, a section of a short and straightforward essay written in 1990 is titled "The Way of the Skeptics," and it begins with a positive reference to Xenophanes:

> To Xenophanes (6th century B.C.) we may credit the insight that even if someone succeeded in describing exactly how the world really is, he or she would have no way of knowing that it was the "true" description. This is the major argument the skeptics have repeated for two thousand five hundred years. It is based on the assumption that whatever ideas or knowledge we have must have been derived in some way from our experience, which includes sensing, acting and thinking. If this is the case, we have no way of checking the truth of our knowledge with the world presumed to lie beyond our experiental interface. . . . These are extremely uncomfortable arguments. Philosophers have forever tried to dismantle them, but they have had little success. (pp. 20–21)

His only criticism of the skeptical tradition "lies in its polemical formulation" (p. 21).

According to von Glasersfeld (1995), then, "knowledge is not passively received but built up by the cognizing subject," and "the function of cognition is adaptive and serves the organization of the experiental world, *not the discovery of ontological reality*" (p. 18, emphasis added). In the introduction to a book on mathematics education he edited a few years earlier he had amplified this position via an attack on the "naïve commonsense perspective" (a sophisticated and far from naïve version of which was attributed above to William James):

> [From] the naïve commonsense perspective, the elements that form this complex environment belong to a *real* world of unquestionable objects, as *real* as the student, and these objects have an existence of their own, independent not only of the student but also of the teacher. Radical Constructivism is a theory of *knowing* which . . . does not accept this commonsense perspective. . . . Superficial or emotionally distracted readers of the constructivist literature have frequently interpreted this stance as a denial of "reality." (von Glasersfeld, 1991, p. xv, emphasis in original)

VON GLASERSFELD AND THE SKEPTICAL TRADITION

The line of reasoning that led von Glasersfeld to reject the "commonsense perspective" started with the same point that Locke and Kant (not to mention James) had accepted, namely, that the knower is only "in direct contact" with his or her own experience that is—as von Glasersfeld (1995) put it—"the reality we live in" (p. 116). However, the next step in his argument is the one where he and James somewhat diverge: As a true member of the skeptical tradition, von Glasersfeld (1996) insists that whatever lies outside our experience—the realm of "things in themselves"—is unknowable, which is not to say that he denies the reality of whatever it is that exists outside of experience, and he certainly recognizes that it can act as a constraint upon our conceptual activities (p. 19). It is on this basis that von Glasersfeld says that he does not reject the notion of "reality," but he is a realist who places the realities in an unknowable realm *outside* experience, whereas James is a realist who places them *inside*. (To complexify matters here, Richard Rorty is an interesting figure whose views are worth comparing with those of James and von Glasersfeld. Following a suggestion from the noted epistemologist Donald Davidson, he advocates that we "stop trying to say *anything* general about the relation between language and reality," for there is no "description independent way the world is"; see Rorty, 1998, p. 90, emphasis added.)

Von Glasersfeld also drew the conclusion (not unlike the one James drew in his pragmatic essays on truth; see Phillips, 1984) that we cannot hold that our so-called knowledge is true, if truth is defined as it usually is, in terms of our ideas "corrresponding to reality"; the best we can do is to discover if our ideas are conducive to our survival and our flourishing, that is, whether they are "viable" (which means they are characterized by the absence of "friction or collision" with each other; see von Glasersfeld, 1995, p.117). Finally, von Glasersfeld (1996) recognizes one other important implication of his position, namely, that other people and "the society they collectively constitute" are things "we construct . . . ourselves on the basis of subjective experience. . . . For whatever things we know, we know only insofar as we have constructed them as relatively viable permanent entities in our conceptual world" (p. 19).

In sum, then, although it is apparent that von Glasersfeld's view is close to that of James in many repects, there is at least this one quite crucial difference that leads the two men along ultimately divergent paths: von Glasersfeld cements the very dichotomy between "inner" and "outer" that James first rejected in the essay on Spencer that he had so admired—for von Glasersfeld, there is experience *and* the reality outside (which is unknowable), but for James there is *no* outside realm, for the real world is *within* the experiental realm that also houses the knower, and James is therefore able to escape epistemological skepticism. For James, but not for von Glasersfeld, the objects of experience are *real*, they are not hypothetical constructs (how we conceptualize these realities is another matter).

A COMPARISON OF THE TWO PHILOSOPHIES

Apparently we have reached an impasse. From rather similar starting points, William James reaches a commonsense position (or rather, perhaps, a position in terms of which he defends common sense) that Ernst von Glasersfeld regards as naïve, whereas von Glasersfeld himself holds a view that James labels as having no supporting "ground whatever." Despite its elaborate metaphysical underpinning, James's view presents us with a simple way of talking: We are interacting with the real things we are experiencing, although our theories about, or conceptualizations of, these things may change or develop over time and with further inquiry (these latter are also commonsense views). Ernst von Glasersfeld, who also seems to hold that his own view is the one that anyone who reflects for a short period (and who is therefore not naïve) will come to accept, talks of our inhabiting a realm that is populated by people and objects of our own construction and to which we attribute reality because these invented constructs allow us to survive and adjust to environmental challenges. Numerous commentators have pointed out that this is well-nigh identical with the idealism of the classic empiricist Bishop Berkeley and others, and it is a position that drew the following wonderful comment from Alfred North Whitehead (1925/1948):

> The bodies are perceived as with qualities which in reality do not belong to them, qualities which are in fact purely the offspring of the mind. Thus nature gets the credit for what should in truth be reserved for ourselves: the rose for its scent: the nightingale for his song: and the sun for his radiance. The poets are entirely mistaken. They should address their lyrics to themselves and turn them into odes of self-congratulation on the excellency of the human mind. (p. 55)

The radical empiricism of William James cannot draw the same satirical comment.

Whose intuitions are sounder—the radical empiricist's or the radical constructivist's? I plan to leave this apparently simple philosophical issue for the reader to decide. But it needs to be pointed out that on this general issue James was somewhat more sophisticated than von Glasersfeld, for he was aware that the issue involves metaphysics—it is not a matter that can be settled simply by appeal to what is "obvious" in our experience itself. Both men are agreed that what we humans experience is, indeed, just our experience; James realizes that it requires an argument—a metaphysical argument—to establish anything further from this, whereas von Glasersfeld apparently thinks he is being straightforward and is *avoiding* metaphysics, whereas in fact—by making a clear distinction between our experience and reality—he is himself relying on a metaphysical theory that, when developed, is at least as complex as that held (and consciously held) by James. As von Glasersfeld (1995) insists, "Radical constructivism is intended as a model of rational knowing, *not as a metaphysics* [italics added] that attempts to describe a real world" (p. 24). Even in epistemology, however, metaphysics is not so easy to escape (see the discussion of this point in Phillips, 1997, esp. pp. 274–275).

At this point a fairly obvious series of questions arise, ones inspired by James's own pragmatism: What "cash value" does the metaphysics have? What difference in practice do the metaphysical differences between the two men make? Do they amount merely to different ways of talking? If the answer to the last question is affirmative, then James would seem to have the advantage, for his way of talking is, indeed, the commonsense way; there is something odd about von Glasersfeld's suggestion that the growing child (to take this as a stark case) is developing in a world entirely of her own creation, and it seems even odder to say that it is our experience that is out to kill us rather than to say it is the things with which we are interacting in our hostile environment. Furthermore, according to von Glasersfeld's account, no individual can be sure that another individual has constructed his universe with the same entities as she has—we are, indeed, each trapped in worlds of our own making. This is not just an idealist mode of speech, it is solipsistic. And it is not just a way of talking: von Glasersfeld and his supporters draw consequences for the conduct of education from their metaphysics and the related epistemology. In a recent commentary on (among other things) the disputes between the radical constructivists and their critics in philosophy of education, the prominent philosopher of education Nicholas Burbules (2000) has suggested that the emphasis on epistemological and metaphysical differences is counterproductive and misguided, and serves only to focus discussion onto issues that are irresolvable; he suggests that the disputants need to move on. The "$64 thousand question," however, is whether they *can* move on, given the central role that metaphysical assumptions, and attendant epistemological ones, play in the disputes.

A COMPARISON BETWEEN JAMES
AND VON GLASERSFELD ON EDUCATION

When we turn to education, however, the tables seem to be turned in favor of von Glasersfeld, although the issues here deserve fuller treatment than can be given here (for further discussion, see the essays in Phillips, 2000).

Despite their origins in a problematic philosophy, his ideas on curriculum and teaching (especially in mathematics and science) have much to commend them, and the constructivism he advocates has produced many interesting although controversial classroom experiments; whereas James's direct remarks on teaching in his *Talks to Teachers* have not aged particularly well, despite a few perennially fresh passages about psychological matters. This may simply be due to the facts that von Glasersfeld is writing many decades after James and has profited from the water that has passed under the educational bridge, and that he has much more experience of this field than his predecessor. After all, James was a consummate public lecturer and writer, and he often addressed teachers, but the fields of curriculum and classroom pedagogy where von Glasersfeld has had such impact were not domains that James had personally studied in any depth (if at all); it is worth noting in this context that the full title of the aforementioned book is *Talks to Teachers on Psychology and to Students on Some of Life's Ideals*, which is a straightforward indication that the book is not, essentially, on the topic of classroom pedagogy. This is not to say that it cannot be read with profit—there is always something to be learned from James!

The point to be stressed is that in the main James's impact on education was not *direct*; rather, it has been via the implications of his philosophy and psychology and also, of course, by way of his impact on Dewey (which was alluded to near the opening of this essay). But to return to von Glasersfeld: Somewhat surprisingly, his work on educational practice seems to be situated squarely in the tradition of Deweyan progressivism, despite the philosophical issues that divide them (see Garrison, 1997a). It is far from clear that Dewey had any direct impact upon von Glasersfeld, and in his 1995 book he says that he does not know enough about Dewey to be able to discuss his ideas (von Glasersfeld, 1995, p. 25); but in an important chapter in this book the resemblances shine through. Von Glasersfeld stresses that there is no one correct way to teach (although he says that constructivist principles suggest what *not* to do), that students learn best if they are convinced the knowledge they are acquiring (or constructing) is of relevance to them and their concerns, and that they must be active inquirers who also regard problem-solving as fun. He states:

> The fundamental principle from which most of my suggestions for the practice of teaching derive is that concepts and conceptual relations are mental structures that cannot be passed from one mind to another. . . . When students are driven to investigate and conceptually grasp a situation, the conceptual changes they are making during the proces of reflection will be far more solid than if they were imposed by a teacher. (von Glasersfeld, 1995, pp. 186, 188; but see all of ch.10)

This passage bears comparison with Dewey's (1916/1966) words in *Democracy and Education*; he refers to knowledge that the teacher "heaps" upon the student as "cold-storage" knowledge, and goes on to say:

> The educational moral I am chiefly concerned to draw is . . . that no thought, no idea, can possibly be conveyed as an idea from one person to another. . . . Only by wrestling with the conditions of the problem at first hand, seeking and finding his own way out, does he think. (pp. 159–160)

There are many other similarities between the educational views of von Glasersfeld and Dewey, but one in particular is worth mentioning because it involves an issue that has drawn both men some sharp criticism. Both of them have faced the issue of what role the teacher should play in directing the young inquirers in his or her charge. This issue, of course, goes back at least as far as the foundational document of modern progressive education, Rousseau's *Emile*. The hero of that book, young Emile, was given what appeared to be complete freedom, including the freedom to suffer the natural consequences of his actions! However, behind the scenes the boy's tutor played a remarkably manipulative role—Emile's freedom was often chimerical. The form in which Dewey and von Glasersfeld inherit the problem is this: Should the constructivist (or progressive) teacher interefere, and be more directive, if it becomes apparent that the students are arriving at ideas that are incorrect? This is a particularly salient concern in science education—should a constructivist teacher stand by and allow a student to construct an incorrect version (incorrect by current disciplinary standards) of, for example, Newton's law of gravitation? As one well-known contemporary essay in science education posed the issue, "when do I tell them the right answer?" (Wadsworth, 1997). Dewey's answer to this conundrum—in which there is at least a little of Rousseau's tutor—was that the teacher must use her knowledge of the subject matter to guide the students, but she must organize it in an appropriate psychologically appealing way—she must, in Dewey's awkward term, "psychologize" this knowledge (the details are spelled out in *The Child and the Curriculum*); it is clear that he did not believe that the students were to be allowed to construct anything they pleased. In somewhat similar vein, von Glasersfeld (1995) in the end comes out also sounding like the subtly directive tutor:

> The teacher cannot tell students what concepts to construct or how to construct them, but by a judicious use of language they can be prevented from constructing in directions which the teacher considers futile but which, as he knows from experience, are likely to be tried. . . . And although his language cannot determine the students' conceptual constructing, it can set up constraints that orient them in a particular direction. (p. 184)

Though there is not much in it, in my judgment Dewey's answer seems rather more acceptable!

It should be noted that there is nothing much in all this with which James would have serious difficulty; after all, insofar as many of von Glasersfeld's ideas about classroom practice converge with those of Dewey, and insofar as James had been such an influence on Dewey, why would there be serious disagreements? It is appropriate to refer once again to the story of the two Marxists with which the discussion began—two thinkers who agree on fundamentals can disagree about implementation, and people who disagree on fundamentals (even while having much in common) can agree on the general issue of what should be done in practice. This is what keeps a pluralistic society from falling apart, as the decision theorist Charles Lindblom (1959) noted many years ago in his classic paper that explains how it is that we are able to "muddle through."

Finally, though, the other issues raised at the outset need to be addressed. Is von Glasersfeld really a 19th-century figure, or is James a late-20th-century one? It will come as no surprise to the reader to learn that my answer to both of these is "yes"! I have gently suggested throughout that von Glasersfeld is squarely located in the skeptical tradition, especially that emanating from classic empiricism. Although there are some striking similarities between him and James, the latter takes the further "giant step" at which von Glasersfeld seems to balk (if he sees it as a possibility at all)— even as early as 1878 in the essay on Spencer, James gave notice that he had leaped into the late 20th century, whereas by maintaining the subject/object (or inner/outer) distinction the way he did, von Glasersfeld indicated that he was remaining in the late 19th century.

CHAPTER 9

Pragmatism's Unfinished Project: William James and Teacher Knowledge Researchers

JERRY ROSIEK

T HIS CHAPTER LOOKS at the methodological challenges facing contemporary teacher knowledge research. The epistemologies underlying two major conceptions of research on teacher knowledge are
examined. The limitations arising from those epistemologies are identified. William James's pragmatism is offered as an alternative epistemology for framing teacher knowledge research that avoids these limitations
and is more germane to the work of teaching.

PRAGMATISM AND RESEARCH

One of the cardinal insights of classical pragmatic philosophy—by which
I mean the work of Charles Sanders Peirce, William James, and John
Dewey—is that intelligence operates by building selective attention to a
person or community's environment. This construction of attention, according to the pragmatist view, is simultaneously an affective, cognitive,
and social process, with real consequences for the individual or community. They can be said to act intelligently insofar as they attend to things
in ways that may bring about desirable forms of continuity and growth.

It is therefore an unfortunate irony that the recent renascence of interest in pragmatic philosophy among social scientists has been so selective in its renewed attention to this philosophical tradition—selective in ways that close off opportunities for new and promising conceptualizations of social scientific research. I am referring to the tendency of occasional readers of the classical pragmatic philosophers to emphasize their insights about the human condition and ignore their ideas about *how such insights should be generated.* For example, John Dewey has long been read by educators for his insights about curriculum and pedagogy but is only rarely read as a source of insight about how to produce knowledge about curriculum and pedagogy. For a description of and a notable exception to this overall trend, see Jim Garrison's (1994, pp. 5–15). More recently, William James has been revisited for his insights about the relation between affect and cognition by contemporary neuropsychologists (Damasio, 1994) and educational psychologists (Prawat, 1997; Rosiek & Iran-Nejad, 2000). Too little attention, however, has been paid to James's radical empiricist conception of what it means to produce knowledge about human experience.

A Research Methodology for the Human Science

Part of this oversight is understandable. Neither Peirce, James, nor Dewey developed anything that could legitimately be called a research methodology. Subsequent writers in the pragmatist vein—the Chicago school of sociology not withstanding[1]—have yet to fill this lack (Manicus, 1998). This lack is remarkable when it is considered that James and Dewey wrote often about a need for reform in the human sciences. For example, in James's (1890/1927) widely read *Principles of Psychology,* the methodological recommendations were sparse and pithy, occurring in one of the shortest chapters (approximately 10 pages) in this two-volume treatise. James's biographer, Ralph Barton Perry (1935), identified this lack of attention to research methodology as a lifelong, though not crippling, feature of James's scholarly practice.

> That [James] did not incline to the use of quantitative methods was due to his non-mathematical cast of mind. That he did not organize experiments and carry them on through years of sustained diligence was due to his impatience. . . . He was an exceptionally acute observer of the natural man [*sic*] in all the varied aspects of his life. He had a lively and veracious imagination. He used whatever facts he could thus find for himself or gather from other observers, interpreted them freely, and constructed an image of human nature which after forty years is not obsolete. (vol. II, p. 24)

This liberal approach to methodological issues led James in directions that presaged contemporary educational research trends. In his classic work on the psychology and philosophy of religion, *The Varieties of Religious Experience*, James (1902/1936) defended an open-ended and interpretive approach to his research in the name of practicality:

> "On the whole"—I fear we shall never escape complicity with that qualification, so dear to your practical man, so repugnant to your systematizer . . . [but our] needs were always many, and the tests were never sharp. So the reproach of vagueness and subjectivity and "on the whole"-ness, which can with perfect legitimacy be addressed to the empirical method as we are forced to use it, is after all a reproach to which the entire life of man in dealing with these matters is obnoxious. (pp. 321–325)

James did not develop this interpretive style into a specific research methodology—one that might be applied by others to diverse phenomena. What he did develop, however, was a general theory of inquiry with three features that make it particularly relevant to contemporary research on education: The theory (1) did not hold a falsificationist view of scientific certainty as its sole ideal; (2) included room for speculative interpretation of events that went beyond the verifiable facts; and (3) sought justification for an interpretation of something in the *reality* of possible future consequences of that interpretation. In other words, James's "pragmatic method" was a metamethodology, a way of evaluating the theoretical frameworks that guide our inquiries; in his own words, he offered it

> less as a solution, then, than as a program for more work, and more particularly as an indication of the ways in which existing realities may be changed. Theories become instruments, not answers to enigmas, in which we can rest. We don't lie back upon them, we move forward, and, on occasion, make nature over again with their aid. (James, 1907/1947, p. 55)

INTERPRETIVE METHODS IN EDUCATIONAL RESEARCH

So why draw attention to James's "metamethodology" in a collection of essays about education? Because educational researchers share many of the frustrations with reductionist methods of social analysis that James wrote about decades earlier. Elliot Eisner (1985) summarized this sense of frustration in his book, *The Art of Educational Evaluation*.

> To my mind the field of education . . . has not searched widely enough for methods of inquiry that will serve education well. We have tried, at least since the turn of the century, to develop a science of education and to employ in practice a technological system that reflects the most efficient methods of industry. The procedures that have been developed have not been a rousing success. (p. 1)

No small part of the push for methodological pluralism in educational research comes from within the field of research on teacher knowledge. Commenting on the influence of behaviorist conceptions of research on teaching, Lee Shulman (1987) expressed a similar concern:

> Assessments of teachers in most states consist of some combination of basic-skills tests, an examination of competence in subject matter, and observations in the classroom to ensure certain kinds of general teaching behavior are present. In this manner, I would argue teaching is trivialized, its complexities ignored, and its demands diminished. (p. 6)

The new conceptions of teacher knowledge that were developed resonate with the emphasis on the *practical* in James's philosophy. Shulman (1987) called for a program of case study research that would capture teachers' *wisdom of practice*. He wrote, "A major portion of the educational agenda for the coming decades will be to collect, collate, and interpret the practical knowledge of teachers for the purpose of establishing a case literature and codifying its principles, precedents, and parables" (p. 8).

This practical knowledge is conceived of as a mediating form of insight, bridging between worlds of theory and practice (Cochran-Smith & Lytle, 1993), between subject matter and student (Grossman, 1990), and across cultural differences (Ladson-Billings, 1994; Sconiers & Rosiek, 2000). Much of the research in this area indicates that teacher practical knowledge is nonpropositional—not reducible to statements of principle. It often exists in tacit habits of experience and is shared by teachers, when it is shared at all, through story telling and other narrative modes of representation (Clandinin & Connelly, 2000; Connelly & Clandinin, 1999; Donmoyer, 1997).

Epistemological Questions

The new approaches to documenting and representing teacher knowledge raise questions about the epistemic status of teachers' knowledge and researchers' insights about teacher knowledge. For most of this century, research on education has been guided by positivist and postpositivist epistemologies, which assume that (1) all knowledge can and must be expressed in propositional form and (2) that only those propositions that are *falsifiable*—can be logically or empirically proven false—can be included in that set of propositions we call "knowledge." These falsifiability criteria pose a problem for the view that teachers' knowledge is often tacit, performative, and narrative in form.

Tacit beliefs are held implicitly in the form of mental and physical habits acquired in the course of practice, as in the way my fingers know my friends' phone numbers by the feel of the keypad, or the way teachers learn to read students' moods and adjust their approach to students accordingly. Such unconscious habits are not always translatable into propositions, and therefore cannot always be adequately described as "true" or "false." Nonetheless they are a form of insight that constitutes an important part of teaching competence. Performative beliefs are held explicitly but play a part in generating their own truth, as in the way a justice of the peace declares "you are now husband and wife," and the utterance makes it so. A teacher may choose to believe a student is smart, despite evidence to the contrary, because such a belief can in fact create the conditions in which the student's performance becomes "smart." Performative beliefs cannot be adequately described as true or false prior to their adoption. Narrative forms of knowledge are contained not in any one proposition but in the complex relations embodied in stories. For example, a story about a student long gone, or who never really existed, can be passed among teachers as a vehicle for sharing practical wisdom. The story may help new teachers react more constructively to new teaching situations, even though no single proposition in the story is literally true or false.

To accommodate nonpropositional forms of knowledge, alternative epistemic criteria are needed. Relatively undeveloped criteria like "plausibility" and "verisimilitude" (Bruner, 1985; Polkinghorne, 1988) have been proposed. D. C. Phillips (1993), a philosopher of educational research with postpositivist leanings, has argued that these are not adequate substitutes for falsifiability where the justification of knowledge claims is concerned. He cautioned, "The fact that a story is credible tells us nothing— *absolutely* nothing—about whether it is true or false" (p. 21). Phillips expressed concern that these new forms of research are being judged solely on their ideological grounds. "From evidence internal to their writings I surmise that researchers who are pro-narrative have tended to have sociopolitical rather than epistemic grounds for their enthusiasm" (p. 29).

There are problems with Phillips's (1993) critique. Foremost among these is his assumption that somewhere somehow we can separate out the epistemological grounds for a belief from the sociopolitical conditions that authorize those standards of judgment. Phillips (1993) is not naïve about the influence of sociocultural factors on processes of knowledge production. He wrote that "to take this position is not to deny that there is a political side to the issue of legitimation of the knowledge-claims of science; it simply is to underscore the point that there is also an epistemological side that might not have been totally undermined by the arguments of Kuhn, Feyarabend, and Rorty" (p. 5). In such a defense, however, Phillips ultimately begs the question. To speak of epistemology as if it is "undermined" by the assertion that it is the product of sociocultural processes is to assume that epistemic judgments can and should be defined as those judgments about knowledge claims that transcend cultural context. Phillips has characterized the views he critiques as antirealist. Phillips is justified in making these objections if our conception of knowledge as a sociocultural production provides for no contact with a reality independent of human mental activity. William James's philosophy, however—specifically his radical empiricist ontology—provides for such contact. Human knowledge constructions, according to James, interact with reality prospectively—they change the future—and those changes conceived of broadly provide the grounds for assessing our interpretations of our experience.

Phillips's uncritical embrace of the idea that all knowledge can be expressed in propositional form is also problematic. Despite these disputable assumptions, the overall question Phillips posed is an important one. He asked, in effect, in what way could a community of inquirers have a critical conversation about the representations of teacher knowledge that it produces—if it does not rely on postpositivist epistemology and critical realism? William James can help teacher knowledge researchers answer this question. To see specifically where and how his philosophy can help, we need to examine more precisely the epistemic binds that teacher knowledge researchers currently face.

JUSTIFYING TEACHERS' PRACTICAL KNOWLEDGE CLAIMS

Teacher knowledge researchers who generate epistemological theory are caught between at least two equally important and frequently conflicting imperatives. On the one hand are demands for clarity and accountability expressed by astute critics of the social sciences like Phillips. On the other hand are demands to honor the complexity and moral drama of the actual experience of teaching. So far, no philosopher of teacher knowledge has produced an epistemic framework that honors both of these imperatives equally.

In an essay entitled "Knowledge and Research on Teaching," Gary Fenstermacher (1994) offered the following formulation of the challenge facing the field of teacher knowledge research: "What is needed to deal with the problem is a more carefully constructed conception of justification, one that makes us more discriminating and discerning than has been typical for the appraisal and judgement of claims of [teachers'] personal and practical knowledge" (p. 39). In his review of the teacher-knowledge research literature, Fenstermacher (1994) identified several different conceptions of knowledge including personal, practical, formal, folk, performance, tacit, and situated knowledge. Fenstermacher acknowledged that some of these conceptions—particularly performance and tacit knowledge—are defined as not occurring in propositional form. Nonetheless, he claimed tacit and performance knowledge must be evaluated if we are to endorse their influence on teachers' professional performance (p. 37). Agreeing with Phillips, Fenstermacher insisted tacit and performance knowledge be translated into some form that resembles propositions if they were to be called knowledge. "Teaching is [a professional] performance, one for which the epistemic merit of any claims to practical knowledge must be both clear and defensible (i.e., such claims are subject to evidentiary or justificatory demands in ways analogous to those of propositional knowledge)" (p. 37).

Fenstermacher (1994) is right, I believe, in insisting that teacher knowledge researchers should make an effort to have clearer conversations about the merit of representations of teacher knowledge. The epistemic commitments Fenstermacher recommended as the means to this end, however, seem self-defeating. They make a mistake that James (1909/1967) warned us against nearly a century ago:

> The treating of a name as excluding from the fact named what the name's definition fails positively to include. . . . It is but the old story, of a useful practice first becoming a method, then a habit, and finally a tyranny that defeats the end it was used for. Concepts, first employed to make things intelligible, are clung to even when they make them unintelligible. (p. 560)

James called this mistake "vicious intellectualism." In this case, the concept clung to is the idea that our understanding of the teaching scene can only be effectively evaluated when that understanding is expressed in something analogous to propositional form. In addition, there is an inevitable drift to a lack of relevance to teaching practice (if not unintelligibility). Responding to the challenge being put to the narrowness of this conception of knowledge, Fenstermacher (1994) proposed a complex hierarchy of knowledge claims that could account for a diversity of knowledge claims. Using "k" to represent a knowledge claim, "T" to represent a teacher, and "R" to represent a researcher, he proposed that researchers use the following breakdown when justifying their knowledge claims:

First level: T expresses k
Second level: T knows k
Third level: R expresses that T expresses k
Fourth level: R knows that T expresses k

Fifth level: *R* expresses that *T* knows *k*
Sixth level: *R* knows that *T* knows *k*

Note the Ptolemaic feel of this model; it proliferates fine-grained qualifications of an original theory in an effort to preserve the viability of that theory. Although it is not difficult to see how the above distinctions follow from Fenstermacher's belief that teacher knowledge must be expressed in propositional form, it is hard to see how any part of the experience of teaching, or the experience of efforts to improve teaching, would have inspired such a model. It is harder still to provide a plausible vision of how the deployment of such distinctions in real conversations about educational practice would bring benefit to that practice.

Again, the value of Fenstermacher's (1994) analysis lies with his affirmation that teacher knowledge needs to fulfill some form of the "justified belief" standard for knowledge that could support a critical conversation about teacher knowledge research among its practitioners. His acceptance of a conception of justification that requires belief to be expressed in something analogous to propositional form, however, is ultimately untenable. Fenstermacher does admit that there might be other ways to think of justification.

EMPHASIZING CONTEXT AND THE PROCESS OF INQUIRY

If Fenstermacher (1994) favored the need for clarity and accountability in his philosophizing about teacher knowledge over the need to represent its complexity and moral drama, many other leading theorists have taken the opposite tack. Jean Clandinin and Michael Connelly (1995, 1996, 2000) have argued that a significant part of teachers' professional knowledge is both experienced and expressed through narrative forms—which better capture the emotional, personal, and moral dimensions of teaching. They responded to four questions Fenstermacher (1994) used to organize his review:

> Though not stated as such, [Fenstermacher's] review, and the work surveyed, implies that valid, reliable, knowledge on the four questions will make possible better educated teachers . . . but we think that answers to these questions are only partially capable of creating understandings that might justify the implication in its full blown sense. We think the narrative context for the ongoing development and expression of teacher knowledge in schools is also of importance. (Clandinin & Connelly, 1996, p. 24)

On the basis of more than a decade of their own empirical studies, Clandinin and Connelly (1996) expressed pessimism about the value of knowledge that can fit into the specific propositional forms that Fenstermacher described.

> We believe we have shown that the professional knowledge landscapes of schools is of such contextual complexity, that the implications [mentioned above]—namely, that knowledgeable responses to Fenstermacher's questions would lead to better teaching—does not hold or, perhaps, to put it more softly, only holds with slight force. (p. 29)

Whereas Fenstermacher spoke of establishing a process of justification for teachers' practical knowledge claims—one that could be used to filter what made it into a personal or profession-wide knowledge base for teaching practice—Clandinin and Connelly are skeptical about the value of such a knowledge base because such justification is always conditional. They explained, "It is simply not possible to use this specific knowledge base to build, with confidence, programs that lead to better teachers and teaching. It always depends [on context]" (p. 29).

Marilyn Cochran-Smith (1999), in a more recent review of conceptions of teacher knowledge, learning, and education, offered a similar critique of establishing a "knowledge base" for teaching. She described three conceptions of teacher knowledge that inform current education reform efforts: (1) *knowledge-for-practice*—when knowledge is produced by (or in collaboration with) university researchers and is intended to become part of a profession-wide knowledge base; (2) *knowledge-in-practice*—when teachers' tacit knowledge about the art and craft of their teaching is made explicit in order that it may be critically reflected upon by teachers and/ or critically discussed in the local and general teaching community; and (3) *knowledge-of-practice*—when knowledge produced by teachers through inquiry on their own practice is intended to inform their own practice.

Cochran-Smith and Lytle (1999) suggested that both *knowledge-for-practice* and *knowledge-in-practice* conceptions of knowing have serious limitations when they are used to inform the design of educational reforms.

> Both derive—or are mistakenly taken to derive—from the distinction between formal and practical knowledge. . . . This distinction works to maintain the hegemony of university generated knowledge for teaching and carries with it the same power and status differentials associated with the disconnections of basic from applied research and theory from practice. (p. 289)

Both, according to these authors, impose a conception of knowledge production and circulation patterned after university academic activity. Knowledge needs to be documented by the select few for the consumption of the many. Like Clandinin and Connelly (1996, 2000), Cochran-

Smith and Lytle (1999) are skeptical about the degree to which teacher knowledge can be broadly and usefully shared. It is the process of inquiry that is of general value they claim.

Inquiry as Stance

This critique leads Cochran-Smith and Lytle (1999) to propose a new conception of teacher education, one focused not so much on documenting and disseminating specific teacher knowledge as on fostering processes of teacher inquiry. They call this conception "inquiry as stance." "Teachers and students who take an inquiry stance work within inquiry communities to generate knowledge and theorize their practice, and interpret and interrogate the theory and research of others" (p. 289).

Clandinin and Connelly (2000) seem to make a similar call for emphasis on teacher inquiry in their book, *Narrative Inquiry*. In the closing chapter, they reflect on what makes for good narrative inquiry into teaching. They consider, but ultimately find lacking, any formal criteria drawn from the fields of literary or cultural criticism.

> One of the problems of being too heavily into the notion of being "I, the critic" is that it has a negative, monitoring sense, the possibility of stifling inquiry. We need to find ways of being aware of what those on either side of the reductionistic or formalistic boundaries might think or say of our work. (p. 182)

This rejection of formalism was not made hastily. For most of their careers Clandinin and Connelly (2000) have endorsed specific criteria for evaluating narrative inquiry, such as "authenticity," "adequacy," and "plausibility" (p. 185). Now, however, they find these conceptions too focused on a final product.

> As we look back on our 1990 question—What makes a good narrative?—we realize that we need to shift the question in order to more adequately address our concerns. Our question is not so much what makes a good narrative—which we feel often implies a question of what makes a good narrative research text—it is rather a question of what makes a good narrative inquiry. . . . It is *wakefulness* that in our view most needs to characterize the living out of our narrative inquiries. (p. 185)

The move here is profound—from considering understanding research on teaching as the central goal of teacher education with teacher inquiry being a means to that end, to a vision of *teacher inquiry as the central goal of teacher education* with examination of research produced by others being a means to *that* end.

Comparing the Two Views

I have a great deal of sympathy with the view that, given a teacher's adequate knowledge of subject matter, the teacher's ability to think critically about his or her practice is more important than any understanding of any specific pedagogical theory. My experience as a teacher and teacher educator tells me that any research product—be it case study, narrative, or statistical analysis—requires extensive teacher thought and inquiry to transform it into real teaching practice. Without the inclination and ability to reflect critically on and learn from their practice, teachers will be unable to benefit from any form of new knowledge.

Some caution is in order, however. Although the move in teacher education toward an emphasis on inquiry seems salutary to me, a move toward an exclusive emphasis on the process of teacher inquiry would be problematic. Dewey (1938) over half a century ago in *Experience and Education*, cautioned against extremes in curricular philosophy. When considering whether to teach inherited understandings of a subject matter versus teaching a discovery process capable of generating its own subject matter, Dewey steered a middle course. Neither alone will do, he said of the education of children. The same can be said for teachers. A scholastic formalism applied to research on teacher knowledge would almost certainly inhibit the generation of genuinely useful teacher knowledge. A theory of critical judgment that applies *only* to the process of teacher inquiry and not to the (tentative) representations produced by that inquiry is not a complete account of how learning from teacher experience actually takes place. Even the most informal teacher inquiry on his or her own practice will result in generating representations of teaching and learning experience. Assessing the quality of these representations is a part of, but is not identical to, fostering a good process of inquiry. Phillips's (1993) concern about how these representations will be judged, which Fenstermacher (1994) shared, remains inadequately addressed by Clandinin, Connelly, Cochran-Smith, and Lytle. Even if teachers adopt an "inquiring stance" and are engaged in "wakeful" inquiry on their teaching practice, *how* will they critique and refine their own and others' interpretations of the classroom scene?

What is needed is a conception of judging representations of teaching and learning that does not require those representations to be in propositional form, and that admits and emphasizes the importance of context to teacher understanding of their work. This conception would need to admit the place of personal biography in teacher knowledge, to resist any final foreclosure into a static and received body of knowledge, and in other ways be germane to the practical experience of teaching. In addition, it would need to provide a response to critical realist philosophy and a critique of the limitations of falsificationist conceptions of knowledge. *Here* is the precise place where James's philosophy can be of use to teacher knowledge researchers.

JAMES AND TEACHER KNOWLEDGE RESEARCH

James's pragmatist epistemology provides a framework for judging human insights that possesses many of the features just mentioned. The most notable and propitious feature of James's pragmatist epistemology, one that has yet to work its way into the fabric of the social sciences, is its emphasis on the future as the primary source of meaning for our representations of experience. John Dewey (1973), writing about James's contribution to American philosophy, summarized the upshot of this epistemology as follows:

> Pragmatism thus presents itself as an extension of historical empiricism, but with this fundamental difference, that it does not insist upon antecedent phenomena, but upon consequent phenomena; not upon precedents, but upon possibilities of action. And this change in point of view is almost revolutionary in its consequences. (p. 96)

What is revolutionary about this emphasis on consequences is the way it reconfigures our most basic notions about the quest for knowledge. First, the scholarly enterprise of naturalistic description ceases to be guided by the regulative ideal of certainty, with meaning clearly terminating in some specific object or event. Instead description takes on more of the character of a tentative prescription for action, with its meaning being drawn from the entire horizon of the conceivable consequences of those actions. Because such horizons are in principle infinite, the meaning of a description does not have an identifiable limit; it terminates only as the result of an arbitrary practical act, but not out of necessity. Second, a pragmatic epistemology is inherently pluralistic. Different emphases and interpretations will recommend different paths of action, which in turn will have different consequences. Although this plurality of meanings may be compared and contrasted one to another, they can never be finally evaluated. The evaluation would always be confounded by the limits of human foresight, and therefore would always retain a certain tentativeness—what James called "an ever not quite." The resonance with the earlier critiques of "knowledge-base" conceptions of teacher knowledge should be clear. James's philosophy would not admit the possibility of the finalized "knowledge-base" that Cochran-Smith and Lytle (1999) find problematic.

Additional parallels to the concerns of teacher knowledge researchers can be found in James's respect for the personal aspect of knowing. For James, the ground or source of knowledge was experience and experience was, ultimately, personal; therefore knowledge was ultimately personal. In his classic work *Varieties of Religious Experience* (1902/1936), he wrote, "So long as we deal with the cosmic and the general, we deal only with the symbols of reality, but as soon as we deal with private and personal phenomena as such, we deal with realities in the fullest sense of that term" (p. 498). Here we can see resonance with the themes in Connelly's and Clandinin's (1999) conception of teachers' personal practical knowledge. They wrote, "Personal practical knowledge is found in teacher's past experience, in the teacher's present mind and body, and in the future plans and actions" (p. 1). James, however, does not relegate the personal and the practical to a subcategory of knowledge. He identifies these as a feature and an ultimate source of *all* knowledge. As such, his epistemology not only promises a sympathetic home for Clandinin's and Connelly's work, but also possible amplification of the themes they develop.

James's philosophy also shares a deep democratic faith in the individual human ability to generate useful knowledge from many contemporary teacher knowledge researchers (e.g., Cochran-Smith & Lytle, 1999; Richardson, 1997; Zeichner, 1998). He preferred to seek amelioration of human affairs at the level of finite individuals, local action, and contingent insight instead of at the level of large institutions, comprehensive plans, and eternal verities. In a letter dated June 7, 1899, he confessed, "As for me, my bed is made: I am against bigness and greatness in all their forms, and with the invisible molecular forces that work from individual to individual, stealing in through the crannies of the world like so many soft rootlets" (McDermott, 1986, p. 42).

For James this preference was not simply temperamental, it was an integral aspect of his overall philosophy. Epistemologically and psychologically, James had respect for the capacity of ordinary experience to provide insights that could be trusted to guide action. In a passage from *Talks to Teachers* (1899/1915), he affirmed the necessity of teachers' own intellectual contribution to an understanding of teaching practice.

> You make a great, a very great mistake, if you think that psychology, being the science of the mind's laws, is something from which you can deduce programmes and schemes and methods of instruction for immediate schoolroom use. Psychology is a science, and teaching is an art; and sciences never

generate arts directly out of themselves. An intermediary inventive mind must make the application, by using its originality. (pp. 7–8)

A Jamesian Conception of Justified Belief

Although James deeply respected the capacity of ordinary folk to produce knowledge, he did not believe that all insights were equally worthy just because they arose out of someone's personal experience. In other words, he was not a relativist. He believed that some ideas, some conceptions, were more likely to positively affect our future experience than others. He described a justifiable belief as one that performs the "function of *a leading that is worthwhile*" and that "sooner or later we dip by that thought's guidance into the particulars of experience again and make advantageous connexion with them" (James, 1907/1967, p. 205). According to James, it is our task as thinkers and citizens to identify those beliefs that are most likely to bring melioration to lived experience. In his books *Pragmatism* (1907/1947), *The Will to Believe* (1897/1947), and *Varieties of Religious Experience* (1902/1936), James laid out explicitly what such an analysis might look like.

James, much like philosophers in the critical realist tradition (Lakatos & Musgrave, 1970; Popper, 1972), took scientific inquiry as his model of efficacious thinking. As has been mentioned, critical realists identified processes of *falsification* as the key feature of scientific inquiry. Because truth and falsity are characteristics of propositions, this meant all scientific knowledge production in the view of critical realists must happen within propositional forms. James (1897/1967) emphasized the practice of empirically testing an idea in the ongoing stream of experience, but his notion of "testing" was more inclusive and robust than Popper's concept of falsification. Although praising the empiricism of science, James warned against indulging the reductionist tendencies of scientific modes of analysis. A commitment to empirically testing one's ideas, James argued, was not equivalent to a rejection of speculative belief that goes beyond the available evidence. In fact, he considered such a rejection both empirically unsupportable and morally problematic.

James maintained throughout his career that "over-belief," belief beyond the immediate physical evidence, was a rationally defensible practice. It is defensible, he argued, insofar as some sort of evidence can be provided that such an overbelief has the potential to bring about amelioration of human experience. In other words, James did not suggest that beliefs can be justified without recourse to empirical evidence. Instead he expands the range of places we can look for such evidence into the future. Seen through James's view, the position taken by critical realists is too synchronic in its conception of justification. It emphasizes only evidence existing in the present and ignores the fact that human belief plays a part in constituting existing and future realities (especially social realities) and occasionally precipitates the evidence that can justify the belief. James had a diachronic conception of justified belief.

James never precisely circumscribed what would count as post-hoc evidence, but indications are that he conceived of such evidence broadly— very broadly—including a perceived increase in the general quality of people's lives. Speaking of the way religious belief recommends sacrifice for the greater good, James (1902/1936) reasoned, "Religion thus makes easy and felicitous what in any case is necessary; and if it be the only agency that can accomplish this result, its vital importance as a human faculty stands vindicated beyond dispute" (p. 19).

Perhaps a better illustration of what James meant by the defensibility of overbelief is his version of the well-known "prisoners' dilemma." Describing a hypothetical train robbery, he observed that if all the passengers believed all the other passengers would stand up with them and resist the looters, then the whole train would in fact stand up and thwart the robbers. The very fact of believing fellow passengers were capable of such solidarity would create the evidence that confirms this belief. James (1897/1967) comments:

> There are, then, cases where a fact cannot come at all unless a preliminary faith exists in its coming. And where faith in a fact can help create the fact, that would be an insane logic which should say that faith running ahead of scientific evidence is the "lowest kind of immorality" into which a thinking being can fall. Yet such is the logic which our scientific absolutists pretend to regulate our lives. (p. 731)

It is here that qualitative researchers may begin to look for a conception of accountability in educational research that may be congenial to their more interpretive work. Phillips (1993) complains that much of the use of narrative modes of representation in teacher knowledge research appears to be driven by ideology. Perhaps it would be more accurate to say that such research is often, implicitly or explicitly, driven by teleological concerns—a desire to generate interpretations that will help in accomplishing some end, be it pedagogical, ideological, or personal. James's philosophy would admit such broadly normative influences into the process of knowledge production. Early in his career, James (1890/1927) expressed this conviction that would color the whole of his life's work, "The meaning of essence is teleological, and . . . classification and conception are purely teleological weapons of the mind" (p. 335).

James's philosophy, however, made this teleological dimension of conceptions subject to the same critical scrutiny as other aspects of research representations. In this way James's philosophy anticipated themes now found in cultural studies scholarship that examines the "motivated" nature of representations generated in popular and scholarly discourse (e.g., Hall, 1997; Said, 1978). James went beyond contemporary cultural studies when he sought to develop a theoretical framework that could hold these representations accountable, not just for their descriptive accuracy but also for their efficacy in accomplishing human purposes.

A Jamesian Response to Critical Realists

James understood that his willingness to respect the teleological or motivated aspects of human thought would sound alien to the general scientific community. In *The Will to Believe* (1897/1967), he admitted with a certain tongue-in-cheek flourish:

> When one turns to the magnificent edifice of the physical sciences, and sees how it was reared; what thousands of disinterested moral lives of men lie buried in its mere foundations; . . . then how besotted and contemptible seems every little sentimentalist who comes blowing his voluntary smoke-wreaths, and pretending to decide things from out of his private dream! Can we wonder if those bred in the rugged and manly school of science should feel like spewing such subjectivism out of their mouths? (p. 720)

Having acknowledged this skeptical sentiment, however, James (1897/ 1967) immediately called into question the logic that underlies it. It is in this response that we can see a direct response to the logic of contemporary critical realism. Decades before Karl Popper put pen to paper, James summarized the critical realist position as "It is wrong always, everywhere, and for every one, to believe anything upon insufficient evidence" (p. 721). He responded by making a crucial distinction between the desire to know the truth and the desire to avoid error.

> Although it may indeed happen that when we believe the truth A, we escape as an incidental consequence from believing the falsehood B, it hardly ever happens that by merely disbelieving B, we necessarily believe A. We may in escaping B fall into believing other falsehoods, C or D, just as bad as B; or we may escape B by not believing anything at all, not even A. (p. 721)

James elaborated on the consequences of, and motivations for, siding with one or the other of these methods of reasoning. His position was that a narrow scientific skepticism, universally applied, is Procrustean of human possibility. Because of the importance of this argument, I quote James (1897/1967) at length:

> Believe truth! Shun error!—these, we see, are two materially different laws; and by choosing between them we may end by coloring differently our whole intellectual life. . . . We must remember that these feelings of our duty to either truth or error are in any case only expressions of our passional life. Biologically considered, our minds are as ready to grind out falsehood as veracity, and he who says, "Better go without belief forever than believe a lie!" merely shows his own preponderant private horror of becoming a dupe. . . . For my own part, I have also a horror of being duped; but I can believe that worse things than being duped may happen to a man in this world. . . . Our errors are surely not such awfully solemn things. In a world where we are so certain to incur them in spite of all our caution, a certain lightness of heart seems healthier than this excessive nervousness on their behalf. At any rate, it seems the fittest thing for the empiricist philosopher. (p. 721)

As can be seen here, James's response to falsificationist conceptions of justified belief was not a simple rejection. It was a rejection of an *exclusive* commitment to such a standard. It is only an emotional and temperamental inclination, and not logic, that advises such exclusiveness James argued, and therefore it is reasonable to entertain other possibilities.

Jamesian Realism

Nevertheless, by what criteria might other standards of epistemic judgment be judged? Phillips (1995) offers that some form of realism needs to be part of any answer to this question. He writes: "My own view is that any defensible epistemology must recognize—and not just pay lip service to—the fact that nature exerts considerable constraint over our knowledge-constructing activities, and allows us to detect our errors about it" (p. 13). James would agree with Phillips on this point. Affirming his realist commitments, James (1907) warned in *Pragmatism*, "Woe to him whose beliefs play fast and loose with the order which realities follow in his experience; they will lead him nowhere or else make false connexions" (p. 205).

The reality against which James would have us check the merit of our ideas, however, included both phenomenological and objective measurable experience. Speaking of teaching, James (1899/1915) affirmed that teachers need to understand the reality of teaching represented in scientific psychological studies as well as the more impressionistic, relational, reality of teaching.

> A science only lays down the lines in which art must fall, laws which the follower of the art must not transgress. . . . And so, everywhere, teaching must agree with psychology, but . . . to know psychology . . . is absolutely no guarantee that we shall be good teachers. To advance that result we must have an additional endowment altogether, a happy tact and ingenuity to tell us what definite things to say and do when the pupil is before us. That ingenuity in meeting and pursuing the pupil, the tact for the concrete situation, though they are the alpha and omega of the teachers' art, are things to which psychology cannot help us in the least. (p. 9)

Writing of teachers' understanding of the art and science of teaching, James (1899/1915) insisted that "the two were congruent, but neither were subordinate" (p. 8) in a competent teachers' practice.

The key difference, then, between James and contemporary critical realists lies not in their respect for knowledge that passes a falsificationist standard of belief—both respect such knowledge. D. C. Phillips (1984) has written an essay entitled "Was William James Telling the Truth After All?" that affirms and explores this affinity between William James's epistemology and Karl Popper's conception of falsification. It lies instead in the respect James gave to those insights experienced as hopes, hunches, and habits that are not strictly falsifiable. Where critical realists exclude such insights from the category of knowledge, James not only included them but considered them of equal importance in our dealings with practical reality, which is the more comprehensive ontological category.

James's Radical Empiricism

James called his more inclusive version of realism "radical empiricism," and the epistemology of consequences based on it "pragmatism." In them we can see a way to substantively address Fenstermacher's (1994) concern that teacher knowledge be subject to some standard of justification. In it we can also see a way to honor the locally contingent, personal, and practical nature of insights produced by teachers' inquiry on their own practice emphasized by Clandinin and Connelly (1995, 1996, 2000) and Cochran-Smith and Lytle (1993, 1999). According to James, some beliefs can be reasonably expected to influence our future phenomenological experience and our actions. These actions in turn can change the conditions in which our future experience will be had. These changing conditions require further refinement of our beliefs, and so on, in an always open-ended, but constrained, process of inquiry. James regarded this influence of our beliefs on future possibilities of experience as ontologically real, epistemically significant, and morally charged. Dewey's

(1973) essay, "The Development of American Pragmatism," affirmed this interpretation:

> Pragmatism thus has a metaphysical implication. The doctrine of the value of consequences leads us to take the future into consideration. And this taking into consideration of the future takes us to a conception of a universe whose evolution is not finished, of a universe which is still, in James's term, "in the making," "in the process of becoming," of a universe up to a certain point still plastic. . . . If we form general ideas and put them into action, consequences are produced which could not be produced otherwise. Under these conditions the world will be different from what it would have been had thought not intervened. This consideration confirms the human and moral importance of thought and of its reflective operation in experience. (p. 51)

By putting an emphasis on the consequences of human belief—a position inspired by the success of scientific modes of inquiry—James avoided advocating both epistemological and methodological relativism. Multiple beliefs are justifiable, but not all beliefs and modes of interpretations are equal, because their conceivable consequences are not all equivalent. James (1897/1967) saw this constrained but open-ended approach to knowledge as the precondition for a truly democratic community. He wrote:

> If we are empiricists, if we believe that no bell in us tolls to let us know for certain when truth is in our grasp, then it seems a piece of idle fantasticality to preach so solemnly our duty of waiting for the bell. . . . No one of us ought to issue vetoes to the other, nor should we bandy words of abuse. We ought, on the contrary, delicately and profoundly to respect one another's mental freedom: then only shall we bring about the intellectual republic; then and only then shall we have that spirit of inner tolerance without which all our outer tolerance is soulless, and which is empiricism's glory; then and only then shall we live and let live, in speculative as well as practical things. (p. 734)

In short, then, a Jamesian response to critical realism has three parts. First is the disclosure that an exclusive commitment to falsificationist standards for justified belief is made on temperamental, not logical, grounds. Second is the assertion that speculative belief that reaches beyond present conclusive evidence can be justifiable without being relativistic. This avoidance of relativism depends on three conditions: (1) such belief remaining within the bounds of what is known with a higher grade of certainty; (2) granting that future possibilities of experience are real, and thus beliefs grounded in an anticipation of those future possibilities are realistic; and (3) that a critical conversation emerges in which comparisons and evaluations of beliefs are made based on reference to their possible future consequences. Third is the celebration of a bounded epistemic pluralism as a precondition for genuine democratic community.

Picking Up the Unfinished Project

This chapter opened with the observation that pragmatism, unlike some other major philosophical traditions of the 20th century, did not inspire the development of a unique research methodology for the human sciences. At best, James left us with a metamethodology, a way for talking about the relative merits of different modes of representing our experience. I offer that his philosophy could provide a better theoretical framework for contemporary teacher knowledge research than any theoretical framework currently being referenced for this purpose. I also believe teacher knowledge research has much to offer this philosophical tradition. We are well positioned to pick up, and further develop, pragmatism's unfinished project of developing a social science methodology focused on the practical consequences of knowledge.

James did not commit himself to in-depth empirical research on the ordinary experiences he philosophically celebrated, and certainly not to the study of the practical experience of teaching. The only model of an empirical study in a pragmatist vein was his classic work of religious philosophy, *Varieties of Religious Experience* (1902/1936), which was focused on extraordinary experience (religious conversion), and did not employ narrative modes of representation extensively. Additionally, James lacked the critical sophistication provided by contemporary poststructuralist and critical theory scholarship that we would now consider essential for evaluating narrative representations of the future. He was not critical enough of the meanings encoded into phrases like "progress," "growth," "cash-value," or of the relationship between market economies, American culture, and his celebration of individuality.

Contemporary teacher knowledge researchers, however, already have more than a decade's worth of experience exploring this intellectual territory. Case studies and narratives have been produced in a wide variety of formats, have been used and tested as curriculum in teacher education classrooms, and have been read and critiqued by educational scholars from a variety of disciplinary backgrounds. In other words, we educators already have many of the things that James's philosophy cannot provide us. This experience makes teacher knowledge researchers remarkably well positioned not only to use James's work to enhance teacher education scholarship but also to add to mainstream pragmatist philosophy. In the same way that sociologists like Foucault extended and invigorated Heidegger's philosophy by applying his ideas to the social sciences, educational researchers might finally give pragmatism its own unique incarnation as a methodology by applying it to educational settings.

In summary then, we find in James's work a long neglected but thoroughly developed theoretical framework, one that will need some work to be of use to us but that is potentially a well-suited home for teacher knowledge scholarship. His philosophical writings point toward a new conception of quality for narrative style representations of teachers' wisdom of practice, one that neither requires the reduction of that knowledge to propositions nor forecloses on the necessity for continuing teachers' inquiry on their own practice. Such criteria, if they were developed, could provide the basis for a scholarship of teaching that is cumulative in character and that locates the final source of legitimation for that knowledge not in the university but in the quality of the experience of teachers, students, and other educational stakeholders.

It is as if long ago, for reasons that have become obscure, pragmatism's deep project of reforming the way we go about knowledge production about human experience was left incomplete. Now, either through happenstance or some inevitability we have yet to fathom, contemporary work in educational research has led some of us back to the site of this unfinished project. Perhaps it is a relic worth noting only in passing, as we make our way to more promising professional and cultural horizons. I believe, however, that teacher knowledge researchers have much to gain by taking a longer look at this project and making it their own. It offers possibilities for amplification of what is best, and for constraint of what is most pernicious, in our conversations about interpretive educational research methods.

NOTE

1. The Chicago school of sociology developed an interpretive approach to sociological research called symbolic interactionism (Blumer, 1969). George Herbert Mead, Herbert Blumer, and Irving Goffman, as well as anthropologists such as Clifford Geertz and Victor Turner, were well known to have been influenced by the writings of James and Dewey. This influence, however, was primarily on their interpretations of how *others* made meaning, not on their own mode of meaning-making as scholars.

CHAPTER 10

James's Concept of Mystical Consciousness: Implications for Curriculum Theory and Practice

AOSTRE JOHNSON

I FIRST ENCOUNTERED William James in the Harvard University building named after him. William James Hall memorialized the man who, in the late 19th century, had founded the university's psychology department, bridging science and philosophy. Although we did not study James's psychological theory in the late 1960s, a passing reference to him by several lecturers in the department was enough to motivate me to search out his work. I read much of it over several years, finding in James what was absent in the department: a serious interest in religious and spiritual dimensions of psychology. James convinced me not only that religion is worthy of sustained psychological study but that it is impossible to understand human consciousness without it. One of the overall themes of his work is the reconciliation of mystical with more "ordinary" experiences.

In my continuing study of psychological theory, I discovered few other references to religious or mystical awareness. I would find it necessary to turn to religious studies and to various mystical traditions for this wider vision of human consciousness. My interest in consciousness also led me to observational studies of children and then to a 12-year career teaching children in schools that merged esthetic, spiritual, and ethical education with progressive, democratic, engaged, participatory methods. As I explored contemporary educational curriculum literature, I noted a similar lack of attention to the religious or mystical dimensions of human experience. I kept James's *The Varieties of Religious Experience* on the front of my bookshelf and in my metaphorical back pocket, returning to him again and again as inspiration in my quest.

When I reentered the academic world in the early 1980s to get my doctorate in curriculum theory, I was delighted to find that my mentor, James Macdonald, had drawn on the work of James in his "transcendental developmental" curriculum theory. Within this framework, Macdonald (1974) noted James's openness to all aspects of human experience, especially the religious and mystical, as well as his methodology of disciplined phenomenological inquiry. He says: "By acceptance of the inner realm as a source of meaning, James only intends that we test it in our lives, that we accept it as phenomenological fact by verifying for ourselves by testing its meaning for us in our human activity" (p. 83).

In the decades following the publication of this article, increasing numbers of theorists and educators have been discussing the relationship between spirituality and education, calling on multiple definitions and approaches. In researching this emerging "subfield," I propose at least 10 categories of definition (Johnson, 1999), all based on some form of "connectedness," including emotion, peace, faith, self-reflection, meaning-making, ecological awareness, creativity, religion, morality, and mystical knowing. Although contemporary curriculum literature engages most of these areas, lines of inquiry concerning the implications of mystical cognition for curriculum theory and practice are largely unexplored. I believe that the mystical theory of William James offers a fertile source of knowledge and inspiration for this endeavor. In this chapter, I discuss James's contemporary relevance, consider James's definition of mysticism in historical context, and outline the elements of his mystical theory. Finally, I examine some of the implications of these elements of his thought for contemporary curriculum theory and practice.

JAMES'S CONTEMPORARY RELEVANCE

Thirty years after I first encountered James, and a century after he worked and lived, I am struck by his prefiguring of 21st-century concerns. Contemporary interest in religion and spirituality proliferates. The global market culture's overemphasis on exteriority—on material consumption and appearance—and the rapid pace of our outer-driven, achievement-oriented society seem to be generating a contrasting fascination with the inner dimensions of life. Although fundamentalist religions are growing rapidly, so too are the numbers of "spiritual seekers," who are searching out mystical wisdom within and across religious traditions.

A popular fascination with spiritual and religious experience characterized the last turn of the century as it does this one. However, 100 years ago in American intellectual life, there was a rising confidence in "modern science" rather than the current ambivalence about it. Although James played a major role in establishing the fledging field of psychology as a science, he did not see belief in scientific method as contradictory to a religious/mystical worldview. His varying roles—head of Harvard's natural history museum, founder of Harvard's department of scientific psychology, lecturer in philosophy, and researcher of religious experience—were not generally a source of conflict for James.

James's scientific colleagues were divided in their responses to his sources of data, which included testimony from controversial psychics, his own mystical experiences, and historical mystical accounts. For some scientists, as Simon (1998) points out: "Psychic phenomena were no less 'real' than invisible natural forces—gravity or electricity, for example—and no less worthy of intellectual inquiry" (p. 141). Other colleagues who reflected the modern shift toward a separation of science and spirit challenged James, but he stood firm, insisting that the fledgling discipline of psychology must be based on scientific method and be open to all sources of data, including and especially direct personal religious and mystical experience.

In addition, James argued that the academic disciplines of science and psychology must be relevant to ordinary people, speaking in their language to their concerns. He believed that although most people wanted to believe in God, the dogmatism of modern science was leading to a lack of faith. He hoped to make philosophical and psychological inquiry bias-free, accessible to all, and based on human questions worthy of consideration. He wanted "to enable individuals who were previously deadened by nihilistic despair to regain a sense of purpose and meaning in their lives" (Barnard, 1997, p. 3). James insisted that a valid philosophy must transform the lives of the people who encountered it.

Apart from his academic acceptance, James achieved a degree of popular recognition of his ideas. However, as his methods and theories were embraced by certain segments of the general public, James worried that he would be seen as more of a popularizing figure of philosophy, "a talker to teachers, religious experiencer or willer to believe" (Simon, 1998, p. 328) than as a serious scientist and thinker. Nevertheless, he persisted in working in all intellectual arenas and in conversing with both philosophers and the general public, including educators.

James was fighting a battle that would apparently be lost to the tides of modernity. Religious consciousness and the type of transformational philosophy that James advocated gradually lost their place in education. For most of human history until the modern era, the spirit had been understood literally as an actual, nonmaterial animating essence of life, connecting self, others, and the world. Teaching and learning were seen as intrinsically connected with spiritual and religious perspectives. But the modernist emphasis on rationality, scientific reductionism, and materialism divided spirit from everyday living in the material world, gradually excluding spiritual and religious perspectives from educational theory and practice. The division was also motivated by the democratic ideal of freedom from a dominant, proscriptive religious ideology, resulting in a formal separation between church and state. Both of these trends led to the taboo or, at the very least, to contention regarding the place of the spirit, religion, and ethics in educational settings.

Now the tides are slowly turning. Widespread popular interest in diverse forms of personally relevant experience is beginning to influence educational theory and practice. The necessity for including spiritual dimensions in education is even more critical than in James's day. The general sense of nihilistic despair that concerned him has intensified. Raised in the increasingly materialistic, hedonistic culture of global capitalism, young people are skeptical, yet yearning for a sense of meaning and purpose. Beaudoin (1998) argues that the apparent "irreverence" of the young is actually a demonstration of and plea for spiritual/religious faith. He suggests that they are suspicious of institutions, hungry for personal religious experience, and comfortable with religious diversity and ambiguity. James's work certainly speaks to these concerns.

In one sense, the postmodern challenge to the modernist worldview has inadvertently opened the doors to spiritual beliefs excluded from the modern academic disciplines of science, psychology, and education. Many contemporary theorists reject previously accepted truth-proclaiming authorities, both the scientific and the religious. Modernist assumptions about the ability of scientific objective rationality to discover and proclaim "truth" are challenged along with religious authorities promoting their own versions of "reality." A loosening of the monopoly of both scientific and religious metanarratives has resulted in the emergence of a diversity of perspectives, including previously marginalized voices (such as women and indigenous peoples) and ways of knowing (such as the imaginative, the emotional, and the intuitive).

But extreme deconstructive postmodern theories also deny the existence of any spiritual or essential reality by proclaiming that *all* "reality" is personal and symbolic, constructed in the context of social and cultural experience. David Griffin (1993) suggests the term "constructivist postmodern" to refer to philosophical perspectives that bridge this socially constructed ideology with nonreductionist natural theism. He refers to James, Peirce, Bergson, Whitehead, and Hartshorne as the "founders of constructivist postmodern philosophy." These philosophers reject two fundamental beliefs of modernism: ontology based on a materialistic understanding of nature and epistemology limited to sensory experience. They embrace the premodern idea that all of nature has consciousness, in the sense of the potential for experience and for some aspect of self-organization. James articulates a transformational mystical philosophy that bridges premodern spirituality, modern rationality, and postmodern diversity.

JAMES'S DEFINITION OF MYSTICISM IN HISTORICAL CONTEXT

Religious scholars have debated the concept of mysticism over centuries. The derivation of the word is unclear but is usually associated with the Greek root meaning "to close," referring to closing the senses to intake and the lips to speech. Thus the mystic is closed to the external world and open to "inner experience." In addition, initiates into an esoteric school of a religion would often be required to take a vow of silence, "to close" the lips to sharing information with the uninitiated. Mysticism has been variously defined as a theory about the nature of reality, a doctrine about how we can feel unified with that reality, a set of spiritual practices, an attitude, and a mode of cognition or perception. Margaret Smith (1980) describes it as neither religion nor philosophical system, but rather "an attitude of mind; an innate tendency of the human soul, which seeks to transcend reason and to attain a direct experience of God, and which believes that it is possible for the human soul to be united with Ultimate Reality, when 'God ceases to be an object and becomes an experience'" (p. 20).

The study of mysticism crosses religious, cultural, and historical divisions, because mystical doctrines are found in virtually all historical periods and religious traditions. These doctrines consist of both personal accounts of individual mystical experience and more philosophical descriptions. In addition, the study of mysticism invites interdisciplinary scholarship, with contributions from religion, history, anthropology, sociology, and psychology. James is generally credited with the founding of the psychological study of religion. In particular, James's *The Varieties of Religious Experience* (1902/1978), based on his Gifford Lectures delivered at Edinburgh University in 1901 and 1902, has often been cited as the original and seminal text in this area.

There is ongoing debate about the extent of the similarities among mystical experiences and the differences between them. Scholars who are interested in particular religions tend to focus on differences between the mystical traditions. Contemporary postmodern trends also lead to an emphasis on differences, with an insistence upon the way in which mystical experience is shaped and bounded by culture and tradition. However, James, along with others who focus on the psychological or epistemological dimension of mysticism, stresses similarities, suggesting a "universal" mystical consciousness, pointing to an underlying commonality in experience and perspective among diverse mystical traditions. Certainly James recognized and valued the significance of difference, but his research and theorizing led him to believe in the existence of a "universal" mystical view of the world.

Under debate is the exact nature of James's definition of mysticism and its centrality to his entire theory of consciousness. This is partly because he discusses mysticism in various contexts, focusing on diverse aspects of its meaning. Sometimes he refers to discrete individual experiences—classical mystical accounts by mystics ranging from Al-Ghazzali to Saint John of the Cross and Saint Theresa to Walt Whitman. In his best-known writing on mysticism (lectures 16 and 17 in *The Varieties of Religious Experience*), James proposes four hallmarks of mystical experience: ineffability, noetic quality, transiency, and passivity. In other words, mystical experiences are brief personal encounters with a state of consciousness foreign to ordinary consciousness that seem to come from elsewhere, are experienced simultaneously as knowledge and feeling, and defy description in words.

Clearly, the "hallmarks" lecture was just one aspect of his view of mystical experience. The tendency of scholars to focus narrowly on these lectures initially led to the recognition of James as an authority. But, as Twiss (1995) says, more recent critics have dismissed James's "hallmarks" view of mysticism as "non-scientific, uncritical, myopic and reductionist," neglecting the larger perspectives contained in *The Varieties* and in his work as a whole.

In many contexts, James makes it clear that he believes that accounts of mystical experiences undermine the authority of rational consciousness, demonstrating that it is only one kind of consciousness. Moreover, he speaks, as do many who focus on the universal similarity of mystical experience, of mystical consciousness as the essence of religion—an "inner fact apart from ecclesiastical or theological complications" (James, 1902/1978, p. 448) that consists of an "active and mutual" relationship with higher powers. Contemporary religious studies scholarship often

challenges the concept of a universal consciousness underlying our social and cultural constructions, and dismisses any suggestion of ultimate
reality or God. This tendency to interpret James through the current
academic bias has contributed further to the marginalizing of James's
authority on mysticism.

Ultimately, James uses the term "mysticism" to refer to an orientation to living based on the implications of mystical experiences and consciousness. As Barnard (1997) notes, "A careful examination of James's
writings reveals that mysticism, for James, is way of life that is centered
around experiences of powerful, transformative, personally interpreted,
contacts with transnatural realities" (pp. 4–5). James's overriding concern
was with the social, ethical, and transformative consequences of mystical
experience, but he did undeniably focus on *individual* mystical experience.
Since much contemporary philosophy underscores the social construction
of experience, contending that the concept of isolated, individual consciousness is a Western invention, this Jamesian emphasis draws criticism. James
does understand mystical experience as arising from a "divine" source
beyond human construction, which is received and interpreted by individuals. But he also emphasizes the ways in which this experience and its
interpretations are molded by social and cultural experiences. James's
mystical way of life, although not communal, is highly relational, based
on an ongoing relationship with the divine and culminating in more ethical, deeply felt connections with others.

A contemporary reassessment of James's mysticism is under way. Twiss
(1995) concludes that James's account of mysticism, taken as a whole, is
"phenomenologically subtle, consonant with historical inquiry, fully supportive of comparative and interdisciplinary inquiry, and identifies many
of the critical issues that still plague the field" (p. 177). Barnard (1997)
argues that James's transformational theory of mysticism offers unex-
pected solutions to contemporary dilemmas in philosophical and psychological theories of mysticism. Ford (1993) demonstrates the significant
role that James's philosophy has played in the turning from modern to
postmodern philosophy and is now playing in offering the possibility of
a deistic postmodern alternative.

JAMES'S THEORY OF MYSTICISM

The central themes of a mystical worldview are embedded in James's
philosophy of radical empiricism, although this has not been widely recognized in philosophical circles. Modernists who altered James's philoso-

phy to fit their beliefs disregarded some of the more mystical aspects of radical empiricism. For example (and of particular interest to educators), Gale (1997) suggests that John Dewey, as both a lover of James and a religious skeptic, focused on James's use of scientific method and natural constructivism and ignored the more mystical elements of radical empiricism. The aim of this "whitewashing" was to "despookify and depersonalize it so it would agree with Dewey's naturalism and socialization of all things distinctively human" (p. 49).

The mystical elements of radical empiricism include the following:

- an emphasis on the primacy of experience, including nonsensory experience.
- a recognition of the nondualistic and interconnected (yet pluralistic) nature of reality.
- the idea that consciousness pervades the universe (panpsychism).

Primacy of Experience

Radical empiricism is based on the idea that "the only universe that is theoretically available to us is manifested within and through the thickness and concreteness of our lived experience" (Barnard, 1997, p. 139). James refers to this lived experience as "pure experience." In other words, our firsthand experience of the world is the ultimate source of all of our knowledge. Ford (1982) and Barnard (1997) both point out that this concept of pure experience really refers to two separate philosophical concepts. On the one hand, pure experience describes the psychological experience of individual persons, for whom all types of experience flow together in consciousness. Our experience of the world is primal and nondualistic. It becomes the basis for our constructed dualities, such as knower and known; mental, physical, spiritual; subject and object. This emphasis on experience is an element of the mystical worldview, but it is also critical to nonreligious constructivist views, such as Dewey's. James argues that all experiences, including mystical ones, have this unitive sense in common. Thus mystical experiences are not exceptional in their subjective/objective ambiguity.

Although experienced with unity, pure experience draws on several sources of data. In addition to sense-perception, each of us has direct, though often unrecognized, experiences of an "unseen world." James believes that, in order to experience our fullest potential as human beings (and as scientists or psychologists), these nonsensory religious or mystical experiences should be included in the data from which we create our theories about life.

Interconnectedness

"Pure experience" also refers to a metaphysical recognition of the non-dualistic and interconnected nature of the universe. By this James does not mean a substance (he declares that there is no general stuff as a universal element) but a possibility or an actuality. Sounding like a contemporary Buddhist, James (1912/1971) says that "the instant field of the present is at all times what I call 'pure' experience . . . it is plain unqualified actuality, or existence, a simple *that*, as yet undifferentiated into thing and thought" (p. 15). "It is made of that of just what appears, of space, of intensity, of flatness, brownness, heaviness" (p. 17). Our discursive reason thinks that its categories correspond to real individual things. But reality is simply that which cannot be broken up. Moreover, James sees reality in terms of systemic connections between objects, events, people, and ideas. Although containing both connections and disconnections, "loosely speaking and in general, it may be said that all things cohere and adhere to each other somehow and that the universe exists practically in reticulated and concatenated forms which make of it a continuous or 'integrated affair'" (James, 1907/1996, p. 68).

Pluralistic Panpsychism

James embraces panpsychism, the premodern and mystical idea that the universe is intrinsically animated. Everything in the universe is conscious; all elements have an inner psychical element or disposition. Consciousness is what organisms *do* rather than *have*. In other words, all things are capable of experience. James further believes that consciousness is an aspect of evolution and was present in the origins of the universe. Ford (1993) and Lamberth (1997) both argue that, although many other James scholars have erroneously claimed that James refuted panpsychism in his later life, in fact, there is opposite evidence from both published and unpublished sources that James remained committed to it.

James adopts a form that he termed "pluralistic panpsychism." Despite the oneness implied in the concepts of pure experience, undifferentiated actuality, and the systemic connections explained above, James rejects the idea of ultimate oneness in the universe as found in both idealistic philosophies and in some mystical views. Reality is as much pluralistic as it is unified. Instead of there being a single "truth" out there waiting to be discovered, the world contains many potential truths that emerge from the undifferentiated actuality. We participate in creating these truths as we discover them, but they are a combination of "that" and ourselves. Radical empiricism is a philosophical/metaphysical system that includes both the all-pervading *that* and the diverse, messy complex world—both unity and disunity.

MYSTICAL EXPERIENCE

In *The Varieties*, James turns to a direct study of religious experience. He sets out to establish a science, or a psychology, of religion. He makes it clear from the outset that he is primarily interested in individual religious experience and its effect on the world. He sees this, rather than philosophy or theology, as the most authentic source of religions. He wants to discuss "religion's existential conditions" rather than the social structure of religion. He deemphasizes the institution and the organization, but he feels that religion is humanity's most important activity. James understands all religions, theologies, and religious organizations as growing out of individual, mystical experiences, based in religious feeling. He describes religious feeling as a "faith-state," a biological and psychological force necessary for a life worth living, the absence of which means collapse. He is most interested in the religious experience of "geniuses," the founders of religions and religious movements, for whom religion is more "fever" than "habit."

> I speak not of your ordinary religious believer, who follows the conventional observance of his country, whether it be Buddhist, Christian, or Mohammedan. His religion has been made for him by others, communicated to him by tradition, determined to fixed forms by imitation, and retained by habit. It would profit us little to study this second-hand religious life. We must search rather for the original experiences which were the pattern setters to all this mass of suggested feeling and imitated conduct. (James, 1902/1978, p. 27)

In looking at these "pattern setters" from a variety of religions, James wants to establish the validity of mystical consciousness and, in doing so, to indirectly establish proof of the existence of God. He also wants to make a case for the consequence of this consciousness to humanity. These four themes in *The Varieties* are the most significant to my study:

- God exists; there is *something more* to human experience than appears on the surface.
- An active relationship with God is the ultimate purpose of human existence and produces real effects; God is both "given" and "cocreated."

- A plurality of mystical and religious expressions is necessary to express the range of human and divine possibilities.
- Mystical experiences have ethical implications.

Something More

James (1902/1978) believes that there is something more than meets the sensory eye to human experience and existence. "The visible world is part of a more spiritual universe from which it draws its chief significance" (p. 468). Mystical experience is definitive proof of the existence of this world of "something more," but not of its exact nature. He leaves plenty of room for a pluralistic, evolving divinity and uses a variety of names for this something, including the wider world, the mystical region, the supernatural region, cosmic consciousness, God—"whichever you choose" (p. 495).

James did not consider himself a mystic, but the few genuine mystical experiences he had affected him deeply. He attached great significance to his own and others' experiences, as they offered a glimpse into this unseen world. However, he suggests that even the ordinary person in everyday life senses the existence of such a realm. James believes that this sense of "something more" is a part of the structure of human consciousness, always present but usually overlooked or ignored, hidden from our waking consciousness by "the flimiest of screens," just waiting for the right circumstances to bring it to awareness.

James explains that this "other" consciousness is actually not other than one's self but a part of one's self. Our "full self" or "wider self" is a whole field of consciousness, the vaster parts of which we may barely or seldom experience. He sometimes refers to our "trans-marginal or subliminal region" consciousness as part of the continuum between visible and invisible worlds. If we travel far enough down the continuum of our wider self, we become aware of "an altogether other dimension of existence from the sensible and merely understandable world . . . we belong to it in a more intimate sense than that in which we belong to the visible world, for we belong in the intimate sense wherever our ideals belong" (James, 1902/1978, p. 495). We sense both that this dimension is utterly strange and inexpressible and that it is our most intimate self.

We experience mystical states of consciousness as both feeling and knowledge, as "states of insight into depths of truth unplumbed by the discursive intellect. They are illuminations, revelations, full of significance and importance" (James, 1902/1978, p. 371). This revelatory experience of communion with our "deepest" self—with "God"—changes us, "marks" us with significance, leaves us both peaceful and energized, profoundly satisfied and yet yearning for more.

Active Relationship With God

Once we have experienced the existence of this unseen world, we feel compelled to continue to communicate with it. For James (1902/1978) and for many who have had powerful mystical experiences, "union or harmonious relation with that higher universe is our true end" (p. 468)— the "very aim and purpose of existence." Prayer, our attempt to communicate, is "the very soul and essence of religion" (p. 448). He defines prayer as "every kind of inward communion or conversation with the power recognized as divine" or "inner communication with the spirit" (p. 468). In other words, for him, prayer is a category that includes meditation on, or contemplation of, the divine.

James (1902/1978) states that prayer or inner communication is a "process wherein work is really done, and spiritual energy flows in and produces effects, psychological or material, with the phenomenal world" (p. 468). This is a key point for the pragmatic James. If there is no change in the "experiencer" as a result of the inner communication, then a "genuine" mystical experience did not occur. Prayer, for James, means an active, mutual, and genuine relationship between human beings and God. As a result of this relationship, "real" energy becomes activated: "Energy from on high flows in to meet the demand and becomes operative within the phenomenal world" (p. 461). For example, James leaves no doubt about his belief in the healing power of prayer: "If any medical fact can be considered to stand firm, it is that in certain environments, prayer may contribute to recovery" (pp. 447–448).

James (1902/1978) believes not only that human beings are affected by God but also that God is changed through the relationship. Our relationship with God is "active and mutual" (p. 448). The divine being communicates with us through mystical experiences, or prayers, and asks something of us in return. Our response plays a role in constructing or cocreating the nature of God. "The universe, at those parts of it which our personal being constitutes, takes a turn genuinely for the worse or for the better in proportion as each one of us fulfills or evades God's demands" (p. 448). In James's universe, we are internal parts of God and not external creations. God is present in all human experience and we are present in all divine experience, contributing to the nature of divinity.

Religious Pluralism

Although James focuses on establishing the existence of a pervasive mystical consciousness, he is also interested in the significance of difference in religious experience. A religious feeling/mystical experience/faith-state may hold a minimum of intellectual content, but when associated with a particular faith, religion, or intellectual content, it gets stamped with it; the feeling or faith latches onto it. This is James's explanation for passionate loyalty to different creeds and religions. In their quest for security, human beings seek to eliminate uncertainty, but in clinging to a particular belief, they oversimplify, which sometimes leads to absolutism and religious dogma.

However, James does not seek to eliminate religion. Rather, he upholds religious diversity. Historical and cultural factors give form and content to mystical experiences, but they do not create them. Not only is the plurality of religious expression a testament to the richness of human diversity, but diversity is necessary in order to express anything nearing the full range of human and divine possibility. James (1902/1978) emphasizes a great variety of "mystical windows" potentially accessible. God can express his/her fullness in this world only through a multiplicity of forms: "The divine can mean no single quality, it must mean a group of qualities. . . . Each attitude being a symbol in human nature's total message, it takes the whole of us to spell the meaning out completely" (p. 470).

James's pluralistic pantheism extends from this world to the "unseen world." He speculates that pluralism is most likely built into the very nature of God. Rather than a place of perfection, the wider world has a mixed constitution, filled with a variety of regions, beings and purposes. We continue to actively construct our experience in that world, as well as this one, "by selecting and subordinating and substituting just as is our custom in this ordinary naturalistic world; we should be liable to error just as we are now" (James, 1902/1978, pp. 416–417).

Ethical Implications

The active, cocreating relationship with God intensifies our moral responsibility. God is made real by the effects she/he produces in us and the resulting impact that we have on the world. As interested as James is in the metaphysics of mystical experience, he is even more concerned with its practical results, as determined by the personality and ethical behavior of the mystic. For James, a mystical worldview demands a higher ethical standard than a materialistic worldview. Using God is even more important than knowing or understanding God.

Religious experience is personal, but it is lived in a social and moral context. James rejects any dogmatic beliefs and argues for a relative morality, with right and wrong emerging in the context of human living. But he does so in the context of a mystical worldview. God has an ongoing, active part to play in the ethics of living. Mystical experiences should produce real effect, regenerative change, and more ethical conduct on our part. Ideally, the experience of, and identification with, our "wider self" jars us out of selfish, egotistical patterns of behavior. The decisions of an ethical life are based on the character traits of the individual, and character is changed by the high emotions of the mystical state or religious inspiration. In these states, we feel peaceful, at rest, and assured of safety, James (1902/1978) says, and we bring this quality to our relations with others as "a preponderance of loving affections." At the same time, we feel highly energized, with "a new zest which adds itself like a gift to life" (p. 468). Mystical experiences give us a sense of "lyric enchantment" and optimism that brings profound meaning to our daily lives. This energy and optimism manifests in the world as heroism. Religious faith based on experience gives individuals the courage and strength to fight for what we believe is right.

James links sainthood to mysticism. Saints are those who live their lives for the welfare of others and, in doing so, provide a model for the rest of us. The saint may begin with brief, episodic mystical experience, but she or he becomes increasingly immersed in a transformational mystical reality, resulting in ever more saintly behavior. After an extended inquiry into saintly behavior, he concludes that, because of the saints, religion does deserve its "towering place in history. Economically, the saintly group of qualities is indispensable to the world's welfare" (James, 1902/1978, p. 368). The unselfish behavior of the saints, in turn, justifies the reality of their mystical worldview. However, James admits that many saints have carried their self-abnegation and religious fervor to extremes and therefore he advocates, in the words of Barnard (1997), "a new improved version—a non-dogmatic, critically aware, tolerant, non-sectarian, non-excessive modern saint" (p. 8). The overall aim of the mystical life is transformation of self and world.

IMPLICATIONS FOR CURRICULUM THEORY
AND PRACTICE

Curriculum theory is ultimately, in the words of Macdonald (1974), "the study of what should constitute a world for learning and how to go about making this world" (p. 137). As such, it seeks to understand assumptions underlying curriculum practices in contemporary culture and to offer alternative theoretical frameworks leading to more liberating curricular decisions. In this sense, curriculum theory is a transformational tool. Recent scholarship in the field focuses on the liberatory potential of political, multicultural, esthetic, and postmodern discourses. Within the smaller

theological/spiritual arena, conversation has centered on historical religious, ethical, ecological, and hermeneutic themes. Postmodern skepticism
toward both unitive religious metanarratives and spiritual reality has im-
peded serious consideration of the implications of mysticism for curriculum.
As we have seen, James's transformative mystical philosophy speaks to
postmodern concerns around pluralism, personal experience, and social
construction of meaning while holding fast to a mystical worldview. Thus I
believe that it has a significant contribution to make to a reconceptualized
curriculum field. The following six themes emerge as central to curriculum
based on this mystical theory:

- Base curriculum in experience
- Integrate and connect curriculum
- Include religious history in curriculum
- Allow mystical experience and perspectives to inform theory and
  practice
- Incorporate pluralistic perspectives and forms of inquiry
- Focus on ethics as a dominant curricular concern

Base Curriculum in Experience

As a professor of philosophy and psychology, James certainly appreciated
and emphasized the education of the intellect, but in its proper place in
the larger educational endeavor. He believed that theoretical knowledge,
divorced from our own experience, has little likelihood of transforming lives,
but that the intellect *can* be developed without impeding our sense of connection with pure experience. Experience, both sensory and nonsensory, is
at the heart of James's philosophy. The source of all information and knowledge is the lived experience of human beings.

All avenues of experience are potentially equally significant for James.
By calling attention to nonsensory experience in his mystical writings,
James is highlighting what has been neglected in the modern world. In
his educational writings, he centered more on the sensory, emphasizing
the significance of focusing student attention. He modeled and advocated
the ongoing practice of describing our full experience in precise detail,
becoming more and more aware of all of the subtle details of thoughts,
feelings, sense perceptions, and intuitions and the way they flow together
to form our full reality. Contemporary mystical theology emphasizes the
mysticism of "ordinary" experience, seeing God in the details of everyday
life in the material world. Perhaps Buddhist religious traditions are attract-
ing so much current interest because of their emphasis on the practice of
presence in everyday experience, of paying attention to sensory reality and

inner emotional experience. This practice of being with our "pure experience" is a type of meditation or contemplation, as well as a scientific skill. A Jamesian curriculum theory is grounded in radical empiricism, in encouraging learners of all ages to pay careful attention to all aspects of their direct personal experience, both sensory and nonsensory. This is a countercultural curriculum focus, in a context that fosters a hurried pace of life, along with reactivity to predominating media influences and consumerism.

Integrate and Connect Curriculum

James's concept of the pluralistic nature of reality coexisted with his belief in a nondualistic, interconnected universe that is also animated and conscious. We participate directly in this interconnected consciousness and experience the unity until our discursive mind divides it into categories. When James asks us to pay careful attention to our experience, he wants us to be able to cut through artificial categories and recapture the world of pure experience, the undifferentiated *that*. In our rush to impose early rationality on children, and to base curriculum in abstractions unrelated to experience, we disengage them from unity of experience, from a feeling of connection between self and the world and among all objects and ideas in the world.

Overall, James points to a lack of continuity in the curriculum as the greatest weakness for educational practice. A Jamesian curriculum theory supports interdisciplinary curriculum, not in a rigid sense but in following the natural connections between ideas and disciplines. Curriculum can be based on themes and questions arising from student questions and concerns and/or from current issues and ethical challenges in both local and global contexts.

An increasing number of scientific theories suggest the ecological interconnectedness of living systems. James recognized both the physical, embodied nature of spirit and the systematic, connected, interdependent, relational nature of all parts of the earth and the universe. We can draw strong support from him for an ecological education based in whole systems thinking, engaging connections between ideas and actions and based in the natural world.

Include the Study of Religions

Religious experience and inquiry represented, for James, the most fundamental concern and function of human existence, a concern largely absent from modern schooling. The "something more" dimension of human experience is one of the central themes of his scholarship and his life. Much of the contemporary discussion concerning religion and education has been framed around the polarization between religious conservatives and liberal defenders of public education. Many people have assumed that the separation of church and state implies that all aspects of religion must stay behind a rigid line drawn around public schooling. This taboo, while undoubtedly protecting children from proselytism, prejudice, and persecution, has also resulted in a distortion of the significant role that religions have played in human history. The taboo also means that many children are not exposed to the way in which religions raise and attempt to answer the profound existential questions of perennial concern to human beings.

However, more recently, voices from across political and religious positions are calling for a reexamination of the place and role of religion in public education. For example, Noddings (1993) states: "There is nothing in the establishment clause of the first amendment that prevents classroom instruction about religion. Further, so long as our presentations are balanced, I see no legal reason why various religious claims and critiques cannot be discussed in all their richness " (p. xv). One proposed solution is a greater emphasis on religion as a central human concern and institution in the history and social studies curriculum. Textbooks in this area have greatly minimized the significant role of religions in history and society. In *Taking Religion Seriously Across the Curriculum*, Nord and Haynes (1998) also suggest ways to include religion in all subject areas, such as religious themes in literature and religious/ethical issues in science.

James's perspectives on religion are synonymous with religious pluralism. Religious curriculum that is inspired by James would include all of the major historical religious perspectives, as well as new religious movements. James believed that the completeness and complexity, the diversity of the divine, need many windows to view and express it. Although religious perspectives have much in common, they also have varying emphases. We could consider the particular gifts that each religion might offer as a source of inspiration for curriculum theory: for example, prophetic justice in Judaism or attentive awareness in Buddhism. We can also consider historical examples of educational practice of varying religions, such as the parables of Christ or the Jewish focus on textual analysis.

Allow Religious/Mystical Experience and Perspective

As I have argued in this chapter, James ultimately defines religious experience in terms of mystical experience. An active, cocreating relationship with God is the "ultimate purpose" of life. According to James's mystical philosophy, transformation stems from direct personal experience with the world around us and with our wider self. Regardless of our own personal religious orientation—atheist, skeptic, seeker, believer, or any combination—putting James's ideas into practice demands an openness to the possibility of entering into an authentic relationship with "something more" than ourselves. For James, communicating with our deepest self/God made life worth living.

Faith as a feeling is prior to and more important than intellectual belief for James. As the basis of both religion and mysticism, it is a biological/psychological experience necessary for a life worth living. James advocated that we cultivate our underlying faith but remain open to new beliefs that will continually shape and change it. Curriculum theorists can explore the connections between faith and the intellectual life. We can investigate the possibilities of using our imaginative capacities to create a world of justice worthy of our children's faith, and we can emphasize the importance of faith-sustaining relationships between teachers and students.

Curriculum could include the question of how others throughout history have cultivated a genuine relationship with "something more." Beyond studying religion, students could be exposed to historical and contemporary mystical literature, including biographies and autobiographies of varied mystics and saints from across history and across cultures.

Drawing on James, Macdonald (1974) uses the word "centering" to refer to activities that engage our preconceptual mystical mode of knowing. He suggests that the aim of an educational ideology based on the spiritual realm should be centering, and by this he means centering in self, in spirit, and in world. Students could learn about, and then empirically test, a whole range of centering activities. The simplest, yet perhaps most profound practices for many, might be opportunities for solitude and silence. James emphasized the significance of prayer, his term for any kind of intentional relationship with the divine. But he referred to many types of mystical practice. In addition to prayer, and the attention practice mentioned earlier, centering practices take forms as varied as the mystical traditions they originate from. These might include mediations on religious figures, breathing practices, meditations on light, or bodily-based exercises such as yoga and tai chi. I believe that James would emphasize the commitment to the relationship rather than the technique used, but that he would also look carefully at intention and results.

Certainly curriculum theorists and teachers must proceed with caution here. The inclusion of mystical and religious experience in the curriculum, while appropriate for many private schools, may prove to be too controversial for public schools in light of first amendment issues. An additional problem arises from the marketplace and its popularization of spiritual experience. In this capitalistic culture, everything, including spirituality and mystical practice, is commodified. Spirituality is sold as a product to inflate personal ego and enhance social standing. Mystical practices that have, for centuries, been taught in a particular religious context and carefully guarded are promoted in the market as secrets of personal power. A curriculum that embraces varying types of mystical experience could easily become superficial. But I believe that James would note the dangers and argue for freedom to seek, along with a commitment to depth of experience. Those educators who work in specific religious contexts can facilitate experiences within their traditions. In pluralistic contexts, students could attempt to locate experiences within their own heritage, when appropriate.

Emphasize Pluralism and Inquiry

William James is a model of open-mindedness, a philosopher who put pluralism at the heart of all theory and inquiry, sometimes risking his professional reputation to do so. He understood the universe, as well as God, as an open system that we are involved in creating. Therefore, knowledge systems and inquiry methods must, by definition, be seen as continuously evolving constructions. To follow in his footsteps, we can cultivate an attitude that invites ideas "from the margins" of our current paradigms, including a receptivity to religious and mystical experiences. Although curriculum theorists do tend to work in opposition to dominant paradigms and to include marginalized perspectives, there are always blind spots in the field that represent current biases. We can be seeking the edges, engaging both in a deep self-reflection that alerts us to our own theoretical and personal limitations and blindness and in an ongoing search for the most fertile sources of ideas in all disciplines. We can also support curriculum methodologies that encourage students' openness to diverse perspectives, especially the active questioning of the sources of knowledge and authority in their education. In contemporary culture, this would certainly include the effects of media and advertising in constructing consumer consciousness.

In *Talks to Teachers*, James discusses the inability of many human beings to understand and sympathize with those who are different: "Hands off: neither the whole of truth nor the whole of good is revealed to any single observer, although each observer gains a partial superior insight from the peculiar position in which he stands. Even prisons and sickrooms have their special revelation" (James quoted in McDermott, 1977, p. 645). This is another version of James's continual message that a pluralistic world needs many perspectives to express itself, and that each human being *is* one of them. Here he encourages us to expose students to people whose experiences and views are very different from their own, including those from less privileged circumstances.

Focus on Ethics as the Overriding Theme

In the current cultural context, it is difficult to balance an individual mystical quest with genuine commitment to authentic relationship, community, and social change. James insists that mysticism be judged ultimately "by the fruits of its action," in terms of its ethical results. The fruit of a mystical relationship with God becomes moral responsibility. According to him, personal relationships with the divine, if they are authentic, lead to greater emphasis on the welfare of others. James believes that profound mystical experience alters our conduct for the better. Although this is a debatable assertion, it is central to a Jamesian understanding of ethics.

A curriculum theory inspired by James will make ethics its most central concern. He urges educators to be clear about the morals they want to engender in their students and then to work consciously toward this goal. Intellectual capacities, though important, are secondary to the value base upon which students' ideas should be tested. Ethical concerns and questions can be emphasized in all areas of the curriculum, including humanities, social sciences, and sciences. Students can discuss ethical dilemmas, participate in democratic school communities, and engage in worthwhile social, ecological, and civic projects.

James noted that morally exceptional individuals are dedicated to their inner ideals, which take precedence over material comfort or worldly success. These individuals demonstrate endurance, determination, steadfastness, fidelity, and courage as they work to make their ideals a reality. By holding up the saints as a model for our behavior, James is advocating for the importance of role models. In a culture that worships fame, youth, beauty, and money, many students idolize movie stars and sports figures. This trend is intensified by the voracious targeting of youth by the advertising industry, weakening family and community ties. Young people spend more time with television and computer realities and with each other than with families or communities. (And we are marketing this trend globally.) They are simply starving for mentors. We can focus curriculum around inspiring ethical models from history and contemporary culture, those whose efforts to make the world a better place are examples of the triumph of the human spirit (including those saints and mystics mentioned earlier).

CONCLUSION: TEACHER AS MENTOR; JAMES AS MENTOR

In a curriculum rooted in mystical and ethical dimensions, the teacher is the first mentor, the living center of centering. According to James, the spiritual realm of existence is actualized as we participate in it. If we do not feel our own spirits, we cannot sense the spirits of others, including those of our students. Our spiritual nature flourishes as we engage with it; our sincere attempts to communicate with the divine activate a powerful latent energy within us. As teachers, our engagement in this dimension allows us to sense it and honor it in our students. This recognition, in turn, helps to actualize their spiritual potential. Kovel (1991) says, "All human beings have the spiritual capacity of a Buddha, or Saint Francis, yet all save a tiny few squander these powers beyond measure" (p. 71). James exhorts us to strive toward the examples of saints, who, within the powerful connection with the spiritual realm of existence, develop the power to do great good. Ultimately, a curriculum rests on the beings of teachers who strive to transform lives by engagement and example.

By all accounts, James was a worthy role model. He was an authentic, encouraging, and inspiring teacher, liked by his students. They described him as sympathetic, patient, sincere, open-minded, and enthusiastic. As a professor, he certainly modeled a deep commitment to the pursuit of truth and the love of learning. The original meaning of the term *profess* is "to affirm, to declare faith, to accept a calling." In order to encourage students to have faith in a life worth living, we must demonstrate an active relationship with issues of faith and a sense of calling to our profession. Although James struggled deeply and openly with despair and doubt in himself and in the world, he also held onto hope and held out hope to those around him throughout his life.

James has inspired me to strive toward becoming a professor of faith and an educator who "leads out" the inner beings of my students. I conclude with his words (adding the feminine in my own words): "Let us be saints, then, if we can, whether or not we succeed visibly and temporally. But in our Father's [and Mother's] house are many mansions, and each of us must discover for [herself] the kind of religion and the amount of saintship that best comports with what [she] believes to be [her] powers and feels to be [her] greatest mission and vocation. There are no successes to be guaranteed and no set orders to be given" (James, 1902/1978, pp. 368–369).

References

Abowitz, K. (1997). Neglected aspects of the liberal-communitarian debate and implications of school communities. *Educational Foundations, 11* (2), 63–82.

Apffel-Marglin, Frederique. (1998). *The spirit of regeneration: Andean culture confronting Western notions of development.* New York: Zed Books.

Bar On, B-A. (1993). Marginality and epistemic privilege. In L. Alcoff & E. Potter (Eds.), *Feminist epistemologies* (pp. 83–100). New York/London: Routledge.

Barnard, G. William. (1997). *Exploring unseen worlds: William James and the philosophy of mysticism.* Albany: State University of New York Press.

Barrett, W. (1978). *The illusion of technique.* Garden City, NY: Anchor Press.

Barzun, J. (1983). *A stroll with William James.* New York: Harper & Row.

Bateson, G. (1972). *Steps to an ecology of mind.* New York: Ballentine Books.

Bateson, G. (1988). *Mind and nature: A necessary unity.* New York: Bantam.

Beaudoin, Tom. (1998). *Virtual faith: The irreverent spiritual quest of generation X.* San Francisco: Jossey-Bass.

Belenky, M., Clinchy, B., Goldberger, N., & Tarule, J. (1986). *Women's ways of knowing.* New York: Basic Books.

Bellah, R., Madsen, R., Sullivan, W., Swidler, A., & Tipton, S. (1985). *Habits of the heart: Individualism and commitment in American life.* New York: Harper & Row.

Bernstein, R. J. (1977). Introduction. *A pluralistic universe.* Cambridge, MA: Harvard University Press.

Bird, G. R. (1986). *William James.* London: Routledge.

Blumer, H. (1969). *Symbolic interactionism: Perspective and method.* Englewood Cliffs, NJ: Prentice-Hall.

Brown, L. (Ed.) (1993). The new shorter Oxford English dictionary: Thumb Index Edition. Oxford, UK: Clarendon Press.

Bruner, J. (1985). Narrative and paradigmatic modes of thought. In E. Eisner (Ed.), *Learning and teaching the ways of knowing* (Vol. 84, pp. 97–115). Chicago: University of Chicago.

Burbules, N. (2000). Moving beyond the impasse. In D. C. Phillips (Ed.), *Constructivism in education: Opinions and second opinions on controversial issues.* 99th Yearbook of the National Society for the Study of Education. Chicago: NSSE/Chicago University Press.

Clandinin, D. J., & Connelly, M. F. (1995). *Teachers' professional knowledge landscapes.* New York: Teachers College Press.

Clandinin, D. J., & Connelly, M. F. (1996). Teachers' professional knowledge landscapes: Teacher stories. *Educational Researcher, 25*(3), 24–31.

Clandinin, D. J., & Connelly, M. F. (2000). *Narrative inquiry*. San Francisco: Jossey-Bass.

Cochran-Smith, M., & Lytle, S. L. (1993). *Inside/outside*. New York: Teachers College Press.

Cochran-Smith, M., & Lytle, S. L. (1999). Relationships of knowledge and practice: Teacher learning in communities. *Review of Research in Education* (Vol. 24, pp. 249–305). Washington D.C.: American Education Research Association.

Code, L. (1991). *What can she know? Feminist theory and the construction of knowledge*. Ithaca, NY/London: Cornell University Press.

Code, L. (1993). Taking subjectivity into account. In L. Alcoff & E. Potter (Eds.), *Feminist epistemologies* (pp. 15–48). New York/London: Routledge.

Cole, M., Engeström, Y., & Vasquez, O. (1997). *Mind, culture, and activity*. Cambridge, UK: Cambridge University Press.

Connelly, M. F., & Clandinin, D. J. (1999). *Shaping a professional identity*. New York: Teachers College Press.

Cormier, H. (1997). Pragmatism, politics, and the corridor. In R. Putnam (Ed.), *The Cambridge companion to William James* (pp. 343–362). New York: Cambridge University Press.

Cotkin, B. (1990). *William James, public philosopher*. Baltimore: The Johns Hopkins University Press.

Croce, P. J. (1995). *Science and religion in the era of William James: Eclipse of certainty, 1820–1880*. Chapel Hill: University of North Carolina.

Curti, M. (1959). *The social ideas of American educators*. Paterson, NJ: Littlefield, Adams & Co.

Damasio, A. R. (1994). *Descartes' error*. New York: G. P. Putnam's Sons.

Darwin, C. (1859/1963). *The origin of species*. New York: Washington Square Press.

Darwin, C. (1889/1904). *The expression of the emotions in man and animals*. London: John Murray.

De Ruyter, D. J., & Miedema, S. (2000). Denominational Schools in The Netherlands. In M. Leicester, C. Modgil, & S. Modgil (Eds.), *Education, culture and values: Vol. 5: Spiritual and religious education* (pp. 133–141). London/New York: Falmer Press.

Dewey, J. (1891/1969). Poetry and philosophy. In Jo Ann Boydston (Ed.), *John Dewey: The early works, Volume 3* (pp. 110–124). Carbondale: Southern Illinois University Press.

Dewey, J. (1910/1997). *The Influence of Darwin on philosophy and other essays*. New York: Prometheus Books.

Dewey, J. (1916/1966). *Democracy and education*. New York: The Free Press, Macmillan.

Dewey, J. (1929/1960). *The quest for certainty*. New York: Capricorn Books.

Dewey, J. (1938). *Experience and education*. New York: Touchstone.

Dewey, J. (1937/1987). The philosophy of William James. In J. A. Boydston (Ed.), *John Dewey: The later works*, (Vol. 11, pp. 105–114). Carbondale: Southern Illinois University Press.

Dewey, John. (1946/1989). Introduction to "The problems of men." In J. A.

Boydston (Ed.), *John Dewey: The later works* (Vol. 15, pp. 154–169). Carbondale: Southern Illinois University Press.

Dewey, J. (1946a). The philosophy of William James. In J. Dewey (Ed.), *The problems of men* (pp. 379–395). New York: Philosophical Library.

Dewey, J. (1946b). *The problems of men.* New York: Philosophical Library.

Dewey, J. (1946c). The vanishing subject in the psychology of James. In J. Dewey (Ed.), *The problems of men* (pp. 396–409). New York: Philosophical Library.

Dewey, J. (1973). *The philosophy of John Dewey* (John J. McDermott ed.). Chicago: The University of Chicago Press.

Donmoyer, R. (1997). Research as advocacy and storytelling. *Educational Researcher, 26*(5), 2–4.

Dronkers, J. (1996). Dutch public and religious schools between state and market. *Zeitschrift fuer Paedagogik, 35*(special issue), 51–66.

Durkheim, E. (1965). *The elementary forms of the religious life.* New York: The Free Press.

Edel, Leon. (1976). *Henry James: The conquest of London, the middle years, the treacherous years* (Vols. 1–3). New York: Avon Books.

Edie, J. (1970). William James and phenomenology. *Review of Metaphysics, 23,* 481–526.

Eisner, E. W. (1985). *The art of education evaluation.* Philadelphia: Falmer Press.

Emerson, R. W. (1982). The American scholar. In L. Ziff (Ed.), *R. W. Emerson: Selected essays* (pp. 83–105). New York: Penguin Books.

Evans, J. (1976). *America: A view from Europe.* San Francisco: San Francisco Book Company.

Flax, J. (1983). Political philosophy and the patriarchal unconscious: A psychoanalytic perspective on epistemology and metaphysics. In S. Harding & M. B. Hintikka (Eds.), *Discovering reality* (pp. 245–281). Dordrecht, The Netherlands/Boston/London: Reidel.

Fenstermacher, G. D. (1994). The knower and the known: The nature of knowledge in research on teaching. In L. Darling-Hammond (Ed.), *Review of Research on Education* (Vol. 20, pp. 3–56). Washington D.C.: American Educational Research Association.

Ford, M. P. (1982). *William James' philosophy: A new perspective.* Amherst, MA: University of New Hampshire Press.

Ford, M. P. (1993). William James. In D. R. Griffin (Ed.), *Founders of constructivist postmodern philosophy.* Albany: State University of New York Press.

Gale, R. (1997). John Dewey's naturalization of William James. In R. A. Putnam (Ed.), *The Cambridge companion to William James* (pp. 49–68). Cambridge, England: Cambridge University Press.

Gale, R. (1999). *The divided self of William James.* Cambridge, England: Cambridge University Press.

Garrison, J. (1994). Realism, Deweyan pragmatism, and educational research. *Educational Researcher, 23*(1), 5–14.

Garrison, J. (1997a). An alternative to von Glasersfeld's subjectivism in science education: Deweyan social constructivism. *Science and Education, 6,* 543–554.

Gates, A. L. (1967). Educational classic: Talks to teachers. *NEA Journal, 56*, 34–35.

Geertz, Clifford. (1983). *Local knowledge: Further essays in interpretative anthropology.* New York: Basic Books.

Gelphi, D. L. (1994). *The turn to experience in contemporary theology.* New York/ Mahwah, NJ: Paulist Press.

Gilligan, C. (1982). *In a different voice: Psychological theory and women's development.* Cambridge, MA: Harvard University Press.

Glasersfeld, E. von. (1990). An exposition of constructivism: Why some like it radical. In R. Davis, C. Maher, & N. Noddings (Eds.), *Constructivist views on the teaching and learning of mathematics* (pp. 19–29). Reston, VA: National Council of Teachers of Mathematics.

Glasersfeld, E. von. (1991). *Radical constructivism in mathematics education.* Dordrecht, The Netherlands: Kluwer.

Glasersfeld, E. von. (1995). *Radical constructivism: A way of knowing and learning.* London: Falmer Press.

Glasersfeld, E. von. (1996). Footnotes to "The many faces of constructivism." *Educational Researcher, 25*(6), 19.

Godfrey-Smith, P. (1996). *Complexity and the function of mind in nature.* Cambridge, UK: Cambridge University Press.

Goodman, R. B. (1990). *American philosophy and the Romantic tradition.* Cambridge, UK: Cambridge University Press.

Griffin, D. (Ed.). (1993). *Founders of constructive postmodern philosophy.* Albany: State University of New York Press.

Grossman, P. L. (1990). *The making of a teacher.* New York: Teachers College Press.

Hall, S. (1997). *Representation.* London: Sage.

Harding, S. (1993). Rethinking standpoint epistemology: What is "strong objectivity"? In L. Alcoff & E. Potter (Eds.), *Feminist epistemologies* (pp. 49–82). New York/London: Routledge.

Hatch, J. A. (2000). Reform, resistance and bad faith. In R. Wisniewski (Ed.), *Reforming a college* (pp. 113–121). New York: Peter Lang.

Hoffman, D. (1998). A therapeutic moment? Identity, self, and culture in the anthropology of education. *Anthropology & Education Quarterly, 29*(3), 324–346.

Howard, H. A., & McGrath, D. L. (1964). *War chief Joseph.* Lincoln: University of Nebraska Press.

Jackson, P. (1986). *The practice of teaching.* New York: Teachers College Press.

James, W. (1878/1992). Absolutism and empiricism. *William James: Writings 1878– 1899* (pp. 1015–1020). New York: The Library of America.

James, W. (1890/1927). *The principles of psychology.* New York: Henry Holt.

James, W. (1890/1950). *The principles of psychology* (Vol. 1). New York: Dover.

James, W. (1890/1952). *The principles of psychology* (Vol. 53). Chicago: Encyclopedia Britannica.

James, W. (1891/1971). The moral philosopher and the moral life. In B. Wilshire, *William James: The essential writings* (pp.). New York: Harper.

James, W. (1892). *Psychology: Briefer course.* New York, Henry Holt.

James, W. (1896/1956). *The will to believe and other essays in popular philosophy.* New York: Dover.

James, W. (1897/1947). *The will to believe and other essays in popular philosophy*. New York: Henry Holt and Co.

James, W. (1897/1967). Excerpts from "The will to believe." In J. McDermott (Ed.), *The writings of William James* (p. 858). New York: The Modern Library.

James, W. (1897/1956). The sentiment of rationality. *The will to believe and other essays in popular philosophy* (pp. 63–110). New York: Dover.

James, W. (1897/1971). The will to believe. In B. Wilshire (Ed.), *William James: The essential writings* (pp. 717–735). New York: Harper.

James, W. (1897/1979). *The will to believe*. Cambridge, MA/London: Harvard University Press.

James, W. (1897/1947). *The will to believe and other essays in popular philosophy*. New York: Henry Holt and Co

James, W. (1899/1915). *Talks to teachers on psychology: And to students on some of life's ideals*. New York: Henry Holt and Co.

James, W. (1899/1958). *Talks to teachers on psychology: And to students on some of life's ideals*. New York: W. W. Norton.

James, W. (1902/1936). *The varieties of religious experience*. New York: The Modern Library.

James, W. (1902/1958). *The varieties of religious experience: A study in human nature*. New York: Mentor.

James, W. (1902/1978). *The varieties of religious experience*. Garden City, NY: Image Books

James, W. (1902/1982). *The varieties of religious experience*. New York: Penguin Books.

James, W. (1902/1985). *The varieties of religious experience*. New York: Penguin.

James, W. (1903/1971). The Ph.D. octopus. In B. Wilshire (Ed.), *William James: The essential writing*. New York: Harper.

James, W. (1903/1987). "The Ph.D. octopus," essays, comments, and reviews. *The works of William James*. Cambridge, MA: Harvard University Press.

James, W. (1907/1967). Excerpts from "Pragmatism." In J. McDermott (Ed.), *The writings of William James* (p. 858). New York: The Modern Library.

James, W. (1907/1975). *Pragmatism*. Cambridge, MA: Harvard University Press.

James, W. (1907/1981). *Pragmatism*. Indianapolis, IN: Hackett.

James, W. (1907/1947). *Pragmatism: A new name for some old ways of thinking*. New York: Longmans Green.

James, W. (1907/1996). *Pragmatism and the meaning of truth*. Cambridge, MA: Harvard University Press.

James, W. (1907/1963). *Pragmatism and other essays*. New York: Washington Square Press.

James, W. (1909/1975). *The meaning of truth*. Cambridge, MA: Harvard University Press.

James, W. (1909/1967). Excerpts from "A pluralistic universe." In J. McDermott (Ed.), *The writings of William James* (p. 858). New York: The Modern Library.

James, W. (1909). *A pluralistic universe*. New York: Longmans, Green.

James, W. (1909/1947). *A pluralistic universe*. London: Longmans, Green.

James, W. (1909/1977). *A pluralistic universe*. Cambridge, MA: Harvard University Press.

James W. (1909/1996). *A pluralistic universe*. Lincoln: University of Nebraska Press.

James, W. (1912). A world of pure experience. *Essays in radical empiricism* (ch. 2). New York: Longmans, Green.

James, W. (1912/1899). *Talks to teachers: And to students on some of life's ideals*. New York: Henry Holt and Co.

James, W. (1912/1947). *Essays in radical empiricism*. London: Longmans, Green.

James, W. (1912/1976). *Essays in radical empiricism*. Cambridge, MA: Harvard University Press.

James, W. (1912/1996). *Essays in radical empiricism*. Lincoln: University of Nebraska Press.

James, W. (1912/1971). *Essays in radical empiricism* and *A pluralistic universe* (R. Bernstein, Ed.). New York: Dutton.

James, W. (1920/1926). *The letters of William James. Two volumes in one*. London: Longmans, Green.

James, W. (1987). *Essays, comments, and reviews*. Cambridge, MA/London: Harvard University Press.

Johnson, A. (1999). A postmodern perspective on education and spirituality: Hearing many voices. *Encounter, 12*(2), 41–48.

Keller, E. (1983). *A feeling for the organism: The life and work of Barbara McClintock*. New York: W. H. Freeman.

Keller, E. (1985). *Reflections on gender and science*. New Haven, CT: Yale University Press.

Ketner, K. L. (1998). *His glassy essence: An autobiography of Charles Sanders Peirce*. Nashville, TN: Vanderbilt University Press.

Kovel, J. (1991). *History and spirit: An inquiry into the philosophy of liberation*. Boston: Beacon Press.

Kulp, C. (1992). *The end of epistemology*. Westport, CT: Greenwood Press.

Laclau, E. (1996). Deconstruction, pragmatism, hegemony. In C. Mouffe (Ed.), *Deconstruction and pragmatism* (pp. 47–68). New York: Routledge.

Ladson-Billings, G. (1994). *The dreamkeepers*. San Francisco: Jossey-Bass.

Lakatos, I., & Musgrave, A. (1970). *Criticism and the growth of knowledge*. Cambridge, UK: Cambridge University Press.

Lamberth, D.C. (1997). Interpreting the universe after a social analogy: Intimacy, panpsychism, and the finite god in a pluralistic universe. In R. A. Putnam (Ed.), *The Cambridge companion to William James* (pp. 237–259). Cambridge, UK: Cambridge University Press.

Lamberth, D.C. (1999). *William James and the metaphysics of experience*. Cambridge, UK: Cambridge University Press.

Larrabee, H. A. (1961). William James' impact upon American education. *School and Society, 89*, 84–86.

Lasch, C. (1986). The communitarian critique of liberalism. *Soundings, 69*(1–2), 60–75.

Levinson, H. S. (1981). *The religious investigations of William James*. Chapel Hill: University of North Carolina Press.

Lindblom, C. (1959). The science of "muddling through." *Public administration review, 19*, 79–88.

Lovejoy, A. O. (1911). William James as philosopher. *International Journal of Ethics, 21*(2), 125–152.

Macdonald, J. (1974). A transcendental development ideology of education. In W. F. Pinar (Ed.), *Heightened consciousness, cultural revolution and curriculum theory* (pp. 85–116). Berkeley, CA: McCutchan.

MacIntyre, A. (1981). *After virtue.* Manchester, NH: University of Notre Dame Press.

Manicus, P. T. (1998). John Dewey and American social science. In L. Hickman (Ed.), *Reading Dewey: Interpretations for a postmodern generation.* Bloomington: Indiana University Press.

Matthews, M. (1994). *Science teaching: The role of history and philosophy of science.* New York: Routledge.

Mayr, E. (1997). *This is biology: The science of the living world.* Cambridge, MA: Harvard University Press.

McCarthy, C. (1997). When you know it, and I know it, what is it we know? Pragmatic realism and the epistemological absolute. In F. Margonis (Ed.), *Philosophy of education 1996* (pp. 21–29). Urbana, IL: Philosophy of Education Society.

McDermott, J. (1977). *The writings of William James.* Chicago, IL: The University of Chicago Press.

McDermott, J. (1986). *Streams of experience.* Amherst: The University of Massachusetts.

Mead, G. H. (1934). *Mind, self, and society: From the standpoint of a social behaviorist* (C. W. Morris, Ed.). Chicago: University of Chicago Press.

Menand, L. (1997). *Pragmatism: A reader.* New York: Vintage Books.

Miedema, S. (1994). The relevance for pedagogy of Habermas's "Theory of communicative action." *Interchange, 25,* 195–206.

Miedema, S. (1995). The beyond in the midst. The relevance of Dewey's philosophy of religion for education. In J. Garrison (Ed.), *The new scholarship on Dewey* (pp. 61–73). Dordrecht, The Netherlands/Boston/London: Kluwer Academic Publishers.

Miedema, S. (1996). Dewey and James on religious experience. In Ch. W. Tolman, F. Cherry, R. van Hezewijk, & I. Lubek (Eds.), *Problems in theoretical psychology* (pp. 351–358). North York, Ontario: Captus Press.

Miedema, S., & De Ruyter, D. J. (1999). Onderwijsvrijheid: een groot pedagogisch goed [Freedom of education as a great pedagogical good]. *Pedagogisch Tijdschrift, 24,* 17–33.

Miller, P. (1968). *American thought: Civil War to World War I.* New York: Holt, Rinehart and Winston.

Murphy, J. P. (1990). *Pragmatism: From Peirce to Davidson.* Boulder, CO: Westview.

Narayan, U. (1989). The project of feminist epistemology: Perspectives from a nonwestern feminist. In A. Jaggar & S. Bordo (Eds.), *Gender/body/knowledge* (pp. 256–269). Rutgers, NJ: Rutgers University Press.

Noddings, N. (1984). *Caring: A feminine approach to ethics and moral education.* Berkeley: University of California Press.

Noddings, Nel. (1993). *Educating for intelligent belief and unbelief.* New York: Teachers College Press.

Nord, W., & Haynes, C. (1998). *Taking religion seriously across the curriculum.* Alexandria, VA: Association for Supervision and Curriculum Development.

Nozick, R. (1981). *Philosophical explanations.* Cambridge, MA: The Belknap Press of Harvard University Press.

Osmer, R. R. (1999). Religion unterrichten in der staatlichen Schule in den USA: Aussichten und Moeglichkeiten [The Teaching of Religion in American Public Schools and Possibilities]. In Ch.Th. Scheilke & F. Schweizer (Eds.), *Religion, Ethik, Schule. Bildungspolitischen Perspektiven in der pluralen Gesellschaft.* [Religion, ethics, school. Perspectives on educational politics in a plural society] (pp. 279–294). Muenster/New York/Muenchen/Berlin: Waxmann Verlag.

Pearson, E., & Podeschi, R. (1999). Humanism and individualism: Maslow and his critics. *Adult Education Quarterly, 50*(1), 41–55.

Peirce, C. S. (1878/1958). How to make our ideas clear. In P. P. Wiener (Ed.), *Values in a universe of chance: Selected writings of Charles Sanders Peirce (1839–1914)* (pp. 113–136). Garden City, NJ: Doubleday.

Peirce, C. S. (1893/1960). Reply to The Necessitarian. In C. Hartshone & P. Weiss (Eds.), *The collected papers of Charles Sanders Peirce* (pp. 390–435). Cambridge, MA: Harvard University Press.

Peirce, C. S. (1905/1958). What Pragmatism is. In P. P. Wiener (Ed.), *Values in a universe of chance: Selected writings of Charles Sanders Peirce (1839–1914)* (pp. 180–202). Garden City, NJ: Doubleday.

Peirce, C. (1905, April/1984). Review of Nichols "A treatise on cosmology," *The Monist, 15.* In H. S. Thayer, *Meaning and action: A critical history of pragmatism.* Indianapolis, IN: Hackett.

Perry, R. B. (1935). *The thought and character of William James.* Boston: Little, Brown.

Perry, R. B. (1979). *In the spirit of William James.* Westport, CT: Greenwood Press.

Phillips, D. C. (1984). Was William James telling the truth after all? *The Monist, 67,* 419–434.

Phillips, D. C. (1993). *Telling it straight: Issues in assessing narrative research.* Paper presented at the Annual Conference of the Philosophy of Education Society of Great Britain, Oxford, England.

Phillips, D. C. (1995). The good, the bad, and the ugly. *Educational Researcher, 24*(7), 5–13.

Phillips, D. C. (1997). Adding nuances: Or copying the perfect country-Western song. *Issues in Education, 3*(2), 273–284.

Phillips, D. C. (2000). *The expanded social scientist's bestiary.* Lanham, MD: Rowman and Littlefield.

Pinker, S. (1997). *How the mind works.* New York: W. W. Norton.

Podeschi, R. (1976). William James and education. *The Educational Forum, 40*(2), 223–229.

Podeschi, R. (1987). Purpose, pluralism and public teacher education. *Journal of Thought, 22*(2), 8–13.

Polkinghorne, D. E. (1988). *Narrative knowing and the human sciences.* Albany: State University of New York.

Popper, K. (1972). *Objective knowledge.* London: Oxford University Press.

Porter, T. (1995). *Trust in numbers.* Princeton, NJ: Princeton University Press.

Posnock, R. (1997). The influence of William James in American culture. In R. Putnam (Ed.), *The Cambridge companion to William James* (pp. 322–342). New York: Cambridge University Press.

Powers, W. T. (1998). *Making sense of behavior*. New Canaan, CT: Benchmark Publications.

Prawat, R. (1997). Response: Problematizing Dewey's views of problem solving. *Educational Researcher, 26*(2), 19–22.

Putnam, H. (1990). *Realism with a human face*. Cambridge, MA: Harvard University Press.

Putnam, R. (Ed.). (1997). *The Cambridge companion to William James*. NY: Cambridge University Press.

Richardson, V. (Ed.). (1997). *Constructivist teacher education: Building new understandings*. Washington DC: Falmer Press.

Reed, E. S. (1997a). The fringing reef: Applying Darwin to the mind. *Times Literary Supplement*, p. 6.

Reed, E. S. (1997b). *From soul to mind*. New Haven, CT: Yale University Press.

Rorty, R. (1979). *Philosophy and the mirror of nature*. Princeton, NJ: Princeton University Press.

Rorty, R. (1989). *Contingency, irony, and solidarity*. Cambridge, UK: Cambridge University Press.

Rorty, R. (1997). Religious faith, intellectual responsibility, and romance. In R. A. Putnam (Ed.), *The Cambridge companion to William James* (pp. 84–102). Cambridge, England: Cambridge University Press.

Rorty, R. (1998). *Truth and progress. Philosophical papers* (Vol. 3). Cambridge, UK: Cambridge University Press.

Rorty, R. (1999). Phony science wars. *Atlantic Monthly, 284*(5), 120–22.

Rosenau, P. (1992). *Post-modernism and the social sciences*. Princeton, NJ: Princeton University Press.

Rosiek, J., & Iran-Nejad, A. (2000). Heeding Prawat and Hruby: Toward an articulation between biofunctional and postmodern theories of human experience. *The Journal of Mind and Behavior, 21*, 1–2.

Rosovsky, H. (1991). *The university: An owner's manual*. New York: W. W. Norton.

Ruddick, S. (1989). *Maternal thinking: Toward a politics of peace*. Boston: Beacon Press.

Said, E. (1978). *Orientalism*. New York: Vintage Books.

Sarason, S. (1996). *Revisiting "The culture of the school and the problem of change."* New York: Teachers College Press.

Schutz, A. (1999). Creating local "public spaces" in schools: Insights from Hannah Arendt and Maxine Greene. *Curriculum Inquiry, 29*(1), 77–98.

Schutz, A. (2000). Teaching freedom: Postmodern perspectives. *Review of Educational Research, 70*(2), 215–251.

Schweitzer, F. (1999). Zivilgesellschaft—Schule—Religion [Civil Society—School—Religion]. In Ch.Th. Scheilke & F. Schweizer (Eds.), *Religion, Ethik, Schule. Bildungspolitischen: Perspektiven in der pluralen Gesellschaft* [Religion, ethics, school: Perspectives on educational politics in a plural society] (pp. 295–307). Muenster/New York/Muenchen/Berlin: Waxmann Verlag.

Sconiers, Z., & Rosiek, J. (2000). Historical perspective as an important element of teachers' knowledge: A sonata-form case study of equity issues in a chemistry classroom. *Harvard Educational Review, 70*(3), 370–404.

Seigfried, C. H. (1978). *Chaos and context: A study in William James.* Athens: Ohio University Press.

Seigfried, C. H. (1990). *William James's radical reconstruction of philosophy.* Albany: State University of New York Press.

Seigfried, C. H. (1996). *Pragmatism and feminism: Reweaving the social fabric.* Chicago: The University of Chicago Press.

Shea, C. (1999, July/August). The department that fell to earth. *Linguafranca: The review of academic life, 9*(5), 24–31.

Shulman, L. (1987). Knowledge and teaching: Foundations of the new reform. *Harvard Educational Review* (57), 1–22.

Siegel, H. (1987). *Relativism refuted: A critique of contemporary epistemological relativism.* Dordrecht, The Netherlands/Boston: Reidel.

Simon, L. (1998). *Genuine reality: A life of William James.* New York: Harcourt Brace.

Smith, M. (1980). The nature and meaning of mysticism. In R. Wood (Ed.), *Understanding mysticism.* Garden City, NY: Image Books.

Soltis, J. (1987). The virtues of teaching. *Journal of Thought, 22*(3), 61–67.

Strike, K. A. (1999). *Liberalism, communitarianism, and the space between: In praise of kindness.* Kohlberg Memorial Lecture at the 25th Annual Conference of the Association for Moral Education (AME), Minneapolis, November 20. [manuscript].

Suckiel, E. (1996). Introduction. In W. James, *Essays in radical empiricism.* Lincoln: University of Nebraska Press.

Taylor, E. (1996). *William James on consciousness beyond the margin.* Princeton, NJ: Princeton University Press.

Thayer-Bacon, B. (1993, Summer). Caring and its relationship to critical thinking, *Educational Theory 43*(3), 323–340.

Thayer-Bacon, B. (1997, Spring). The nurturing of a relational epistemology. *Educational Theory, 47*(2), 239–260.

Thayer-Bacon, B. (1997). The power of caring. *Philosophical studies in education* (pp. 1–32). Ohio Valley Philosophy of Education Society. Atlanta, GA.: Georgia State University.

Thayer-Bacon, B. (2000a). *Transforming critical thinking: Thinking constructively.* New York: Teachers College Press.

Thayer-Bacon, B. (2000b). Caring reasoning. *Inquiry: Critical thinking across the curriculum, 119*(4), 22–34.

Townsend, K. (1996). *Manhood at Harvard—William James and others.* New York: W. W. Norton.

Twiss, S. B. (1995). Revisiting and revisioning William James's account of mysticism. *The Journal of the Psychology of Religion,* 4–5, 123–180.

Vanden Burgt, R. J. (1981). *The religious philosophy of William James.* Chicago: Nelson-Hall Publishers.

Van Peursen, C. A. (1994). *Na het postmodernisme. Van metafysica tot filosofisch sur-*

realisme [After postmodernism. From metaphysics to philosophical surrealism]. Kampen/Kapellen, The Netherlands: Kok Agora/Pelkmans.

Wadsworth, P. (1997). When do I tell them the right answer? *Primary Science Review, 49,* 23–24.

Wardekker, W. L., & Miedema, S. (in press). Identity, cultural change, and religious education. *British Journal of Religious Education.*

Weber, M. (1946). Bureaucracy. *Max Weber: Essays in sociology.* New York: Oxford University Press.

Weiss, P. (1995). Feminist reflections on community. In P. Weiss & M. Friedman (Eds.), *Feminism and community* (pp. 3–18). Philadelphia: Temple University Press.

West, C. (1989). *The American evasion of philosophy.* Madison: The University of Wisconsin Press.

West, C. (1993). *Keeping faith.* New York/London: Routledge.

Westbrook, R. B. (1991). *John Dewey and American democracy.* Ithaca, NY: Cornell University Press.

Whitehead, A. (1925/1948). *Science and the modern world.* New York: Mentor.

Wild, J. (1969). *The radical empiricism of William James.* Garden City, NY: Doubleday.

Wilshire, B. (1971). *William James: The essential writings.* New York: Harper & Row.

Wilshire, B. (1990). *The moral collapse of the university: Professionalism, purity, and alienation.* Albany: State University of New York Press.

Wilshire, B. (1998). *Wild hunger: The primal roots of modern addiction.* Lanham, MD: Rowman and Littlefield.

Ziebertz, H. G. (1995). Religioese Identitaetsfindung durch interreligioese Lernprozesse [Religious identity formation via interreligious processes of learning]. *Religionspaedagogische Beitraege, 36,* 83–104.

Zeichner, K. M. (1998). *The new scholarship in teacher education.* Paper presented at the Annual Meeting of the American Educational Research Association, San Diego, CA.

(especially James and Dewey), on constructivism in epistemology and education, and on philosophical and methodological issues in social science and educational research. His latest books are *The Expanded Social Scientist's Bestiary* and *Postpositivism and Educational Research*, with Nick Burbules.

Ron Podeschi is professor-emeritus of educational policy and community studies at the University of Wisconsin-Milwaukee, having earned an M.A. in philosophy and a Ph.D. in philosophy of education at Northwestern University. He has been an active scholar with an interdisciplinary approach that integrates philosophical assumptions and cultural values. His activities have centered in the American Educational Research Association, American Educational Studies Association, Adult Education Research Conference, and the Society for Intercultural Education, Training and Research. His 36 years of teaching include three decades in Milwaukee, where he was involved with inner-city schools, minority communities, and graduate and undergraduate programs in urban education.

Jerry Rosiek is an assistant professor of educational research methodology at the University of Alabama, where he teachs a three-course sequence in qualitative research methodology. His current research interests include (1) efforts to document the emotional dimension of teacher knowledge, (2) exploring the modes of representation that can convey these emotional content of teacher insights, and (3) considering the epistemological, ontological, and ideological questions raised by the use of such representations in social scientific discourse.

Barbara Thayer-Bacon is an associate professor in the Department of Educational Leadership and Cultural Studies, University of Tennessee. Her primary areas of scholarship are philosophy of education, critical thinking, epistemology, feminist theory, and educational reform. She is the author of several chapters in essay collections, numerous journal articles, and two books, *Philosophy Applied to Education: Nurturing a Democratic Community in the Classroom*, with Dr. Charles S. Bacon as contributing author, and *Transforming Critical Thinking: Constructive Thinking*. Her third book, *Relational "(e)pistemologies,"* is currently under review.

Bruce Wilshire is professor of philosophy at Rutgers University. Among other works, he has authored *William James and Phenomenology: A Study of "The Principles of Psychology," The Primal Roots of American Philosophy: Pragmatism, Phenomenology, and Native American Thought*, and *The Moral Collapse of the University: Professionalism, Purity, and Alienation*. He is the editor of *William James: The Essential Writings*.

Index

Abowitz, K., 59, 70
Absolutism, 33, 98–99, 108
Activity theory, 16
Affirmative postmodernism, 62
Agassiz, Louis, xviii, 7–8
All-form, 30
Alternative communities, 72
American Educational Research
    Association (AERA), xi
American Philosophical Association, 50,
    51, 55
American Pragmatism, 109–110
American Psychological Association, 56–
    57
American Scholar, The (Emerson), 56
Anguish, 63–64
Apffel-Marglin, Frederique, 47–48
Aristotle, 43, 44, 107
Arnold, Matthew, 54–55
Art of Educational Evaluation, The (Eisner),
    132
Associationism, 11, 14

Barnard, G. William, 153, 157, 164
Bar On, B-A., 111–112
Barrett, W., 65
Barzun, Jacques, xviii–xix
Bateson, Gregory, 23
Beaudoin, Tom, 154
Behaviorism, 25
Belenky, M., 108
Bellah, R., 64
Bergson, Henri, 106–107, 155
Berkeley, George, 122, 125
Berlin, Isaiah, 52
Bernstein, R. J., 106
Bird, G. R., 75
Black Elk, 54–55, 57 n. 3
Blumer, Herbert, 150 n. 1
Bohr, Niels, 52
Borges, Jorge Luis, 52

Brain, 13
Breaking rules, 69–70
Bredo, Eric, xiii–xiv, xvii–xviii, 1–26
Brown, L., 91
Bruner, J., 134
Buddhism, 159, 165–166, 167
Burbules, Nicholas, 126
Bureaucracy, 71

Cather, Willa, 52
Cherryholmes, Cleo, xvi, 89–96
Child and the Curriculum, The (Dewey), 128
Civil society, 84–86
Clandinin, D. Jean, 133, 137–140, 142,
    147
Clinchy, B., 108
Cochran-Smith, Marilyn, 133, 138–142,
    147
Code, Lorraine, 109
Cole, M., 16
Collaboration, 71–72
Collective action, 71–72
Community, xv, 60–62
    professional, 70, 71–72
Conant, James, 52
Connelly, Michael F., 133, 137–140, 142,
    147
Construction of "reality," 122–123
Constructivist postmodernism, xvii, 154–
    155
Context, in process of inquiry, 137–141
Continental thought, 53, 60
Cormier, H., 66–67
Cotkin, B., xviii, 60–62, 66, 73
Courage, 70
Creativity, 32
Critical realist tradition, 143–146, 148–
    149
Critical social theory, 84
Croce, P. J., 8, 10
Cultural assumptions, 68–69

Culture
    multicultural education, 34, 38–39
Curriculum
    and education as pragmatic experience,
        96
    mysticism and, 164–170
    nature of, 95
Curti, M., 24

Daly, Mary, 48
Damasio, A. R., 131
Darwin, Charles, xiv, 3–4, 6–10, 9, 11, 12–
    13, 15, 16, 20, 22–23, 52, 118, 122
Davidson, Donald, 124
Death, 49–50
Decontextualization, xvii
Deism, 21
Democracy and Education (Dewey), 110,
    127–128
Deprivatization of religion, 75, 82–84, 87
De Ruyter, D. J., 82
Determinism, 7, 100
Dewey, John, xi, xii, xvi, 4, 5, 8, 9, 13,
    16, 18, 24, 43, 51, 54–55, 57 n. 3, 61,
    67, 93, 95, 98, 102, 105, 108–113,
    118, 119–120, 127–131, 140, 141,
    147–148, 158
Differentiation thesis, 75, 81–82
Diversity, 61, 71–72
Donmoyer, R., 133
Dostoevsky, Fëdor, 43, 46, 50, 57 n. 1
Dronkers, J., 82
DuBois, W. E. B., 66
Durkheim, E., 23, 82

Each-forms, 30–35
Economic individualism, 67
Eddy, Mary Baker, 64
Edel, Leon, 51
Edie, J., 63–65, 68
Educare, 51
Education
    as a living affair, 25–26
Educational research, 130–150
    context in process of inquiry, 137–141
    interpretive methods in, 132–135
    James and, 141–150
    justifying teachers' practical knowledge
        claims in, 135–137
    pragmatism and, 130–132

Ego psychology, 14
Einstein, Albert, 52
Eisner, Elliot, 132
Eliot, Charles, 56
Emerson, Ralph Waldo, 50, 53–54, 56
Emile (Rousseau), 128
Emotional concerns
    of James, 4–5
Engeström, Y., 16
Enlightenment, 102
Epistemology, 33–36, 142
    metaphysics and, 126
    questions in teacher research, 133
    relational, 98
    standpoint, 98
Essays in Radical Empiricism (James), 18,
    76–77, 103–104, 117, 119, 121,
    122
Essentialism, 95
Ethics
    ethic for strangers, 85
    humanistic, 64
    as overriding theme, 170
    religious education and, 163–164
Evans, J., 63
Evolutionary thought, 6–10, 118–119
    Darwinian ideas in, 9–10
    Darwinian influences on, 6–8
Existentialism, 28, 47
    "jungle of experience" and, 59–60
Experience
    education as pragmatic experience, 96
    "jungle of experience," 59–60
    pure experience, 78–80, 120–121
    radical empiricism and, 158
Experience and Education (Dewey), 140
Expressive individualism, 64
Externalism (Spencer), 120

Falsification, 143, 146–147
Feminist approach, 97–114
    absolutism and, 98–99
    individualism and, 111–112
    pluralism and, 98
    pragmatism and, 99–103, 109–110, 113
    radical empiricism and, 98, 103–105
    radical pluralism and, 106–108
    relativism and, 98–99, 102–103, 108–
        112, 113
    subjectivism and, 101, 103

Fenstermacher, Gary D., 135–138, 140, 147
Flax, Jane, 109
Ford, M. P., 157–159
Formalism, scholastic, 140
Foucault, Michel, 149–150
Freud, Sigmund, 52
Functional psychology, 1

Gale, R., 59–61, 64, 67–68, 73, 158
Garrison, Jim, xiv, 27–41, 54, 127, 131
Gates, A. L., xi
Geertz, Clifford, 48, 150 n. 1
Gelphi, D. L., 75
Gemeinschaft, 85
Gendered self, 69
Genetic theory of truth, 17–18
Gesellschaft, 85
Gilligan, C., 108
Gimbutas, Marija, 52
Glasersfeld, Ernst von, xvi–xvii, 116–117, 118, 119, 121, 122–129
Globalization, 83
Godfrey-Smith, Peter, 118, 120
Goffman, Irving, 150 n. 1
Goldberger, B., 108
Goodman, R. B., 28, 37
Griffin, David, 154–155
Grossman, P. L., 133

Habermas, Jürgen, 82, 84
Habit formation, 25
Habits of the Heart (Bellah et al.), 64
Hall, S., 145
Harding, Sandra, 109, 111–112
Harrison, Jane Ellen, 52
Harvard University, xviii, 7, 8, 151, 153
Hatch, J. A., 70
Haynes, C., 167
Hegel, G. W. F., 5, 7
Heidegger, Martin, 43, 46, 149–150
Heisenberg, Werner, 52
Hocking, William Ernest, 48–49
Hoffman, D., 68
Holographic theory of memory, 16
Howard, H. A., 43
How the Mind Works (Pinker), 45–46
Hudson, W. H., 49
Humanism, 64
Humanistic ethics, 64

Idealistic theory of the mind, 11
Ideal manhood, 69
Ideal self, 68–69
Illich, Ivan, 48
Individualism, 33–34, 64, 66–68, 110, 111
  economic, 67
  expressive, 64
  intentional self and, 67–68
  moral, 66–67
  utilitarian, 64
Individuation, 44
Inner self, 64–65, 68
Intentionality, 65–66
Intentional self, 67–68
Interconnectedness, 159
In the Spirit of William James (Perry), 47
Intrinsic values, 66
Iran-Nejad, A., 131
Irigary, Luce, 52

Jackson, P., xi
James, Henry, xviii, 8, 51
Jastrow, Joseph, 56–57
Johnson, A., 152
Johnson, Aostre, xiv, xvii, 151–171
Joy, 39–40, 50–51
Jung, Carl, 52
"Jungle of experience," 59–60
Justified belief, 143–145

Kant, Immanuel, 122, 123
Keller, E., 108
Ketner, K. L., 56–57
Kierkegaard, Sören, 42, 50, 57 n. 1
King, Martin Luther, 38
Knowledge-for-practice (Cochran-Smith), 138
Knowledge-in-practice (Cochran-Smith), 138
Knowledge-of-practice (Cochran-Smith), 138
Kovel, J., 171
Kristeva, Julia, 52
Kuhn, Thomas, 56
Kulp, C., 120

Laclau, Ernesto, 93, 94
Ladson-Billings, G., 133
Lakatos, I., 143
Lamberth, David C., 74, 76–80, 159

Langer, Susanne, 52
Larrabee, H. A., xi
Lasch, C., 66
Leiter, Report, 52–53
Levinson, H. S., 76, 87
Lindblom, Charles, 129
Local Knowledge (Geertz), 48
Locke, John, 18, 122, 123
Logical positivism, 45
Lovejoy, A., 2–3
Lytle, S. L., 133, 138–142, 147

Macdonald, James, 152, 164, 168
MacIntyre, A., 66, 70
Madsen, R., 64
Mandarinism, 54
Manicus, P. T., 131
Mann, Thomas, 52
Marginalized lives, 111
Marxism, 115, 129
Masgrave, A., 143
Materialism, 29
Matthews, M., 122
Mayr, E., 9–10
McCarthy, C., 104
McDermott, John, 57 n. 3, 142, 169
McGrath, D. L., 43
Mead, George Herbert, 16, 110, 111,
     150 n. 1
Meaning of Truth, The (James), 103
Melville, Herman, 50
Menand, Louis, 93, 94
Mentoring, 170–171
Metamethodology, xvii, 132–135
Metaphysics, 27, 91, 126
   mature, of James, 121–122
   of pure experience, 78–80, 120–121
Methodolatry, 48
Methodological postulate, 19
Miedema, Siebren, xv–xvi, 74–88, 75, 82,
     84, 85–86
Miller, P., 6
Minimal realism, 80
Modernism, 62, 154–155
Monism, 29–33
Moral choice, 65–66
Moral Collapse of the University, The
     (Wilshire), xv
Moral individualism, 66–67
Morrison, Toni, 52

Multicultural education, 34, 38–39
Murphy, J. P., 18
Mysticism, xvii, 20, 151–171
   active relationship with God, 162
   curriculum theory and practice and,
     164–170
   defined, 155
   in historical context, 155–164
   James on, 157–161
   radical empiricism and, 158–160
   "something more" and, 161

Naïve relativism, 98–99
Narayan, U., 111–112
Narrative Inquiry (Clandinin and
     Connelly), 139
Natural selection, 16
Neo-Hegelianism, 6–7, 19
Nervous system, 13
Newcomb, Simon, 56
Newton, Isaac, 118, 128
Nietzsche, Friedrich, 42–43, 57 n. 1
Noddings, N., 108, 167
Nord, W., 167
Nozick, R., 73

Objectivity, 62–63
Occam's razor, 10
Off-task activities, 39–40
"On a Certain Blindness in Human
     Beings" (James), 33, 34, 49
Ontological reality, 123
Optimism, 63–64
Organismic metaphor, 23
Osmer, R. R., 81–84
Other, the, 105, 110
Over-belief, 143–144

Panpsychism, 159–160
Pauli, Wolfgang, 52
Peale, Norman Vincent, 64
Pearson, E., 64, 67
Peirce, Charles Sanders, xi, xvi, 6, 18,
     55, 56, 91–95, 99–103, 105, 106,
     108, 109–110, 113, 130, 131,
     155
Performative beliefs, 134
Perry, Ralph Barton, 2, 4–8, 21, 22, 47,
     131
Personal identity formation, 86

Personalization
  James and, 5, 75–80
  of religious education, 75–80
Phenomenology, 14–16
Phillips, Denis C., xvi–xvii, 115–129, 130,
    134–135, 136, 140, 144, 146–147
Philosophy
  Continental thought, 53, 60
  epistemology of reaching out to others,
    33–36
  of James, 16–23
  nonanalytic approaches to, 53
  pluralism and, 21–23
  psychology and, xviii
  radical empiricism and, xv–xvi, 18–21,
    61, 76, 87, 103–105, 106–108, 116,
    147–149
  scientism and, 45
Physiology
  psychology and, 12–13
Piaget, Jean, 122
Pinker, Steven, 45–46, 52–54
Plato, 107
Pluralism, 21–23, 27–30, 35, 40–41, 71,
    107–108
  creativity and, 32
  feminist approach and, 98
  "jungle of experience" and, 59–60
  panpsychism, 159–160
  prescribing, 61–62
  radical, 76, 106–108
  religious, 83–84, 162–163, 166, 169
  spiritualism and, 29, 30–33
Pluralistic empiricism, 76
Pluralistic Universe, A (James), 18, 76–77,
    106
Plurality of religiosity, 83–84, 162–163,
    166, 169
Podeschi, Ron, xv, 58–59, 58–73, 64, 67
Polkinghorne, D. E., 134
Popper, Karl, 143, 145, 147
Porter, T., 58, 59, 62, 71
Posnock, R., 66
Postmodernism, xiv, xvii, 62, 69–70, 154–
    155
  affirmative, 62
  constructivist, xvii, 154–155
Powers, W. T., 13
Practical knowledge, 135–137
Practical reasoning, 35

Pragmatism, 1–26, 89–96, 99–103, 116
  assumptions of, 94–96
  basic strategy of, 2
  of Dewey, 147–148
  education as pragmatic exercise, 96
  as guide to experimentation, 95
  of James, 17–18, 141–150
  Peirce as father of, 91–94, 99–103, 113
  Peirce's maxim and, 91–94
  pragmatic method, 90–91
  squirrel story, 89–93
  teacher knowledge research and, 130–
    150
Pragmatism (James), 101, 143, 146–147
Prawat, R., 131
Prayer, 162, 168
Pre-reflective knowing, 68
Principles of Psychology, The (James), xi, 1,
    8, 13, 63, 118–119, 131
Prisoners' dilemma, 144
Privatization
  of religious experience, 74–79, 80
Professional community, 71–72
Professionalization, xv, 42–57
  ecological approach to education and,
    47–50
  failure of awareness and, 48–50
  joy and, 50–51
  notion of "social ills," 54–55
  overlap between philosophy and cognitive
    science departments, 52–54
  philosophy and, 43–47, 52–54
  reorganization of university and, 51–54
Professional practice, 69–72
Progress, 65–66, 87–88
Progressivism, 127
Protestant Christianity, 81–82
Psychology
  of James, 10–16
  phenomenology and, 14–16
  philosophy and, xviii
  physiology and, 12–13
Psychology: The Briefer Course (James), 122
Pure experience, metaphysics of, 78–80,
    120–121
Putnam, Hilary, 47, 122
Putnam, R., xii, 61, 63

Qualified relativism, 98–99, 102–103,
    108–112, 113

Radical constructivism, xvi–xvii, 116–117
  construction of "reality" and, 122–123
  radical empiricism versus, 125–129
  skeptical tradition and, 123–124
Radical empiricism, xv–xvi, 18–21, 61, 76,
      87, 103–105, 106–108, 116, 147–149
  feminist approach and, 98
  mysticism and, 158–160
  radical constructivism versus, 125–129
Radical pluralism, 76, 106–108
Radical relativism, 102
Rationalism, 104
Realism
  of James, 146–147
Reed, Edward S., 7–8, 11
Relational epistemology, 98
Relativism
  naïve, 98–99
  qualified, 98–99, 102–103, 108–112,
      113
  radical, 102
  vulgar, 102
Religious education, 74–88
  in curriculum, 166–167
  deprivatization of, 75, 82–84, 87
  differentiation thesis in, 75, 81–82
  focus on personal experience in, 75–80
  fundamentalist religions, 152–153
  privatization of, 74–79, 80
  religion as transformative resource, 84–
      86
  secularization and, 82, 83–84
  transformational philosophy and, 153–
      154
Research. See Educational research
Resistance, 69–70
Richardson, V., 142
Romanticism, 28–29
Rorty, Richard, xv–xvi, 10, 63, 74–75, 80,
      81, 93, 120, 124
Rosenau, P., 62
Rosiek, Jerry, xvii, 130–150, 131, 133
Rosovsky, Henry, 51
Rousseau, Jean Jacques, 128
Royce, Josiah, 6, 51, 55
Ruddick, S., 108

Said, E., 145
Sainthood, 164

Santayana, George, 66
Sarason, S., 65
Scholastic formalism, 140
School and Society (Dewey), 118
Schutz, A., 69–72
Schweitzer, F., 84
Science wars, 63
Scientific reductionism, 154
Scientism, 45
Sconiers, Z., 133
Secularization, 82, 83–84
Seigfried, Charlene Haddock, 63, 67, 98,
      99, 101, 110
Self, 64–69
  cultural assumptions and, 68–69
  fluidity of selves, 64–65
  gendered, 69
  ideal, 68–69
  idea of, 64
  individualism and, 66–68
  inner self, 64–65, 68
  moral choices and, 65–66
Self-regulation, 25
Shea, Christopher, 53
Shulman, Lee, 133
Siegel, H., 98–99, 103
Silko, Leslie Marmon, 52
Simon, L., 153
Skeptical tradition, 62, 123–124, 145, 165
Smith, Margaret, 155
Social analogy, 22, 23
Social self, xv
Socrates, 49
Soltis, J., 70
Some Problems of Philosophy (James), 43
Spectator theory of knowledge (Dewey),
      119–120
Spencer, Herbert, 6–7, 118–119, 120, 121,
      129
Spirit of Regeneration, The (Apffel-Marglin),
      47–48
Spirituality, 28–33, 168–169
  monism, 29–33
  oneness and inclusion in, 36–41
  pluralism, 29, 30–33
  prayer and, 162, 168
  theism, 29
Squirrel story, 89–93
Standardized tests, 57

Standpoint epistemology, 98
Stanton, Elizabeth Cady, 52
Stephenson, R. L., 49, 50
Stevenson, Robert Louis, 35–36
Strager, Bev, 40
Stream of thought, 14–15, 16
Strike, K. A., 85, 86
Subjectivism, 62–63, 71–72, 101, 103
Suckiel, Ellen Kappy, 121
Sullivan, W., 64
Supernaturalism, 76, 80
Swidler, A., 64

*Taking Religion Seriously Across the
    Curriculum* (Nord and Haynes), 167
Talks to Teachers on Psychology (James), xi,
    33, 47, 61, 97, 118–119, 121–122,
    127, 142–143, 169
Tarule, J., 108
Taylor, E., xii, 61
Thatness of being, 104–105, 107
Thayer-Bacon, Barbara, xvi, 97–114, 99, 108
Theism, 29
Tipton, S., 64
Tolstoy, Leo, 50
Townsend, K., 69
Transcendency-in-immanency, 88
Transcendental developmental
    curriculum, 152
Truth, theory of, 113
Turner, Victor, 150 n. 1
Twiss, S. B., 156, 157

Ultimate agreement, 100
University, The (Rosovsky), 51
Utilitarian individualism, 64

Vanden Burgt, R. J., 75
Van Peursen, C. A., 88
Varieties of Religious Experience, The (James),
    20, 48, 75–80, 131–132, 142, 143,
    149, 152, 155, 156–157, 160–161
Vasquez, O., 16
Vicious intellectualism, 106, 136
Vico, Giambattista, 122
Violence, 35
Vitiation, 54
Vulgar relativism, 102

Wadsworth, P., 128
Wardekker, W. L., 85–86
War metaphors, 97–98
Weber, Max, 43, 50, 57, 82
Weiss, P., 72
West, Cornel, 66–67, 80, 88, 99, 100
Westbrook, R. B., 75
"What Makes Life Significant" (James), 33
Whatness of being, 104
Whitehead, Alfred North, 125, 155
Whitman, Walt, 28–29, 37, 49
Wild, J., 62, 67–68
Will to Believe, The (James), 143, 145
Wilshire, Bruce, xv, 42–57, 44, 45, 55, 68
Wilson, E. O., 52
Wisdom of practice, 133
Wittgenstein, L., 43, 93
Wordsworth, William, 28–29, 37
Wyman, Jeffries, 7–8

Xenophanes, 123

Zeichner, K. M., 142
Ziebertz, H. G., 82–84